Catalogue Foster + Partners

The Deutsche Bibliothek
holds a record for this
publication in the Deutsche
Nationalbibliografie;
detailed bibliographical
data can be found under
http://dnb.ddb.de

Library of Congress Control
Number: 2005900731

©2008, Foster + Partners,
London, and Prestel Verlag,
Munich · Berlin · London ·
New York

Prestel Verlag
Königinstrasse 9
80539 Munich
Germany
Tel +49 (089) 381709-0
Fax +49 (089) 381709-35
www.prestel.de

Prestel Publishing
900 Broadway, Suite 603
New York, NY 10003
USA
Tel +1 (212) 995-2720
Fax +1 (212) 995-2733

Prestel Publishing Ltd
4 Bloomsbury Place
London WC1A 2QA
United Kingdom
Tel +44 (020) 7323-5004
Fax +44 (020) 7636-8004
www.prestel.com

Printed in Italy
on acid-free paper

ISBN 978-3-7913-3973-3

Catalogue Foster + Partners

PRESTEL

MUNICH · BERLIN · LONDON · NEW YORK

Contents

Foreword
Mouzhan Majidi
Chief Executive

This new Catalogue marks an exciting moment in the evolution of the practice. We have just celebrated our fortieth anniversary, so in one sense it documents our history. But it also looks to the future, with many new projects that we are currently developing. Looking through the book, you see that the scale of that work is growing and its nature changing. It's clear that the challenges of the next forty years are going to be quite different from those we've been familiar with in the past; and so it's natural that we as a practice should grow and evolve accordingly.

We are engaged in a wide variety of projects – at a range of scales. However, much of our new work goes far beyond the way that architecture has been practised traditionally. These projects have moved beyond the scale of the individual building to encompass major infrastructure and city masterplanning. There is also a focus on the public realm – on transport, bridges, streets and squares – everyday places that are easily taken for granted but have a real impact on the way that we live. We really are at the point where it's possible to consider the design of the built environment as a totality – for the first time to be able to have a holistic approach to design.

The steady growth of the practice over the years is one factor in allowing us to address projects on this scale. Although we have a global reach, with the support structure that can only come with a certain size, we retain the flexibility and other advantages of a small studio, with a strong set of core values. We maintain close contacts between the design team and the client and pride ourselves on offering a highly personal service.

Something that we have always done as a company is to 'think global and act local'. That has been true, for example, in terms of our approach to sustainability. It applies in another sense too. Although our main studio is in London, we are an international practice, with a network of offices around the world. We will always have a local presence for any new project wherever it may be.

If our outlook is completely international, so too is our team – to the extent that between us we speak forty-five languages. That is something that has been very important in terms of building close relationships; it transforms the level of creative dialogue we are able to have with clients – and that goes to the very heart of what we do. We all know that good architecture requires the support and encouragement of a good client. This book, therefore, is as much a record of the involvement of our many clients as it is the creativity of the consultants – especially the engineers – who have shared our endeavours. It is a celebration of 'the team' in its widest sense.

Introduction
Norman Foster
Founder and Chairman

When I present our work, I often say to my audience that I want to share with them some of my experiences and those of my colleagues – our combined endeavours. That ambition is the foundation for this new edition of our Catalogue – which highlights the increasing scale and variety of the many projects we have completed and takes a look into the future with a 'preview' of things soon to come.

This book also records a period of unprecedented growth and change for the practice. It was compiled at the end of 2007, a landmark year in which we celebrated our fortieth anniversary. During that year we won thirteen international competitions and forty-one awards for design excellence to add to the seventy-nine competitions and 459 awards that we have gathered since our birth in 1967. The same year also saw us expand the ownership of Foster + Partners to embrace nine senior partners, who average around twenty years each with the company, increasing the number of shareholders from four to fourteen. I appointed Mouzhan Majidi, who joined us in 1987, as a new chief executive, to work alongside me in my very active role as chairman and founder. A further step was to broaden the company's financial base in order to expand our client services, continue our worldwide expansion and open up to new markets. In that spirit, we invited 3i to take a minority shareholding – a natural synergy given that their profile, global network and long-term interests are complementary to our own.

The combination of these moves has liberated me and my senior colleagues to be able to concentrate more on our core strength which is quality of design, in the broadest sense of that word. One manifestation is a strengthening of the design board which I chair. Spencer de Grey and David Nelson, as heads of design, steer the board on a day-to-day basis and with younger members we review every project at each stage of its evolution.

In one respect the Foster studio is close in spirit to one of those schools of architecture which is open around the clock and thrives on a jury system of outstanding critics united by a consistent code of design ethics. In another sense it is blended with the model of an international consultancy, driven by a belief in the importance of research. Those few such global consultancies will typically explore the workings of the client organisations that they serve. Objective research on our part is a critical part of our design strategy. In that approach we can optimise the potential of new buildings and infrastructure for progressive change, not only for

the private world of the occupants but also in the public domain. Small is indeed beautiful. However, we frequently need the strengths that size can bring. In our company the marriage of these two qualities is achieved by the group system. We have six groups, each with its own leader, and they can operate on any kind of project anywhere in the world – subject only to the condition that they do not compete for the same project!

This code of sharing opportunities is also literally reflected in sharing the present success and future prosperity of our company. To that end, at the time of writing in early 2008, we have further extended the shareholding of Foster + Partners to embrace an additional thirty-three equity holders – making forty-seven in all. The youngest, Narinder Sagoo, is thirty-two and is also a member of the design board.

When it was first established, the office was only a handful of people. Over the years, as its horizons have expanded, it has grown to become a global practice, currently a team of 1,250 with projects in fifty-one countries. My close colleagues have all helped to guide the practice's evolution. Together we are fortunate to have the support of an extraordinary team and so many generous collaborators – the consultants, particularly engineers of diverse skills – and, not least, our many clients, without whom nothing is possible. This new Catalogue is in no small part a reflection of all of their creative contributions.

Although design is largely generated in London and management flows out from there, it is impossible to think of the London studio in isolation from our network of overseas offices, which ensures that we have a physical presence on the site of every project, wherever it is being built in the world. The dynamic of Riverside owes much to the interaction and movement between these different places and cultures. The practice relies on a creative blend of youth and experience and it is completely cosmopolitan: the average age is a little over thirty and together we speak some forty-five languages.

Looking back over the past few years we have witnessed huge social and technological transformations. That is as true of the practice of architecture as it is of the world at large. We see also that this pattern is accelerating rather than diminishing, and that is reflected in many of the new projects illustrated here. It might be said in this context that the only constant is change. However, reviewing our work highlights a number of themes and concerns that have guided us consistently from the beginning, and we see those projected forward into our new work as

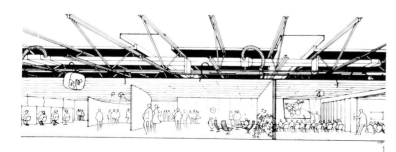

1

2

1. Newport School, Wales (1967); sectional perspective drawing by Norman Foster.

2. Thomas Deacon Academy, Peterborough, England (2003–2007); looking down into the central concourse.

3. McLaren Technology
Centre, Woking, England
(1998–2004).

4. Electronic Arts European
Headquarters, Chertsey,
England (1997–2000);
a view along the internal
'street' that lines the
lakeside.

points of continuity. Design for me is all encompassing. It is about values. I believe that we have a moral duty to design well and responsibly – whether that is at the scale of a door handle or a regional or city masterplan. Design can explore the new and build on the past. It can transform patterns of health, living and working. To design is to question and to challenge.

Tracing a line from my early passions and influences to our work today, I found myself writing down some key words. The first of these was 'inspiration'. There are so many sources that inspire design. For me there have been people and places, the work of other architects and artists, as well as natural forces and the achievements of technology. Being affected by what we see, and then moved to create, is the starting-point for all original work. 'Fascination' was the word that next came to mind, suggesting curiosity and the urge to learn and understand. Then came 'motivation' – the passion, the constant search for perfection that drives the designer. That mix of inspiration, fascination and motivation can be complex and contradictory, so perhaps in the end 'integration' is the key word and the first of the themes I would highlight. Integration, for me, can mean bringing disparate elements into harmony, or breaking down conventional social and spatial boundaries.

For example, in one of our earliest projects we pioneered the idea of a school building that would be open-planned, filled with light, democratic and flexible, without corridors or institutional barriers. Today we can see that idea at work in a family of new schools we have recently completed in cities around the UK, beginning with the Bexley Business Academy, and continuing most recently in Folkestone and Peterborough. The Academies represent a new direction in secondary education. Often replacing failing schools in under-privileged areas, they are designed to create inspirational environments in which to teach and to learn, and to create exciting new opportunities for pupils. Importantly, they also break down barriers between school and community by offering after-school social and educational facilities. These ideas were pioneered in our Lycée Albert Camus at Fréjus in the south of France completed in 1993. They can also be traced back to my research studies in the late 1960s.

Integration – in the sense of bringing people together and encouraging communication – is an idea that we have applied in university buildings for scientific and medical research, first at Imperial College in London, and again at Stanford University in California. More recently we have

begun work on a new School of Management at Yale University in New Haven. In this context communication is one of the most valuable qualities. We continue to hear tales of medical breakthroughs happening not in the rarefied atmosphere of the laboratory but by people getting together over a coffee. In the Center for Clinical Science Research and the Clark Center, both at Stanford, the social spaces are every bit as important as the laboratories.

That willingness to challenge accepted responses or solutions is something that has always underpinned our work. It means trying to ask the right questions, allied with a curiosity about how things work – whether that is an organisation or a mechanical system. I have characterised that tendency to look at a problem afresh, from first principles, as 'reinventing'. Often that process can be seen to unfold through a series of projects.

If we take an early building like our headquarters for Willis Faber & Dumas – which questioned the conventional office tower and reinvented the concept of workplace – you see how it sparked ideas that we continue to develop and refine. Above all, we were concerned with the quality of life and light, with introducing more joy into the workplace. We find those ideas re-explored in other low-rise projects – such as the European Headquarters for Electronic Arts and the McLaren Technology Centre – as well as a family of high-rise office projects, most recently the headquarters for Hearst in New York. There, the lobby with its company restaurant is conceived on the scale of a town square – a social focus for the Hearst community.

We took an equally radical approach with another formative project – the Sainsbury Centre for Visual Arts. It is a gallery without walls in the conventional sense. Galleries, teaching spaces, students, academics and visitors are brought together under a single roof. Traditionally, this range of facilities would have produced several buildings. But by integrating everything in this way we encouraged creative interaction between different departments and activities. It is also a celebration of light and space. The use of natural toplight is an important part of the energy equation, but it goes beyond that to impact on the spirit of the place. We would probably not have conceived Stansted Airport without the experience of the Sainsbury Centre; and Stansted in turn gave us a strategy that informed the design of much larger terminal buildings at Chek Lap Kok in Hong Kong and Beijing International.

5. Center for Clinical
Science Research,
Stanford University, USA
(1995–2000). The central
courtyard: a focal space for
the building's users and the
wider university community.

6. James H Clark Center,
Stanford University, USA
(1999–2003). The central
courtyard is animated by
the movement of people
throughout the day.

1. Hongkong and Shanghai
Bank Headquarters, Hong
Kong (1979–1986); the
north facade, seen from the
waterfront.

2. Hong Kong International
Airport, Chek Lap Kok,
Hong Kong (1992–1998).
The Stansted model was
expanded and developed by
Chek Lap Kok.

1

With Stansted, we went back to the roots of air travel, to try to recapture the clarity of the early terminals. It has none of the maze-like routes or changes of level that typified the airport terminal at that time; and all the heavy services that usually clog the roofspace are instead placed in an undercroft so that the roof can become a lightweight canopy, admitting daylight. Significantly, our reinventing of the airport terminal through the Stansted model has long been adopted by airport planners worldwide and is 'coming home' again to inform the design of our new Heathrow East terminal, which will replace long outdated facilities there.

One of the things that most excites me about our approach to practising architecture today is the mobility we enjoy, not just in moving around the world, but also in our ability to respond very quickly to new challenges. Chek Lap Kok and Beijing illustrate this in both senses, having moved very fast indeed. In the case of Beijing, we were commissioned in mid-November 2003; by the end of that month we had mobilised thirty-eight staff in London, and set up an office of eleven in Beijing; over the next four months the team completed 2,500 preliminary design drawings, in time for the groundbreaking ceremony on 28 March 2004. At the peak of construction there were an astonishing 50,000 workers on site. Consider that this is a building of 1.3 million square metres, capable of handling up to 50 million passengers per annum. Yet remarkably it was commissioned and completed in a little over four years.

Although Chek Lap Kok and Beijing are among the largest airports in the world, the experience of the traveller is considered paramount. Beijing provides, under one roof, all the facilities and passenger-handling capacity currently provided by five terminals at Heathrow – plus another seventeen per cent of that total. We strove to make the building friendly and accessible. Walking distances are short, public transport connections are fully integrated, and transfer times are minimised. Like Stansted, both terminals are open to views to the outside and are planned under roof canopies whose skylights are both an aid to orientation and sources of daylight. I call this an analogue experience in a digital world. Interestingly, despite their scale they are also very efficient in energy terms because they are compact, with relatively small footprints when compared with a proliferation of separate terminals. Both are also compelling examples of how political will can produce a long-term solution to a problem, on an unprecedented scale, and at a pace inconceivable in the West.

Hong Kong is also significant in terms of the history of the practice in that it gave us our first major opportunity to build overseas. Conceived during a sensitive period in Hong Kong's history, the headquarters for the Hongkong and Shanghai Bank was intended as a statement of confidence. Our brief was to create 'the best bank building in the world'.

In the process we reinvented the high-rise office building, by questioning the conventional office tower with its centre core of circulation and services. We pushed the cores to the perimeter to create flexible, open office floors; and vertical movement combines high-speed lifts with escalators to reduce travel times and increase connectivity between floors. To aid flexibility we designed demountable partitions and installed raised 'aircraft' floors. Significantly, the Bank attributes a measure of its tremendous growth as a company over the past twenty years to the ability to reconfigure its headquarters building quickly and easily as its needs have changed. For example, unlike any of their competitors they were able to introduce a dealing floor directly into their headquarters.

Shifting technological, social and economic patterns mean that the work patterns and lifestyles of building users are continually evolving. Being aware of those changes and being able to predict future trends is fundamental to the way that we work as designers. As the Bank demonstrates, gaining a clear understanding of a client's needs at the outset can increase an organisation's long-term effectiveness and improve the well-being of its staff. Going forward, to help us explore alternative working and living patterns we have a specialist workplace consultancy team in the studio whose role is to analyse new trends. They will also visit a project after everyone has settled in, talk to the different user groups and report back on how it works and what we might do better in future. That information will feed into the design of the next project, as part of a constant process of questioning and learning.

Although the design team from one project to the next might be different, the design board, and the broader structure of the office, ensure that we have a strong collective memory. That holds true whatever the building type. The Sage Gateshead, for example – our first building for the performing arts – involved a very steep learning curve. But that experience widened our knowledge base and helped us to achieve

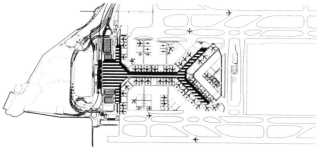

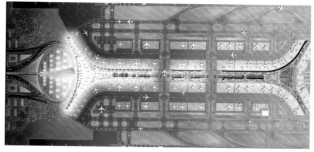

2

3

4. Wembley Stadium, London, England (1996–2007); sketch by Norman Foster exploring the symbolic role of the arch on the London skyline.

5. The Wembley arch illuminated at night; the dome of the British Museum's Great Court can be seen in the foreground.

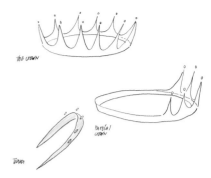

4

5

3. Beijing International Airport, Terminal 3, China (2003–2008). Chek Lap Kok in turn informed the design of Beijing – the world's largest and most technically advanced airport building.

1, 2. Gomera Regional Planning Study, Canary Islands (1975). A 'green' project long before the term had gained common currency, the Gomera masterplan explored strategies for sustainable, energy self-sufficient tourist development on the island, including harnessing wind and solar power.

commissions for new performing arts buildings in Dallas, New York and St Petersburg. Similarly, the success of our Wembley Stadium led to the commission to design the Camp Nou Stadium in Barcelona just four months after Wembley's opening in 2007.

Our collective memory impacts in other ways too. Our forty-storey headquarters for Swiss Re at 30 St Mary Axe in the City of London is rooted in a radical approach – technically, architecturally, socially and spatially. But it synthesises and takes forward ideas we explored in projects such as the Commerzbank in Frankfurt, and before that in the Hongkong Bank and experimental projects with Buckminster Fuller in the early 1970s.

The Commerzbank stemmed from a desire to reconcile work and nature within the compass of an office building. Although the climate is controlled for 80 per cent of the year it uses natural ventilation for energy reduction, making it the world's first ecological skyscraper. It is also responsive to its city-centre location, emerging as it does from the centre of a large traditional urban block. As with Swiss Re, we developed a strategy that allowed us to place such a tall building in the city and yet to break down its scale and to improve the quality and amount of public space at street level.

Similarly, the 'gardens in the sky' that we first proposed for the Hongkong Bank and realised in the Commerzbank can be seen at work again in Swiss Re, where our environmental strategy focuses on a series of atria, designed to be greened with plants, that spiral up around the perimeter of the building. These spaces are natural points for social exchanges and function as the building's 'lungs', distributing fresh air drawn in through the facade. This system reduces the demand for air-conditioning and together with a range of other energy-saving measures means that the building consumes just half the energy of its environmentally sealed neighbours. The internal environments of Commerzbank and Swiss Re are also literally fresher and for the occupants therefore more desirable.

The design strategies that underpin these projects highlight another significant theme in our work. Sustainability is a word that has become fashionable over the last decade. However, sustainability is not a matter of fashion, but of survival. The United Nations, in its latest Global Environment Outlook, outlined a series of possible environmental scenarios for the next thirty years. At worst, it foresaw crises triggered

by increasing water shortages, global warming and pollution. It suggested that these trends might be slowed, but only if nations work together to address radically the global consumption of natural resources and energy, and to halt man's degradation of the environment.

It is generally accepted that global warming is due to rising atmospheric concentrations of 'greenhouse' gases – most significantly carbon dioxide and methane. But in our experience few people are aware that in the industrialised world buildings consume half the energy we generate and are responsible for half the carbon emissions, the remainder being divided almost equally between transport and industry. Architects clearly have a role to play in challenging this equation. Sustainability requires us to think holistically. The location and function of a building; its flexibility and lifespan; its orientation, form and structure; its heating and ventilation systems and the materials used; together impact upon the amount of energy required to build and maintain it. However, as I will explore later, the only way we can truly achieve a sustainable future is by simultaneously addressing the infrastructure that binds together the stock of individual buildings.

To help us make new advances in sustainable design we have our own research and development group, which includes a sustainability forum. The forum was established to consolidate and develop the practice's knowledge base and has allowed us to improve access to information on new products, materials, and research findings. In many of our projects we have pioneered solutions using renewable energy sources, which offer dramatic reductions in pollution. Examples are not confined to buildings. Working with industry we have created a new generation of super-efficient wind turbines and new forms of cladding systems that can harvest solar energy.

The ambition of that thinking can be seen at work in the world's first regional-scale conservation and sustainable development project, which we are developing in Libya following the launch of the Cyrene Declaration in 2007. Located in the Green Mountain region, our planning study embraces an area of 5,500 square kilometres, including some of the most spectacular natural landscape on the Mediterranean coast.

The strategies we are exploring in Libya can in turn be traced to the planning study we undertook in the mid-1970s for Gomera, in the Canary Islands – where we pioneered sustainable patterns of tourist development. Gomera was a 'green' project long before the environmental

3. Green Mountain Regional Plan, Libya (2007–). The Green Mountain region of Libya has the potential to become one of the world's most desirable tourist destinations; as with Gomera, the challenge is to develop in a sustainable way, moving towards carbon neutrality on a regional scale.

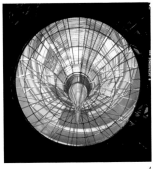

4. New German Parliament, Reichstag, Berlin, Germany (1992–1999); looking up into the lantern – a source of daylight and natural ventilation.

4

agenda was seriously being discussed. We investigated the use of indigenous building techniques, together with alternative energy sources – wind and solar power, water conservation and gas production from domestic waste – to minimise the island's reliance on diminishing natural resources.

Many of the 'green' ideas that we explored in early projects are only now becoming a reality because of the new technologies at our disposal. In the early 1970s, our collaboration with Buckminster Fuller prompted the development of the 'Climatroffice', an experimental project that brought the office into the garden and the garden into the office, creating a microclimate within an energy-conscious enclosure. Then, however, we lacked the technological tools to realise it within a realistic timeframe. Today our computer-modelling techniques allow us to research and design structures in greater depth and far more rapidly. We can see that in the design of the Swiss Re building, where the building's complex curvature was encoded using sophisticated computer software. It should be noted, though, that in parallel many of the aesthetic decisions for this building were explored through the medium of physical models and pencil sketches.

Similarly, the Chesa Futura apartment building in the Swiss Alps married advanced computer-aided design tools with state-of-the-art prefabricated timber construction and handcrafted shingles to create a building that is environmentally benign and visually 'of its place'. By increasing the density of its own site in an urban centre it demonstrates that we do not have to build housing on the fringes of towns and cities, consuming precious land and suburbanising nature. It also shows that we do not need to consume large amounts of energy, even in a cold climate.

We also understand the importance of studying the 'whole life' energy patterns of our buildings – which takes into account not just how much energy they consume, but also how much is embodied in their fabric. Chesa Futura is a low-energy structure not just in terms of its consumption, but also in terms of the life cycle of the materials used. Wood is an entirely renewable resource and it absorbs carbon dioxide during its growth cycle. Additionally, in this part of Switzerland, building in timber is culturally sympathetic, reflecting local architectural traditions; and it contributes to the local ecology of harvesting older trees to facilitate forest regeneration. These are sustainable systems that work with, rather than against, nature.

In a very different context, our building for Hearst in New York takes bold steps in terms of sustainability, beginning with its construction. Its diagrid frame uses twenty per cent less steel than a conventional post and beam structure and eighty-five per cent of that steel is recycled, which is highly significant in terms of the building's embodied energy. A host of other passive environmental measures, including the use of natural ventilation for nine months of the year, ensure that its energy consumption represents a twenty-three per cent improvement on the standard set by state and city energy codes. Significantly, it is the first new tower in Manhattan to be awarded a gold rating under the US Green Buildings Council's Leadership in Energy and Environmental Design Program (LEED).

Environmentally friendly construction is in keeping with Hearst's philosophy as a company. Hearst places a high value on the notion of the healthy workplace and it is not alone in believing that providing such an environment is set to become an important factor in future recruitment. As a private corporation occupying the entire building, Hearst also had the benefit of making decisions unencumbered by outside interests. It reinforces our experience that it is enlightened owner-occupiers – companies such as Willis Faber, Commerzbank and Swiss Re among others – that can be relied upon to offer a lead for the market to follow.

Sustainable strategies can be applied in the context of old buildings as well as the new. With our transformation of the Reichstag in Berlin we developed a radical new energy solution, using renewable bio-fuel – refined vegetable oil from rape or sunflower seeds – which, when burned in a co-generator to produce electricity, is remarkably clean compared to fossil fuels. Together with a raft of energy saving measures, and the increased use of daylight and natural ventilation, this has led to a ninety-four per cent reduction in the building's carbon emissions. Significantly, the Reichstag today creates more energy than it consumes, allowing it to act as a local power station for other government buildings nearby. If a nineteenth-century structure can be transformed from an energy-guzzler into a net energy provider, how much easier is it to design new buildings that make responsible use of precious resources?

The Reichstag highlights another important theme in our work: how new architecture can be the catalyst for the revitalisation of old buildings. An old building on this scale, especially one with a complex history, is like a city in microcosm, with many layers of intervention over time. Just as

5, 6. Chesa Futura, St Moritz, Switzerland (2000–2004). The project combined state-of-the-art computer design tools with centuries-old construction techniques – including hand-cut larch shingles – to create a building that is both environmentally sustainable and contextually apt.

5

6

Opposite: Hearst Headquarters, New York, USA (2001–2006). The main spatial event is a lobby that occupies the entire floor plate of the old building – a civic space for the Hearst community on the scale of a town square.

1. The Great Court at the British Museum, London, England (1994–2000). A new kind of urban space – a cultural plaza.

2. Smithsonian Institution Courtyard, Washington, USA (2004–2007). The roof above the grand central courtyard has transformed the visitor experience of the museum.

the experience of a city can be enriched when there is a creative dialogue between old and new, so too can that of a building. We began that dialogue between old and new with the Sackler Galleries at the Royal Academy, and we see it again in a more recent project, the Great Court at the British Museum.

The Great Court was once one of London's lost spaces, largely filled by book stacks and storage areas around the circular Reading Room. The departure of the British Library gave us the opportunity to reclaim the nineteenth-century courtyard. By clearing away the book stacks and casting a glazed canopy over the space we were able to reinvent the court as the organisational heart of the Museum and enhance the experience of the five million people who visit it each year. The Great Court was the first of a new kind of civic space – a cultural plaza – which pioneered patterns of social use hitherto unknown within this or indeed any other museum.

More recently, we have been able to explore this concept further at the Smithsonian Institution in Washington DC. The enclosure of the building's grand central courtyard has transformed the public's experience of the Smithsonian's galleries and provided the institution with one of the grandest event spaces in the city. By integrating acoustic layers into the structural web of the roof it offers new levels of performance for speech and music.

At the British Museum, as part of a related series of interventions, we freed the forecourt of parked cars and restored it to provide an appropriate formal reception space for the Museum and a major new amenity for London. Our approach was rooted in the belief that it is not only individual buildings but also their wider urban context that affects our well-being. In that sense, it relates to our 'World Squares' masterplan, which makes detailed proposals for the environmental improvement of Trafalgar Square, Parliament Square and Whitehall in the centre of London. Its goals are to enhance pedestrian access and enjoyment of the area for Londoners and the thousands of people who visit each year, and to address public transport and create more sympathetic settings for its historic buildings and monuments. I have described that task as a 'balancing act' – a search to promote a genuinely integrated solution able to satisfy the often conflicting needs of residents and visitors; something that holds true for any historical urban environment attempting to sustain contemporary activities.

The first phase to be implemented has been the transformation of Trafalgar Square. The northern edge of the square, in front of the National Gallery, has been closed to vehicles and paved to create a broad pedestrian plaza that is linked by steps to the main body of the square. Although a relatively discreet intervention, its effect has been radical, changing completely the visitor's experience of the space – and with none of the traffic chaos predicted by the sceptics. To implement these local changes involved metropolitan wide surveys of traffic and pedestrian movements.

Frequently when I share a project with others I find myself talking about the importance of the social focus, the heart of the building, the way in which it can change the quality of people's lives. As we can see in Trafalgar Square, that applies equally to urban infrastructure – the squares, parks and public spaces, the bridges and transport systems, the 'urban glue' that holds a city together. Indeed, I would argue that the quality of life in a modern city is influenced more by the quality of its infrastructure than by the nature of its individual buildings. Infrastructure can also have a powerful impact in other ways. For example, if you look at our Millennium Bridge in London or our Millau Viaduct in rural France you find that in terms of the prosperity they are bringing to their local communities, and their powerful symbolic role, their value far exceeds that of the connection itself.

It is also interesting to observe how an individual project, linked to an enlightened political initiative, can help to regenerate the wider fabric of a city. The Carré d'Art in Nîmes is an early example. It looks out on to a space once choked by parked cars and unfriendly to visitors. Go there today and you find a different world. There is a thriving outdoor café life, new shops have opened and the ripple effects are visible far beyond the site. A similar objective drove the Sage music centre, which has provided a catalyst for the regeneration of Gateshead's riverside and a key element in helping to establish Tyneside as an arts destination in its own right. In each case, a concern for the physical context has produced projects that are sensitive to the culture and climate of their place.

What these projects tell us is that the holistic thinking that underpins sustainable strategies for architecture must equally be applied at the scale of the city. We know that attractive, sustainable localised communities can be created when transport connections, workplaces, schools, shops, parks and recreation spaces are all within walking or

3. Carré d'Art, Nîmes, France (1984–1993). The renewal of the space in front of the building has reinvigorated this quarter of Nîmes.

4. Trafalgar Square, London, England (1999–2003). The square's transformation results from the 'World Squares for All' masterplan.

3. Milano Santa Giulia, Milan, Italy (2004–). Located on a former industrial site, strategically between city centre and suburban fringes of Milan, the scheme aims to combine the best of both worlds to create a sustainable urban community.

1

cycling distance of home. This is also the essence of so many traditional settlements which are like magnets on the tourist trail. The clean nature of much post-industrial work also means that workplaces can be combined with housing in mixed-use development – 'clean' industries, such as microelectronics and new service-sector offices and studios are completely compatible with residential areas. In our continuing work in Duisburg, in the former German 'rust belt' of the Ruhr, we have demonstrated that inner cities can be revitalised by introducing these newer industries and locating them alongside housing and schools – even creating more green spaces in the process.

However, while we know that virtually every new building can be designed to run on a fraction of current energy levels, or make use of renewable energy sources, the bigger global picture is dominated by two further crucial issues: population growth and the shift towards living in cities. The world's population stands at 6.7 billion; by 2050 it is expected to reach nine billion. In less than ten years there will be fifty-nine 'megacities' – cities with populations of ten million or more. Two thirds of them will be in so-called developing countries, especially in South-East Asia, where up to half the population will be urbanised. But what will those cities look like?

One of the chief problems facing the world today is urban sprawl. As cities grow horizontally rather than vertically, people are forced to travel greater distances between home and work, bringing consequent increases in energy consumption and carbon emissions. There is a direct correlation between urban density and energy consumption – denser communities promote walking rather than driving – and high density does not automatically mean overcrowding or economic hardship. Significantly, two of the world's most densely populated communities, Monaco and Macao, are at opposite ends of the economic spectrum; and in London some of the most desirable areas are also the most densely populated. Mayfair, Kensington and Chelsea, for example, have population densities up to three times higher than those found in many of the capital's poorer boroughs.

Working within the context of existing cities we can increase densities and improve urban quality using both high-rise and low-rise solutions. Our Tokyo Millennium Tower was ahead of its time in proposing a radical new model for the vertical city. It took a traditional horizontal city quarter – housing, shops, restaurants, cinemas, sporting facilities, green spaces

2

1. Millennium Tower, Tokyo, Japan (1989); a super-tall tower, with a resident population of 60,000 people, the building was conceived as 'city in the sky'.

2. Russia Tower, Moscow, Russia (2005–). A mixed-use, super-dense vertical city for 25,000 people, the building combines offices, a hotel and residences with a wide range of public amenities.

3

5. Masdar, Abu Dhabi, UAE (2007–). A pioneering development, Masdar will create a carbon-neutral, zero-waste, urban community – a blueprint for sustainable development worldwide.

Overleaf: Milano Santa Giulia; sketch by Norman Foster.

and public transport networks – and turned it on its side to create a super-tall building. Capable of housing a community of up to 60,000 people – some 20,000 more than the population of Monaco – it would have occupied less than one hundredth of the land. It was a virtually self-sufficient, self-sustaining community in the sky.

This sounds like future fantasy. But in fact we are currently constructing a similar tower in Moscow. Located in Moscow City, 5.5 kilometres from Red Square, it will be a mixed-use, super-dense vertical community of 25,000 people. Standing 600 metres tall, it encloses some 520,000 square metres and provides everything from offices, a hotel, public spaces, shopping and leisure facilities to residences with private gardens. At its pinnacle the final seven storeys are devoted to public viewing galleries, restaurants and exhibition spaces. The base with its shopping and leisure venues connects directly into the Moscow metro system.

Elsewhere in the world we are developing schemes for high-density, sustainable communities that address a variety of cultures and climates. In Milan, our Santa Giulia masterplan is reclaiming a former industrial area that lies close to the heart of the city, yet near to leafy suburbs. Our starting point was to ask: is it possible to have the advantages of the city and suburbia without the problems of either? As with World Squares, the answer is a series of balancing acts – urbanity with parks, pedestrians with traffic, old with new, public transport with private cars – to create a 'city within a city'. The focus of the scheme is a new 37-hectare public park, which will be a place for leisure pursuits and relaxation for the 12,000 people who will live and work in Santa Giulia, as well as a 'green oasis' for metropolitan Milan as a whole.

In Abu Dhabi, the enlightened Masdar Initiative will be the world's first attempt to produce a zero-carbon, zero-waste community. To achieve this would be a challenging task anywhere in the world. In a desert environment this has been likened to the equivalent in past times of putting a man on the moon. It has led to the creation of a 6-million-square-metre new town of 90,000 people that re-explores the planning principles of a traditional walled city. Driven by Abu Dhabi's Future Energy Company, it will also be a centre for the development of new ideas for energy production, with a university and special economic zones. Ground was broken in January 2008 with completion planned for 2018. The project has already been boosted by a $15 billion investment programme.

Abu Dhabi has also given us the opportunity to explore sustainable ways of building for leisure as well as for work, with a mix of low-rise and high-rise elements. A modern version of the traditional souk, the city's Central Market is being reinvented as a mixed-use complex – a 'city in microcosm' – that will translate the Gulf vernacular into a modern day urban architecture that is friendly, human-scaled and ecologically responsible.

On the Abu Dhabi waterfront, at Al Raha Beach, the Al Dana Precinct combines offices, apartments, a hotel and shops in a mix designed to encourage activity throughout the day. The building's form has evolved in response to sophisticated computer environmental analysis, which has helped us to resolve the contradictions of the site, so that it creates shade yet also admits daylight, encourages cooling air currents yet provides shelter against the desert wind.

As these projects demonstrate, we have a vital role as advocates to encourage sustainable solutions. But architects in turn need more progressive developers and politicians with courage to set goals and incentives for society to follow. Some countries have given a lead. Germany, for example, was among the first to understand the need to reduce consumption and promote renewable energy sources, and it is no coincidence that some of the practice's most advanced environmental thinking has been encouraged by the attitudes of German clients and the State.

The more we examine our work over time, the more themes begin to emerge and overlap with each another. There is a high degree of 'interconnectivity'. If I had to summarise I would say that our work represents an approach that is inclusive and all-embracing. The best architecture comes from a synthesis of all the elements that separately comprise and inform the character of a building: the structure that holds it up; the services that allow it to function; its ecology; the quality of natural light; the symbolism of the form; the relationship of the building to the skyline or the streetscape; the way we move through or around it. Above all, I believe that architecture is rooted in the needs of people – material and spiritual, measurable and intangible. It must have the ability to transcend function, to add beauty as well as value to lift the spirits, to move us in some way. That is what we continue to strive for.

4. Central Market, Abu Dhabi, UAE (2006–). Inspired by the vernacular architecture of the Gulf, this scheme reinvents the traditional market form to create a densely planned mixed-use complex.

4

5

MF
26-2-06

Museum of Fine Arts, Boston
Boston, USA 1999–

Founded in 1870, the Museum of Fine Arts, Boston, is one of the world's finest art museums, visited by more than one million people every year. However, in common with many such institutions, the sheer scale of this audience places a great strain on its facilities. This scheme for the Museum's renewal presents a strategic framework within which its current accommodation will be doubled to provide new galleries, a study centre, and temporary exhibition and education spaces. In the process, the visitor experience will be transformed.

Architecturally, the project echoes themes explored in the Reichstag and the Great Court at the British Museum, establishing a creative dialogue between old and new, and strengthening links with the local community by making the building more open and accessible. At the core of the scheme is the restoration of the logic of the Museum's original Beaux-Arts plan, devised by the American architect Guy Lowell. Following Lowell's intentions, the central axis of the main building is reasserted with the reintroduction of the main entrance to the south and the reopening of the north entrance. At the heart of this axis is a new information centre, from where visitors will begin their tour. A glazed structure – 'a crystal spine' – provides new accommodation and partly encloses the two existing grand courtyards in a glass 'jewel box', creating new spaces for visitor orientation, cafés, sculpture and special events.

The Museum's new buildings will be highly energy efficient; the courtyards will be naturally lit, and the galleries and study centre will have state-of-the-art climate control, the gallery spaces configured to allow art to be displayed with a more obvious sense of clarity and light. Surrounding the Museum, new landscaping is designed to strengthen links with the adjacent Back Bay Fens, laid out by Frederick Law Olmsted, architect of New York's Central Park. The landscape design follows Olmsted's Romantic tradition of winding paths and informal planting to draw the greenery of the Fens into the building.

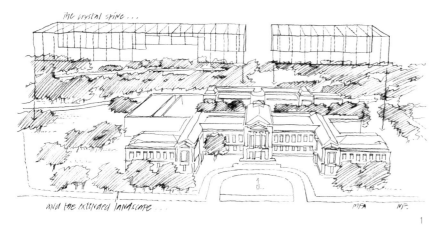

1

3

2

1. Sketch by Norman Foster explaining the concept of the new 'crystal spine'.

2. Cross-section through the east courtyard, one of two such spaces created by the 'crystal spine'.

3. A visualisation of the east courtyard.

Winspear Opera House
Dallas, USA 2002 –

The Dallas Opera Company is internationally renowned for its dedication to excellence and innovation and that commitment is evident in its plans to build an opera house in the new Performing Arts District of Dallas. Representing a radical rethinking of the traditional opera experience, the design addresses the questions: 'What is the nature of the opera house in the twenty-first century; and how can we create a building that offers a model for the future?'

The design of the opera house follows on from the practice's formulation of a masterplan for the Performing Arts District, which will eventually contain buildings by other Pritzker Prize winners: Rem Koolhaas, IM Pei and Renzo Piano. Designed to ensure accessibility and legibility within a pedestrian-friendly environment, these new buildings will relate to one another along the 'green spine' of Flora Street. The Winspear Opera House faces the Grand Plaza and the Annette Strauss Artists Square performing space and will provide a focal point for the entire district.

Organisationally, the Winspear reinvents the conventional form of the opera house, inverting its closed, hierarchical structure to create a transparent, publicly welcoming series of spaces, which wrap around the rich red-stained drum of the 2,200-seat auditorium. The ambition is to create a building that will not only be fully integrated with the cultural life of Dallas, but will become a destination in its own right for the non-opera-going public, with a restaurant, café and bookstore that will be publicly accessible throughout the day. In elevation the building is transparent, its soaring glass walls revealing views of the public concourse, upper-level foyers and grand staircase. Entered beneath a deeply overhanging canopy, which shades the outdoor spaces from the harsh Texan sun, the transition from the Grand Plaza, through the foyer, into the auditorium is designed to heighten the drama of attending a performance – in effect, 'to take the theatre to the audience'.

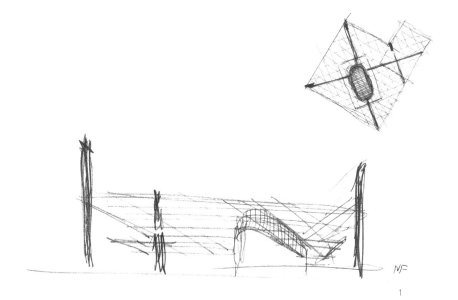

1

3

2

1. Early sketches by Norman Foster.

2. A visualisation of the auditorium, looking towards the proscenium.

3. The building will form the focal point of Dallas' new Performing Arts District. It is designed to be a welcoming presence, with a range of activities that will draw people in throughout the day.

New Globe Theater
New York, USA 2003 –

Heralding the reopening of Governors Island, which has been closed to the public for 200 years, this proposal for the New Globe company will form the focus of a new cultural hub in New York Harbor. Housed within the massive masonry walls of Castle Williams – built to defend America against the British in the War of 1812 – the project aims to bring this national monument to new life as a state-of-the-art contemporary performance venue. In combining old and new it continues the practice's clear philosophy about the sensitive treatment of historical structures and builds on a body of work that ranges from the Reichstag in Berlin to the Great Court at the British Museum.

The design of the theatre is inspired by the circular form of the traditional Elizabethan playhouse. It was discovered that the internal dimensions of Castle Williams are identical to those of the renowned Elizabethan Globe Theatre in London. The new theatre is thus conceived as an 'insert' – set beneath a new roof canopy – that matches the existing castle structure in both plan and section, allowing the character and integrity of the original building to be preserved. In weaving together the physical history of the castle with Shakespeare's theatrical legacy, the New Globe is offered as a symbol of a common cultural heritage.

The theatre can seat 800 people, distributed through three gallery levels, with 400 'groundlings'. Extensive modelling studies were undertaken with Arup Acoustics to ensure that the space will evoke the 'feel' of an Elizabethan theatre, but with improved acoustic performance. A significant element of the scheme is its environmental strategy, which deploys a range of passive controls: the thermal mass of the castle is used as a 'heat sink' to minimise the energy required to heat or cool the auditorium; a sun-tracking shading device shelters the glazed circulation zone between the new and old structures; and heat pumps use water from the Hudson River to eliminate the need for cooling towers.

2

1. The historic Castle Williams – built to defend New York against the British in 1812 – stands on the tip of Governors Island, overlooking lower Manhattan.

2. A view of the auditorium, which is evocative of an Elizabethan playhouse.

3. Cutaway drawing showing how the auditorium is contained within the massive masonry walls of the old fortress.

4, 5. Cross-sections through the auditorium and entrance foyer, respectively.

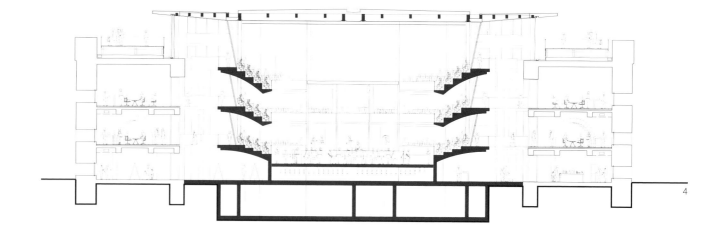

4

1

3

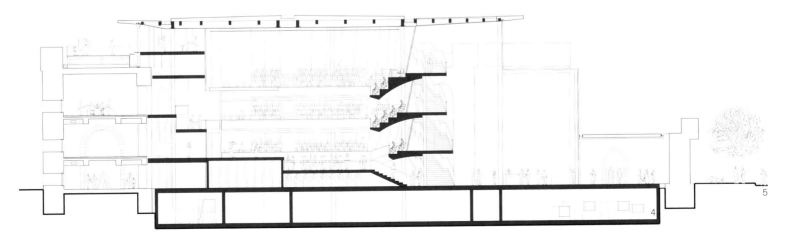

4

5

Zenith

St Etienne, France 2004–

A state-of-the-art music and cultural facility for Saint-Etienne, the Zenith will be the first such cultural venue to be built in the Rhône-Alpes region of central southern France. Won as the result of an international competition the project has two aims: to be a catalyst for the major cultural and regeneration initiatives being planned for this formerly industrial city; and to challenge sister city Lyons' historical monopoly on staging regional arts events, putting Saint-Etienne Métropole firmly on the cultural map.

The building's distinctive cantilevered roof structure was developed in response to aerodynamic studies. It is designed to act as a wind scoop to channel and intensify the flow of air through the building and reduce energy use. Cold air currents through the auditorium at night-time are harnessed, utilising the exposed concrete finishes in the auditorium as a radiant cooling surface, thereby reducing energy consumption. This system is fully reversible to take advantage of prevailing winds from both northerly and southerly directions. Additionally, the deep overhang of the roof canopy ensures that the glazed foyer is shaded from direct sunlight.

Access to the concert hall is via a broad ramped podium, incorporating artists' and backstage facilities, which bridges the busy Rue Scheurer Kestner and allows audience members to enter and exit quickly and efficiently. A glazed foyer organises internal circulation and provides access to all floors and visitor amenities. The auditorium is designed to be highly flexible and can be configured for audiences ranging from 1,100 to 7,200 people. Backstage facilities include changing and production spaces, staff refectories and delivery areas; there is also a VIP reception suite. A comprehensive landscape strategy links the Zenith to 1,200 car parking spaces and to a proposed landscaped pedestrian network leading to other leisure and cultural facilities and existing public transport connections.

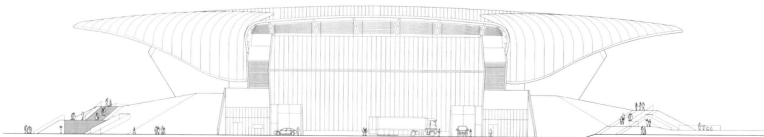

3

1, 2. Construction images taken in spring 2008.

3. Drawing of the north elevation.

4. Competition section through the auditorium and foyer. Artists' quarters, backstage facilities and set storage are incorporated into the landscaped podium on which the building sits.

1

2

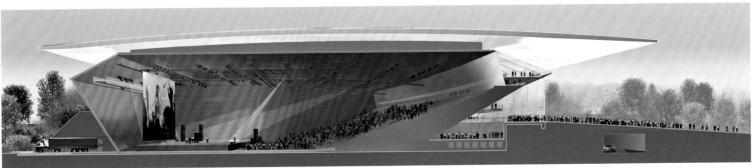

4

New Holland Island

St Petersburg, Russia 2006–

Edged by canals, and covering an area of 7.6 hectares, New Holland Island was created in the time of Peter the Great as a centre for shipbuilding. Over succeeding centuries it has served as a naval prison, been home to a naval radio station, and from Soviet times accommodated high-security naval and military facilities. The military recently ceded the island to the city, thus creating the opportunity for New Holland's dramatic reinvention as both a major cultural centre and a self-sufficient city district.

Reflecting a creative dialogue between old and new, the historic warehouses, originally built for timber storage, are reinvented as hotel and retail space and complemented by a range of amenities for the visual and performing arts. An office complex, which completes the missing side of the 'triangle', will establish the island as a venue for business as well as pleasure. An outdoor arena follows the contours of the dock basin to provide a venue for open-air performances, which can be flooded for regattas or frozen as a skating rink. The historic rotunda is adapted as a 400-seat recital hall for more traditional theatre, opera and dance and the main performance venue – the 2,000-seat Festival Hall – forms the centrepiece. An art gallery links the three performance venues at basement level. Using a sophisticated system of natural ventilation and an energy strategy that maximises the insulating properties of snow and the cooling potential of the surrounding canals, the island will be energy efficient and sustainable.

Crucially, the scheme provides the infrastructure to connect with the city at an urban scale. There will be a prominent gateway into the site from the major city artery of Nevsky Prospect and new bridges and routes will tie the island into a wider cultural quarter that includes the Mariinsky Theatre and the Hermitage Museum to establish a thriving, accessible centre for the arts. The project has the regenerative power to lift the fortunes of the surrounding areas, while locking itself into the heart of one of Europe's most dynamic cities.

1. An aerial model view looking west across the island.

2. Visualisation showing the central courtyard with existing warehouse buildings and hotels on the left and the main performance venue ahead.

3. The outdoor performance arena.

4. An aerial view of the scheme showing the dock basin in summer with a raised stage at its centre. In winter, the basin freezes to become an ice rink.

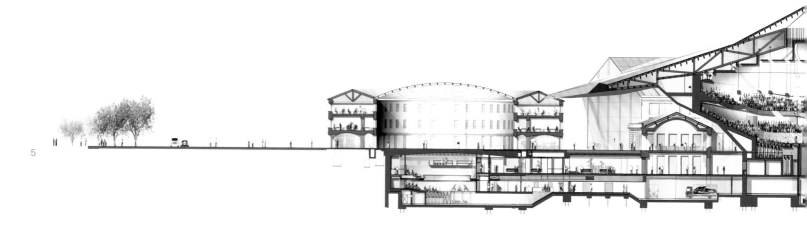

5

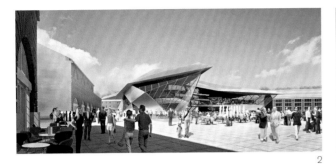

2

5. Section demonstrating the relationship between the three performance venues – the recital room beneath the rotunda, the festival hall and the outdoor arena. Gallery space is provided in the basement levels beneath.

3

4

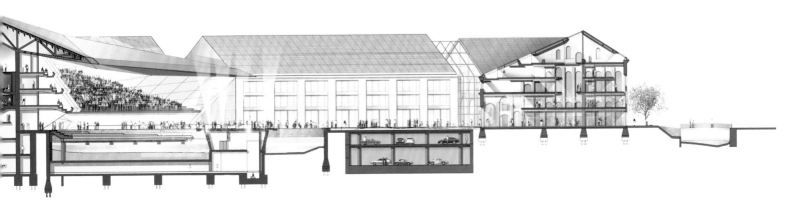

Pushkin Museum Cultural Quarter
Moscow, Russia 2007 –

The Pushkin is the finest museum of European art in Moscow and one of the world's great cultural institutions. Building on the experience of projects such as the Carré d'Art in Nîmes and the Great Court at the British Museum, in which cultural buildings were explored as part of a wider urban programme, this masterplan aims to establish a thriving cultural quarter focused on the Pushkin. Combining the best of old and new, the project is another step in the museum's evolutionary growth. It encompasses the restoration of the museum itself, the acquisition of surrounding villas and the creation of new buildings to more than triple the museum's exhibition and archive spaces and provide state-of-the-art facilities.

Located close to urban landmarks, including the Kremlin and the Cathedral of Christ the Saviour, the scheme celebrates connections to its wider urban context. Streets in the new quarter will be pedestrianised and its boulevards, courtyards and gardens unified with hard and soft landscaping. New connections will be forged by a covered axial network, which will allow visitors to move freely whatever the weather. Punctuated by light-wells, which draw in daylight and open up views, this underground route will enjoy a strong relationship with the environment above ground. There will also be discreet below-ground access for vehicles; and links to the nearby metro station will be improved.

The grand neoclassical museum building will have its formal entrance reinstated and its spectacular glazed roof restored. Two existing courtyards will be glazed, the west courtyard becoming a new focal point with access to subterranean exhibition spaces and other parts of the quarter. Among a range of new facilities are an administration building, a library and a 600-seat multi-functional concert hall. There will also be new shops, cafés and restaurants, and a boutique hotel. When it is completed, the new quarter will see the Pushkin's visitor numbers increase five fold to approximately 5 million a year, comparable with the British Museum or the Louvre in Paris.

1, 2. Visualisations of the courtyard that provides access to a network of subterranean walkways; and a pedestrian route along the tree-lined boulevard to the east of the museum.

3. The grand main approach to the museum building will be re-established.

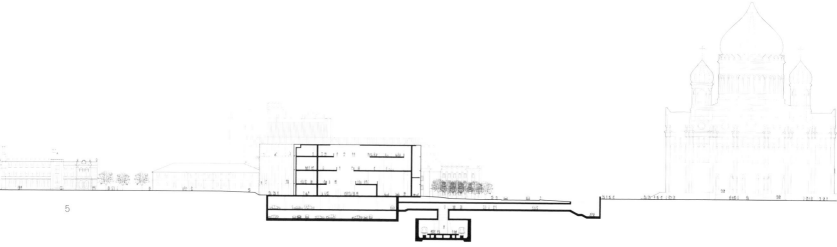

5

3

4. Model of the new cultural quarter; the restored museum building is in the centre, with the new exhibition space to the east and concert hall and library to the west.

5. Long section through the main building showing the relationship with St Basil's Cathedral and the Kremlin.

4

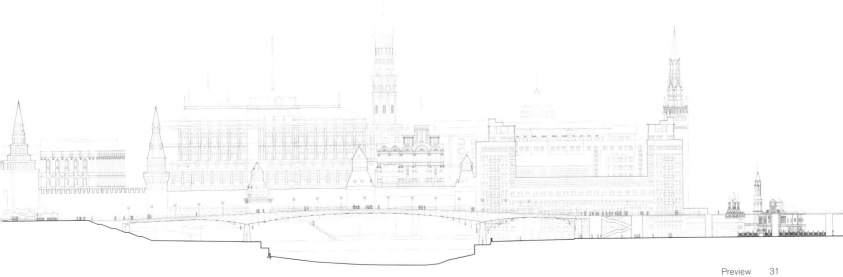

IM Valery Gergiev Cultural Centre

Vladikavkaz, Russia 2007 –

This scheme for the Maestro Valery Gergiev cultural complex, in the historic heart of the northern Caucasus city of Vladikavkaz, will create a new focus for the city, adding to its rich cultural heritage and bringing world-class performance spaces to the region. With Mount Kazbek and the Caucasus mountains forming a dramatic backdrop, and located next to the fast-flowing River Terek, the sculptural forms of the concert hall buildings are designed to echo the region's glacial mountainous landscape.

The main 1,200-seat hall is a natural acoustic philharmonic concert hall. It faces on to Svoboda Square, forming the termination of the axis generated by the Boulevard of Peace. Located next to it is a smaller, 500-seat flexible multi-purpose hall, which reaches into the riverside park along the East bank of the Terek. These two halls are connected at river bank level by a concourse that unites the whole complex. The concourse acts as a foyer for both halls and forms the spine of the commercial facilities that spread along the riverside park. The organic form of the concourse extends further into the park landscape to create a new outdoor theatre and areas for cafés and outdoor dining.

The complex is to be extended across the River Terek on to the west bank by a new pedestrian bridge, giving access to school, library, youth and cinema facilities that will be constructed in a second phase of development. These facilities will be housed in similar but smaller forms to those housing the two performance halls. When it is completed, it is hoped that the Gergiev cultural complex will become a thriving, sustainable centre for the arts and culture for Vladikavkaz and for the whole North Ossetian-Alanian Republic, of which the city is the capital, providing a catalyst for further development and becoming an important tourist attraction in its own right.

4

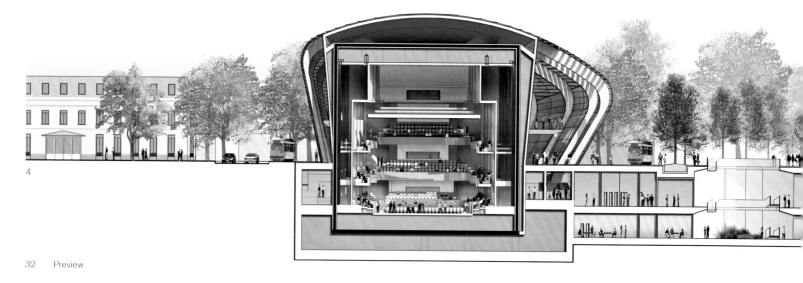

1, 2. The complex seen from Freedom Square and from across the Terek river.

3. Visualisation of the entrance foyer of Hall 1.

4. North-south section through Hall 1, the 1,200-seat philharmonic concert hall, and Hall 2, a 500-seat multi-purpose venue, with the artists' entrance between.

1

2

3

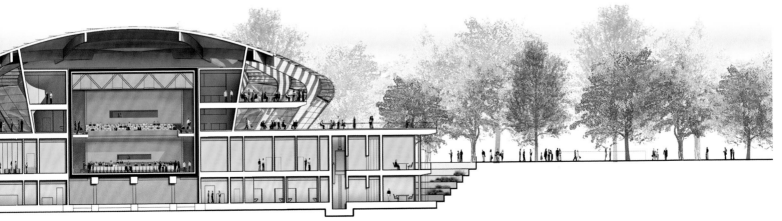

Quartermile Masterplan
Edinburgh, Scotland 2001–

The Quartermile development is one of the largest and most comprehensive regeneration schemes in Scotland. Formerly the home of the historic Edinburgh Royal Infirmary, the 8-hectare site is located within a conservation area on Edinburgh's Victorian fringes and includes nine listed buildings. It lies between the heart of the city and the parkland of the Meadows and falls within the central area of Edinburgh designated a World Heritage Site by UNESCO in 1995. This scheme for its renewal extends the practice's investigations into the creation of sustainable, mixed-use urban communities, continuing themes first explored in schemes such as the King's Cross and Duisburg Inner Harbour masterplans.

The Royal Infirmary hospital campus was originally open and accessible, but a cumulative series of additions had the effect of rendering it impenetrable, isolating it physically and visually from the surrounding city. The starting point for the Quartermile scheme, therefore, was to open the site up, creating a network of pedestrian routes and landscaped public spaces that draw the park directly into its heart, creating a strong sense of place and reinforcing pedestrian connections to the centre, allowing it to become a vibrant, integral part of the city once again.

New construction is combined with the selective refurbishment of the historic buildings, with the new woven carefully into the grain of the old. The scheme provides housing, high-quality office space, a five-star hotel, restaurants, cafés and shops. Apartment buildings are located at the quieter edges of the site while offices and shops are concentrated in the centre. The commercial buildings frame a new public plaza – the 'Quartermile' – which accommodates a performance space for concerts and other events. The first phases include the construction of three residential buildings, an underground car park, and the completion of Number One Quartermile Square, a seven-storey office building that offers dramatic views of Edinburgh Castle to the north and Quartermile to the south and forms a striking gateway to the development.

1

1. A completed Quartermile apartment building overlooking Middle Meadow Walk; retail spaces occupy the ground floor.

2. Drawing indicating how the new buildings are inserted between the historic structures.

Right: aerial visualisation of the masterplan area looking north; The Meadows is in the foreground; in the distance are Edinburgh Castle and the new town.

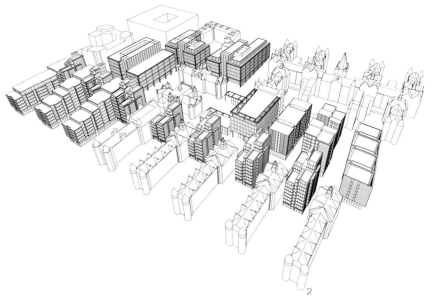

2

Crystal Island
Moscow, Russia 2006–

Located on the wooded Nagatino Peninsula, 7.5km from the centre of Moscow, Crystal Island is conceived as a compact, diverse urban quarter – a city in microcosm – sheltered against the winter and summer extremes of Moscow's climate. Rising from a large public square, the entire development is enclosed within a vast tent-like superstructure, with one of the tallest enclosed public spaces in the world at its heart. It comprises a mix of apartments, offices, hotels, a school and shops, together with a range of cultural, exhibition and performance venues – places to live, work, relax and be entertained – all within easy walking distance. High in its peak – 300 metres above ground level – is a viewing platform with a panoramic view of the Moscow skyline.

The scheme is located in a landscaped park, edged by the Moscow River. The park itself forms another key amenity, providing a range of activities throughout the year, with cross country skiing and ice skating in winter and cycling and jogging in summer. The building's spiralling geometry generates a diagonal grid structure, 450 metres high, which combines economy of form with optimum structural rigidity. The underlying geometry extends out into the park to provide a framework for future development, while the arrangement of the accommodation at the perimeter allows the scheme to grow organically over time.

Efficient energy management is at the heart of the design. The external envelope creates a thermal buffer and performs as a breathable second skin, able to seal itself in winter to minimise heat losses, and to open up in summer so that the interior spaces can be cooled naturally. Passive strategies include organising the different elements of the programme to achieve an overall energy consumption balance. Sustainable initiatives include on-site renewable and low-carbon energy generation; and a wind farm is integrated within the top of the superstructure to exploit the high wind speeds at this elevation and maximise yields, enabling the scheme to meet a proportion of its own energy needs.

1

3

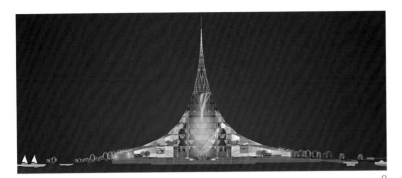

2

1. Sketch by Norman Foster.

2. Cross-section through the atrium – the tallest enclosed public space in the world.

3. Looking north over the Moscow River towards the city. The building's spiral structure is integrated seamlessly with the landscape of the surrounding park. Russia Tower is visible in the distance.

Milano Santa Giulia Masterplan
Milan, Italy 2004 –

Like many large cities, Milan is bordered by former industrial areas that can be reclaimed and brought to life as attractive, sustainable urban communities. The Santa Giulia site is blessed by a combination of size, location and excellent transport connections. It lies close to the heart of the city, yet near to leafy suburbs. The question was: is it possible to have the advantages of the city and suburbia without the problems of either? The answer is a series of balancing acts – urbanity with parks, pedestrians with traffic, old with new, public transport with private cars – to create a 'city within a city'.

The success of the traditional city is its vertical layering – for example, shops and cafés at street level with housing or offices above – which is recreated here. The urban core of Santa Giulia is organised around a broad boulevard – the Promenade – which combines offices and apartments with restaurants and shops. These, and the other residential and commercial buildings, are integrated with formal public spaces and gardens. Uniquely in the context of Milan, the focus of the scheme is a new 37-hectare public park. A place for leisure pursuits and relaxation for the 12,000 people who will live here, it will also serve metropolitan Milan as a whole – a 'green oasis' in the city.

Environmental and ecological issues have been addressed at every level, from the creation of green space to the orientation of the buildings; their flexibility and life span; the materials used to build them; and the energy they consume. By balancing the vitality of urban life against the calming influence of nature, Santa Giulia will offer a welcoming environment with a strong sense of place. Within the vision of the masterplan, architects, artists and sculptors from around the world are being invited to contribute individual buildings and works of art. The aim is to create a project that will be a beacon to other cities facing sustainable development challenges of this kind. It's about 'thinking global and acting local'.

4

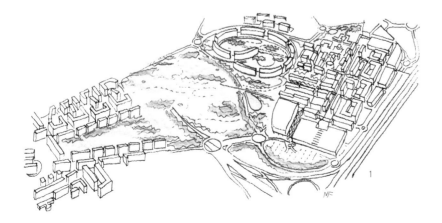

1

1. Axonometric sketch by Norman Foster showing the masterplan area viewed from the south.

2. The living room of the Santa Giulia show flat.

3. Cross-section through the main promenade illustrating its vertical layering – shops and cafés line the street level with housing and offices above.

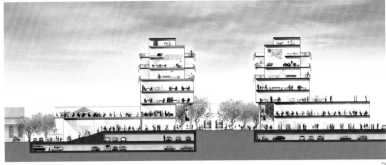

4. An aerial rendering of the masterplan area, showing the park, the crescent housing and the commercial district.

5. A view of the promenade with its shops and cafés.

Russia Tower
Moscow, Russia 2005–

Located in Moscow City, 5.5km from Red Square, Russia Tower will be a mixed-use, super-dense vertical city for 25,000 people, with offices, a hotel, shopping and apartments with private gardens. At 600 metres high, with 118 occupied floors, it will be the tallest naturally ventilated tower in the world and one of the greenest new buildings in Europe. Continuing themes first explored in the Tokyo Millennium Tower, the project extends the practice's investigation into the nature of the tall building, taking structural, functional, environmental and urban logic to a new level.

Based on a highly efficient geometry derived from a triangular plan with an open 'green' spine, the building's primary structure comprises three 'arms' that taper as they rise. They create a slender pyramidal form that achieves maximum stability with minimum structure and allows the most effective distribution of space. The higher floors containing residential and hotel accommodation are designed as a series of modular units that can be configured individually. Apartments benefit from fresh air, natural light, double- or triple-height volumes and access to sky gardens. At the summit, public viewing decks with cafés and bars create a magnetic new attraction for visitors and residents, while an ice-rink and shops add vitality to life at street level.

The environmental strategy harnesses a range of passive techniques and controls. Strategically, mixed-use offers a strong starting point, allowing energy balance throughout the day as people move between office and home. Structurally, the tower's slender profile creates shallow floor plates that maximise daylight penetration and increase the potential for natural ventilation. The triple-glazed, high-performance facade reduces heat loss; photovoltaics supply the building's energy needs and feed electricity back into the city grid; energy recycling reduces heating demand by 20 per cent; and snow and rain water harvesting is expected to cut fresh water consumption for toilets by a third. Socially and environmentally, Russia Tower offers a sustainable new solution for contemporary living.

1

2

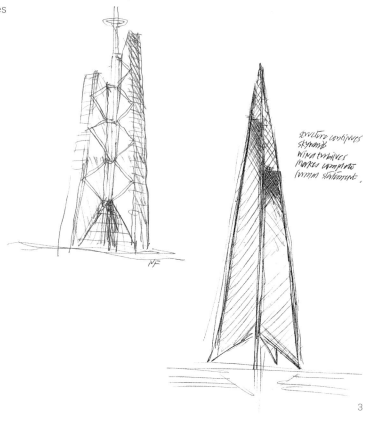

3

1. Looking into the pyramidal entrance atrium space. There are separate entrances for each 'arm' of the building – containing residential, commercial and hotel elements – and each has a separate address. The efficiency of the structural geometry allows the atrium to be fully glazed, ensuring that the space is flooded with light.

2. A view of the tower's summit with its observation decks and solar collectors.

3. Early sketches by Norman Foster exploring two structural options and the possibility of varying the heights of the building's three 'arms'.

4. A visualisation of the tower at night. The building's reverse fan structure gives it great strength and stability; the relatively shallow 21-metre-wide floor plates of each 'arm' are the key to bringing natural light into the building.

4

Central Market

Abu Dhabi, UAE 2006–

The historic Abu Dhabi Central Market is one of the oldest sites in the city. Inspired by the traditional architecture of the Gulf this scheme aims to reinvent the market place as a contemporary mixed-use complex and give the city a new civic heart. By offering an alternative to the globalised 'one-size-fits-all' shopping mall it offers a distinctive modern interpretation of the regional vernacular. As a shopping experience it combines luxury goods shops with food markets and craft-based trades. Like the traditional souk, these different experiences are brought together in an interior architecture of dappled sunlight, vibrant colours and running water, with a changing rhythm of squares, courtyards and alleyways.

Rising above this dense, close-grained 'mat' are three towers, each with a separate address, which vary in height and bulk depending on whether they contain offices, residences or a combination of a hotel and serviced apartments. Visually they form a family, with smooth reflective facades designed to need little maintenance in this dusty desert environment. To maximise the ground plane, the towers are grouped together, but spaced sufficiently apart to enhance privacy and views. The effect is a harmonious cluster – a symbol for this central site and a new landmark on the Abu Dhabi skyline.

The development has a strong sustainable agenda, with solar collectors and layers of internal shading on the towers to control glare and solar gain. Continuing the characteristic greenery of Abu Dhabi, the site is generously landscaped, the roofs of the lower buildings forming a series of terraced gardens. For four months of the year the climate here is very pleasant – comfortable enough to stroll and sit outside. This has inspired a sequence of public routes and spaces in which barriers between inside and outside are dissolved. Cooling naturally when conditions allow, for the remainder of the year these spaces can be enclosed by roofs or walls that slide into place to enable the internal environment to be more closely controlled.

1

1. Model view, showing the publicly accessible roof gardens arranged above the souk.

2. An early sketch by Norman Foster, showing the shaded route through the souk.

3. Visualisation of one of the courtyards; the shading system comprises movable shutters that track the path of the sun.

4. Looking along one of the malls, which contain more traditional shops selling things such as arts and crafts and spices.

2

3

4

Masdar
Abu Dhabi, UAE 2007–

This pioneering new development explores sustainable technologies and the planning principles of the traditional walled city to create a desert community that will be carbon neutral and zero waste. The 640-hectare project is the first to result from the Masdar Initiative, which was established by the government of Abu Dhabi to promote renewable energies in the Gulf. It will be a centre for the development of new ideas for energy production in the region and attract the highest levels of international expertise and commerce.

Masdar offers a benchmark for the carbon-neutral city of the future. Its environmental ambitions are not only unrivalled internationally, they have also provided a highly challenging design brief that promises to turn conventional urban wisdom on its head. A mixed-use, low-rise, high-density city designed for a population of 90,000 people, the programme includes a new university and the headquarters for Abu Dhabi's Future Energy Company, together with special economic zones and an Innovation Centre. Strategically located for Abu Dhabi's principal transport infrastructure, Masdar will be linked to surrounding communities and the international airport by a network of existing road and new rail routes. The city itself will be car-free. With a maximum distance of 200 metres to the nearest rapid transport links and amenities, the city is designed to encourage walking, while its compact network of shaded streets and alleyways evoke the strong architectural identity of Abu Dhabi, creating an attractive pedestrian environment, sheltered from the extremes of the harsh climate.

Masdar will be built in several phases over a seven-year period. Expansion has been anticipated from the outset, allowing for urban growth yet avoiding the problem of sprawl that besets so many cities. The city comprises two walled quarters, the larger of which will be completed first. The surrounding land will contain wind and photovoltaic farms, research fields and plantations, so that the community will be entirely energy self-sufficient.

1. A visualisation of one of the public courtyards within the city, which resonate with the traditional architecture of the region.

2. A detailed view of the university quarter, emphasising the city's layering and mix of uses. Laboratory buildings are seen on the left, with apartments on the right.

3. A rooftop view of the city looking south.

Opposite: an aerial view of the entire development, showing the relationship between the two city quarters and the central spine that connects the city to Abu Dhabi's principal transport infrastructure. The photovoltaic field seen in the foreground will contribute to the city's power generation.

Projects in Libya
Libya 2007–

The practice is working on a range of projects in Libya, from a waterfront and marina in Tripoli, to a masterplan for the Green Mountain region of Eastern Libya. Although these projects are programmatically diverse, they share an underlying theme which is to find ways of developing – or repairing the scars of earlier development – that will be environmentally sensitive and sustainable.

Covering some 5,500 square kilometers, the Green Mountain region is an area of outstanding natural beauty and biodiversity, described as 'one of the ten last paradises of the Mediterranean'. The region is also rich with archaeological remains, including the UNESCO World Heritage Site at Cyrene. The Green Mountain Conservation and Development Authority has been established to oversee the creation and management of a National Park and other archaeological conservation areas; and it has identified locations for compact, mixed-use development that will combine commerce with amenities for cultural and environmental tourism. Currently, the studio is developing three such projects. The emphasis is on sustainable infrastructure, including renewable power generation, waste management and recycling facilities, and closed-loop water systems, with the goal of moving towards carbon neutrality on a regional scale. A further challenge is to establish sustainable industries, including fishing, organic agriculture and manufacturing based on new technologies.

The waterfront scheme near Tripoli is designed to reinforce the city's historic relationship with the coastline. Located on the Mediterranean coast, east of the walled medina, it is a lively, mixed-use quarter informed by the existing compact urban grain of the city. Arranged in dense city blocks the buildings are set around traditional internal courtyards and semi-private gardens, overlooked by balconies and verandas. The active fishing harbour is adjacent to new shops, cafés and restaurants lining a waterside promenade. Constituting a substantial extension of Tripoli's sea frontage, the project is designed to respect and connect with the historic medina while creating a dynamic new urban quarter for the social and economic development of the city.

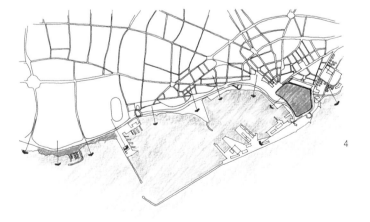

4

1. Canyon Resort – view from the hotel.

2. Temple of Zeus, Cyrene.

3. With its rich archaelogical heritage, the Green Mountain region has great potential as a tourist destination.

4. Drawing of Tripoli's waterfront highlighting the Medina (the old city) and the Marina.

5. Aerial model view of the Marina; new city blocks are set around courtyards.

6. Night-time view of the Marina looking inland.

1

2

3

5

6

Circle Hospital
Bath, England 2006–

There is a wealth of evidence to suggest that a well-designed hospital environment can reduce recovery times and contribute to better outcomes for patients, while providing a more attractive workplace for medical staff. Circle is a privately funded initiative which plans to build a chain of health campuses in the UK that will place patients at the centre of a new approach to healthcare. Patients will be treated irrespective of whether they are paid for by private insurance or through the National Health Service (NHS) under the UK Government's 'Choose and Book' scheme.

Circle Bath is among the first of these new centres to be designed. The architectural ambition is to re-cast the hospital building as a humane and civilised place for all those who use it. Everyone in the hospital – whether a surgeon, nurse or porter – is regarded as a 'partner' in the delivery of healthcare, with a common goal of promoting patient well-being. The building provides operating theatres, bedrooms, consultation, treatment and recovery spaces, and offers both inpatient and outpatient accommodation. It is relatively small in scale – with a floor area of 6,000 square metres – which lends it an intimate atmosphere and avoids the confusion and disorientation common in larger hospitals. Divisions between departments are minimised, easing the stress involved in consultation, treatment and recovery for patients and reducing walking distances for staff. A shared double-height atrium – which contains a café, nurses' station and reception point – provides a central focus for patients and staff alike.

The building is dug into its hillside site, its profile kept low, with public entry arranged at the higher level and service access below. Throughout the building, there is an emphasis on natural light and views: recovery spaces on the lower level are fully glazed, as are the operating theatres, and both look out on to a private garden. Balconies line the building's northern and southern edges, oriented to maximise views across the surrounding rolling countryside. Sympathetic landscaping further emphasises the therapeutic natural environment – an overall approach very different from more familiar hospital surroundings.

1

2

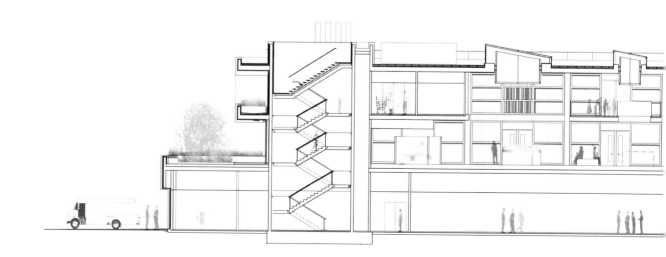

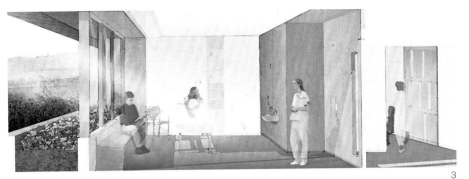

3

1. An outpatient consultation room.

2. Inpatient bedroom, with views over the landscape.

3. Perspective section of an inpatient bedroom.

4. The atrium forms the focal point of the hospital.

5. Long section through the atrium.

4

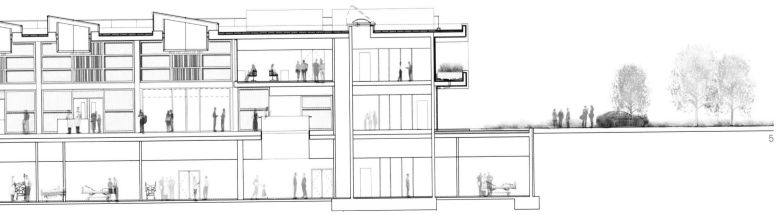

5

City of Justice
Madrid, Spain 2006 –

The Campus of Justice at Valdebebas Park is part of a wider masterplan to redevelop this area of Madrid into a thriving new commercial and residential community. This scheme aims to reinvent the judicial process in the region, bringing all the relevant buildings together to create the largest campus of its kind in Europe. The design of the first two elements – the Audiencia Provincial (Regional Appeals Court) and the smaller Tribunal Superior de Justicia (High Court) – is intended to articulate the values of transparency and accountability that lie at the heart of the judicial system.

Circular in form, and designed to avoid the conventional hierarchy of 'front' and 'back', the two buildings address each other across an open plaza. The larger building, the Audiencia Provincial, is organised around a soaring central atrium that rises through all six levels. On the ground floor a shallow pool – reminiscent of the use of water in traditional Spanish architecture – reflects daylight and helps to cool and humidify the air. The first two levels are occupied by courtrooms, which are clustered in groups that relate to the division of the courts into criminal, civil and mercantile. On the upper levels, offices line the perimeter and meeting rooms look into the atrium, while the president's suite is raised symbolically at the top of the building. The smaller Tribunal Superior de Justicia opens into a central triangular atrium which looks up to the courtrooms at the top of the building. Here, the lower floors are occupied by offices, with a section adjoining the atrium that provides information and help to the public.

The environmental strategy has been a key driver of the design. Interior gardens play an ecological role, bringing in daylight and fresh air and enhancing a sense of openness and lightness. The scheme also takes advantage of Madrid's abundant sunshine by incorporating photovoltaics to harness solar energy; and the facades maximise translucency, while incorporating natural shading to minimise solar gain.

1

2

1. A courtroom in the Tribunal Superior de Justicia.

2. One of eight patios in the Audiencia Provincial.

3-5. Sketches exploring, from left: the relationship between the Tribunal Superior de Justicia and the larger Audiencia Provincial; the atrium of the Tribunal Superior; and the atrium in the Audiencia Provincial.

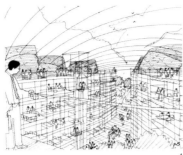

6. The two buildings face each other across a public plaza; the Audiencia Provincial is to the right.

7. Cross-section through the two buildings; the Superior de Justicia is on the left.

3

4

5

6

YachtPlus 40 Boat Fleet
2005 –

This series of 40-metre, long-range cruising yachts for the YachtPlus fractionally owned luxury fleet is the latest in a line of nautical commissions that began with the design of the 58-metre motor yacht *Izanami* in 1993 and continued with the sailing yacht *Dark Shadow* in 2002. In exchange for a share in a specific yacht, YachtPlus owners will acquire year-round access to a fully crewed and serviced fleet in the Mediterranean in summer and the Caribbean in winter. Each yacht can carry twelve guests, with a crew of eight, and has a maximum speed of 17.5 knots. Cruising at a steady 16 knots it will have a range of 950 nautical miles – a voyage, say, from Monte Carlo to Capri.

The yachts are being built and fitted out in the yards of Rodriquez Cantieri Navali's high-tech luxury yacht division near La Spezia in Italy. Like *Izanami*, the hulls are of aluminium alloy, with composite used for the superstructure. While the yachts have a conventional semi-displacement hull and diesel propulsion systems, their overall form represents a striking departure from precedent. The superstructure is placed far forward to maximise outdoor terrace space, and the interiors are opened up to daylight and views. The owner's suite is located at the prow, arranged so that it points the course of the yacht, articulating the thrill of living on the water.

Fully glazed bulkheads and wide window openings dissolve divisions between inside and outside, and the teak planking of the main deck runs through the length of the main saloon, creating a sense of continuity from the decks to the living spaces. The different deck levels are connected by a glass spiral staircase, designed to draw daylight down through the guest accommodation, while reflective wall finishes will maximise the spread of light. At night, state-of-the-art lighting systems integrated into scene-setting ceilings can change the mood and atmosphere of every space, adding a further dramatic dimension to life at sea.

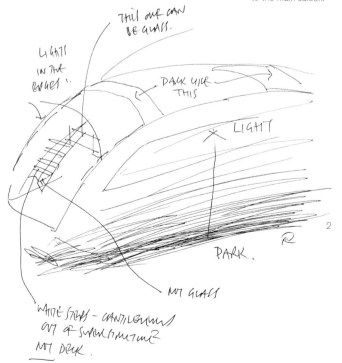

1

1. Aft visualisation showing the Hollywood stair connecting the beach deck, main deck, panoramic deck and sun deck.

2. Sketch study of the yacht's curved form by David Nelson.

3–5. A yacht under construction in the shipyard at La Spezia.

6. Visualisation of the boat in motion.

7, 8. Construction views looking up the circular stair well and along the main deck to the main saloon.

2

3

4

5

6

7

8

The Khan Shatyr Entertainment Centre
Astana, Kazakhstan 2006 –

Astana, the new capital of Kazakhstan, is being constructed in an austere eastern landscape with an inhospitable climate that can generate temperatures of -35°C in winter and +35°C in summer. The Khan Shatyr Entertainment Centre will provide the city with a range of civic, cultural and social amenities sheltered within a climatic envelope – a 'world within' – that offers a comfortable microclimate and lush landscape, year round, whatever the weather.

Located at the northern end of the new city axis, the masted structure soars 150 metres from an elliptical base to form the highest peak on the Astana skyline. Enclosing an area in excess of 100,000 square metres it comprises an urban-scaled park, along with a wide variety of shopping and leisure facilities, including cafés, restaurants and cinemas, and entertainment spaces that can accommodate a varied programme of events and exhibitions. The park steps up the height of the building in undulating terraces. A tropical water park, weaves its way through the landscape and its wave pools, river and waterfall are lit by roof-lights that are seamlessly integrated into the design. The highest terrace forms a viewing deck with dramatic views over the city and the Steppes beyond.

The tent-like cable-net structure is clad in a three-layer ETFE envelope, a material that allows daylight to wash the interiors while sheltering them from weather extremes. While the buildings within the envelope are fully conditioned, the target temperatures in the landscaped areas are +15°C in winter and +30°C in summer. In winter, a key challenge is to prevent the formation of ice on the inside of the envelope. This is achieved by a combination of temperature control and directing warm air currents up the inner fabric surface, a strategy that also prevents downdraughts. In summer, fritting on the outermost foil layer provides solar shading. Inside, low-level jets direct cool air across the space, while opening vents at the apex induce stack-effect ventilation.

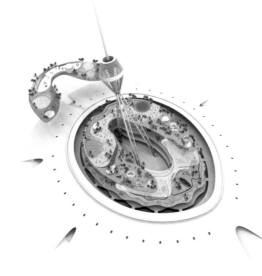

1. An early study model showing the internal landscaping.

2. Drawing showing the steel cable net encircling the building's central steel mast.

3. Model illustrating how the five entrances are impressed into the sloping landscape.

1

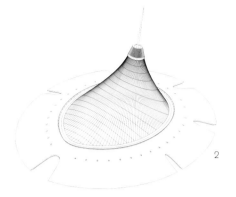

4. Visualisation of the complex at night; the lower two levels in the podium will house retail spaces.

5. A view of the aqua park and indoor beach.

6. Looking up through the building from the central events space at ground level.

Resorts and Hotels

2003 –

Ideas for a sustainable resort community were first developed by the practice as far back as 1975, with a study for the Canary Island of Gomera. Yet it is only more recently that projects have provided the opportunity to develop some of these early concepts. These projects illustrate the benefit of a truly integrated approach, where everything is considered, from the views, the terraces and the impact on the environment down to the quality of finishes. Another theme is the creation of highly flexible, boundary-free spaces, where for example, pools continue from external terraces through to living spaces; or bathrooms are integrated within the main bedroom suite.

The Silken Hotel in London, the New Dolder Grand in Zurich and the Clarence Hotel in Dublin are examples of city retreats, where the fabric of the existing historic structures has been celebrated and complemented with a modern intervention. These three hotels combine a sensitive approach to the historical legacy of their respective sites, while creating a contemporary hotel experience. Whether the soaring atrium at the Silken, the Steinhalle at the Dolder or the 'sky catcher' at the Clarence, these central spaces bring a sense of drama to the hotel experience and continue the practice's investigation into the idea of the 'urban room'.

In contrast to the urban nature of these hotels, the practice is developing environmentally discreet resorts in Mauritius and Turkey. The strategy for the former is driven by the need to generate reforestation and minimise the visual and physical impact of the resort on this beautiful coastal stretch. Designed as a series of gardens within a garden, water is a dominant theme with pools and fountains establishing a sense of calm. The resort is car free and uses sustainable strategies for water collection. Similarly, the resort in Bodrum, Turkey, is self-sustaining, conceived as a year-round community. It employs indigenous construction techniques and is planned around traditional courtyards that resonate with its wider cultural and architectural context.

4

5

1, 2. Renderings of the Sentosa Island Resort, Singapore (2003–).

3. A villa within the Bodrum Sustainable Resort Community with panoramic views over the Aegean Sea (2007–).

3

6

4, 5. The luxury Corniche Bay villas in Mauritius look out to sea (2006–).

6. The Marina Hotel in Bodrum is set in the hillside behind the promenade.

1. The quayside facade of the Clarence Hotel in Dublin (2006–).

2. A cross-section through the 'sky catcher' of the Clarence Hotel.

3, 4. A hotel room in the Hotel Puerta America, Madrid (2004–2005).

5. Plan study of the Puerta America hotel room by Norman Foster.

1

2

6

8

9

10

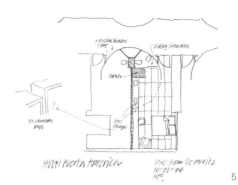

3

4

5

6. The Dolder Grand Hotel in Zurich; two new wings frame the central tower and spire of the historic hotel (2004–2008).

7. Winding stone walls that begin in the landscape wrap inside to define a pool in the Dolder's spa.

7

11

12

8. Sketch by Norman Foster exploring the approach to the Dolder, which exploits the panoramic views over Zurich.

9, 10. Stencil-cut aluminium balustrades line the Dolder's new wings, their design resonating with the forms of the surrounding forest.

11. The Silken Hotel, London at the intersection of the Strand and Aldwych (2004–).

12. The bar on the tenth floor of the Silken Hotel.

Aldar Al Raha Beach Development
Abu Dhabi, UAE 2006–

The Al Dana Precinct is the centrepiece of Al Raha Beach – a new waterfront city east of Abu Dhabi. The design strategy is a highly specific response to the climate and topography of this dramatic coastal site and the building has evolved through a process of sophisticated environmental computer analysis. The resulting scheme resolves the contradictions of the site: it provides shade yet also admits light; it is cooled by a natural flow of air yet is buffered against the strong desert wind; it is asymmetrical and sculptural yet it is environmentally and functionally coherent.

Al Dana sits at the eastern end of the semi-circular marina of Al Raha, extending outward to include a peninsula which will accommodate a new convention centre. The project brings together a carefully chosen mix of offices, apartments, hotel and shops to encourage a constant pattern of economic and social activity throughout the day. The building's sinuous form rises up to a tower to the east and is wrapped in a shimmering, undulating louvred shading system that is angled to minimise solar gain depending on orientation. The main entrance to the south connects to a soaring central atrium, which is buffered from the climatic extremes by the apartments and the conditioned offices that line the perimeter.

Although the form of the building appears to be intuitive, its logic is rooted in a sustainable environmental strategy that relies on a series of passive controls. To the south, the building is indented to reduce the area of the building most vulnerable to direct sunlight, with the services and circulation cores occupying most of the remaining exposed areas. At ground level, the overhang of the roof creates a shaded walkway that wraps around the site, and the roof is streamlined according to the prevailing winds to encourage cooling air currents around and through the building.

2

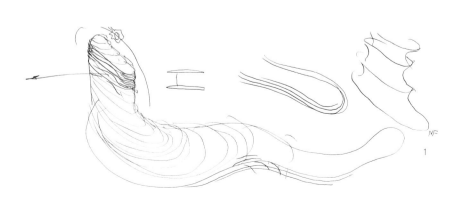

1

1. Concept sketch by Norman Foster.

2, 3. Visualisations of the scheme in the context of the Al Raha marina.

4. Model view; the new buildings extend from the hotel tower in the east to retail spaces in the centre of the marina.

3

4

Johnson Wax Company – Project Honor
Racine, USA 2006–

In 1935 H F Johnson Jr – chairman of S C Johnson – embarked on a remarkable 15,000-mile flight to Brazil in a Sikorsky-38 amphibious plane in search of a sustainable source of natural wax: the Carnaúba palm tree. Sixty-three years later, Johnson's son Sam retraced that flight in a replica of the Carnaúba plane to complete a historic family journey. Located on the S C Johnson headquarters campus in Wisconsin, Project Honor creates two companion buildings: Fortaleza Hall, which will form a permanent home for the replica Carnaúba and convey the extraordinary story of H F Johnson's flight; and the Community Building, which will give the campus a new social heart.

An initial masterplanning study of the campus revealed the ideal development site, adjacent to Frank Lloyd Wright's celebrated Johnson Wax office building and research tower. The new buildings anchor an area conceived as a 'town square', the Community Building being close in spirit to a collegiate 'commons'. In contrast to the more solid and internalised Wright buildings, Fortaleza Hall is completely transparent, with an oval form designed to give a 360 degree view of the Carnaúba. Visitors will view the aircraft suspended in mid-air, as if in flight. Alongside it will be photographs of the original plane and mementoes of the two expeditions.

The Community Building accommodates a wide range of staff facilities, including a restaurant, shops and gymnasium. It is conceived as a gathering place, where Johnson's staff will meet and spend time together. Essentially a rectangular building, it curves in on one side to follow the form of Fortaleza Hall. With its load-bearing Kasota stone walls, it forms a visual counterpoint to the steel and glass structure of the hall, echoing the surrounding masonry buildings. The two buildings are linked by a glazed atrium and lift lobby, which connects via an undercroft to the matrix of tunnels that form the principal communications network through the campus.

1

1. Site plan, showing the location of the new building within the S C Johnson headquarters campus.

2. An early sketch study by Norman Foster.

3. Visualisation at dusk, showing the approach to the hall from the campus, with the new Community Building curving round to the right.

2

3

4

5

6

4. The exterior of Fortaleza Hall at ground level, with Frank Lloyd Wright's Research Tower visible in the background.

5. The glazed wall of the Community Building viewed from the first floor balcony.

6. Looking into Fortaleza Hall, with a replica of H F Johnson's Sikorsky-38 aircraft suspended overhead.

Motor City
Alcañiz, Spain 2007–

La Ciudad del Motor – Motor City – will be a major mixed-use leisure and cultural destination within a new motor sports centre in the city of Alcañiz, in the Aragon region of Spain. The project was won as the result of an international competition, and is one of a number of significant new schemes in Spain, which include Madrid's City of Justice, the Torre Caja Madrid, a winery for Faustino and a masterplan for Seville. Motor City is conceived as a centre of excellence for motor sport, a dynamic counterpoint to this historic city and an exemplar of sustainable design. The wider development includes a technological park – complete with extensive vehicle testing facilities to rival any Grand Prix circuit – and a world-class grandstand.

The building comprises a hotel tower and a series of four double-height enclosures, which will accommodate shops, restaurants and cafés and a range of galleries and public event spaces. The pebble-like form of these enclosures is inspired by the contours of the surrounding landscape and by the sleek aerodynamic aesthetic of the racing car. Rooted in an environmental strategy that uses passive controls as well as harnessing renewable energy to enable the entire complex to be broadly carbon neutral, the building's smooth forms are sculpted in response to solar and wind patterns. The corridors between the enclosures draw natural ventilation and light deep inside the complex and their orientation welcomes visitors through to the grandstand while maximising views.

Integrated within the lightweight canopy that floats over the entire scheme are photovoltaic cells and solar thermal tubes, which together with an array of wind turbines will provide the development with zero-carbon heat and power. The roof appears as a single element which sweeps up to meet the hotel tower that gives the development its identity. When illuminated at night, the tower will become a beacon for Motor City, echoing the nearby Parador of Alcañiz, and herald a new era of sustainable development for the region.

3

4

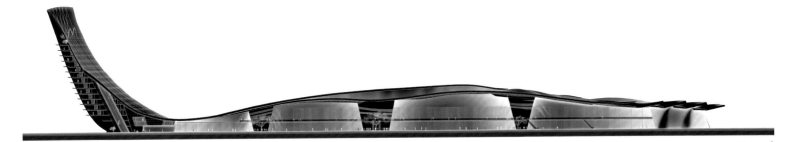

1. Cross-section through the
hotel tower and roof canopy.

2. Visualisation of the
Grand Prix circuit in use.

3, 4. Two views of the
interior; versatile drum-like
spaces can be used as
exhibition spaces or shops.

5. Openings in the roof
canopy allow natural
ventilation.

6. The central circulation
spine bathed in natural light.

5

6

Camp Nou Stadium

Barcelona, Spain 2007–

Home to FC Barcelona, Camp Nou Stadium is already the largest in Europe, with over 98,000 seats. The challenge of this project is to reinvent the existing stadium, enlarging it to accommodate 106,000 fans and provide greatly enhanced public areas and increased hospitality facilities. The project goes beyond a simple refurbishment to impact on the spirit of the place. El Barça is 'more than a club', and in that sense Camp Nou is 'more than a stadium': it is a symbol of the pride the fans feel for their team; a landmark for the city of Barcelona, and beyond that for the Catalan people.

The original stadium was designed by architects Mitjans-Miró, García Barbon and Soteras Mauri and inaugurated in 1957. It was expanded for the 1982 World Cup Finals when the asymmetric upper tier was added, completing the seating bowl as its architects had intended. While the remodelled stadium retains the essential elements of the original, importantly it introduces many improvements including escalators to the upper tier and a new roof that covers the seating bowl (it is currently roofed only on the west side). Central to the design concept is the intention to build around the existing stadium while it remains in use by FC Barcelona for all its matches, something that represents a real technical challenge.

If the new Wembley can be seen as a model for FC Barcelona's aspirations in terms of stadium amenities, in every other respect Camp Nou will be very different. Inspired by Barcelona's rich architectural heritage and Gaudí's distinctive use of tile, the enclosure that wraps the building forms an overlapping mosaic of translucent tiles in the club's colours – blue and maroon, interwoven with white, yellow and red. The tiles continue over the stadium's roof, supported on a cable-net structure that spans the seating bowl. On match nights, this mosaic will glow vividly, providing a bright new architectural icon for the city and a defining emblem for the club's thousands of fans.

1

2

1. Rendering showing the approach to the stadium with its 'mosaic' facade.

2. A view of the internal concourse looking out to the city to the right and the stadium bowl to the left.

3. East-west cross-section through the stadium bowl.

Opposite: the stadium by night; the Torre de Collserola glows on the hillside in the background.

3

Jameson House
Vancouver, Canada 2004 –

Rising above two existing Art Deco buildings, Jameson House is a new tower located at the heart of Vancouver's heritage district. The scheme continues the practice's investigation into contemporary interventions within historic structures, explored previously in a high-rise context with the Hearst Tower in New York. The project is also an example of a building that combines living and working in one location, encouraging social activity and balancing energy consumption between its mix of daytime and night-time uses.

The project involves the restoration of the A-listed 1921 Ceperley Rounsfell Building – returning the entire internal double-height volume to its original configuration – and the retention of the facade of the B-listed Royal Financial Building, dating from 1929. The new tower comprises ten storeys of offices, including shops and a restaurant, and twenty-six storeys of apartments with underground parking. The relatively even twenty-four-hour spread of energy demands has enabled full advantage to be taken of a central cogeneration plant – the first of its kind to be used in Vancouver. It is planned to run on bio-diesel as primary fuel and combined with an absorption cooling plant can supplement both cooling and electricity requirements for the building.

Developed in response to the local climate, the concept for Jameson House has been sensitive to seasonal sun paths, prevailing winds, humidity levels, air temperatures and precipitation rates specific to the location. Directional wind profiles and solar exposure have been used to help determine the facade design and external building form to achieve lower thermal loads and opportunities for open balconies and natural ventilation. Jameson House will also be a green building in a more literal sense. The top of the tower, the balconies, and a roof terrace at level 4 will be green spaces, introducing planting and trees to the precinct area, irrigated naturally via a rainwater harvesting system.

1

2

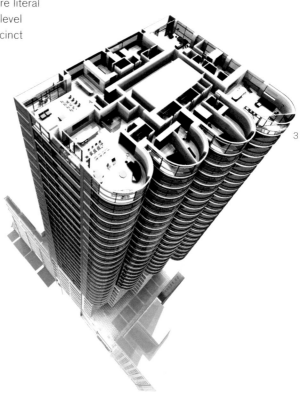

3

1, 2. The living spaces in a typical Jameson House apartment.

3. Sectional perspective showing the upper floor layouts.

4. Visualisation showing the building from West Hastings Street. The new tower sits atop two historical buildings that have been refurbished and incorporated into the scheme.

4

The Troika
Kuala Lumpur, Malaysia 2004 –

Located at the north-eastern corner of the Park, within the precincts of Kuala Lumpur City Centre – Kuala Lumpur's 'city within a city' – the Jalan Binjai development combines apartments, offices, shops and restaurants within a single complex, with the aim of promoting a more sustainable, densely planned approach to living and working in the twenty-first century city. The project comprises three apartment towers – of thirty-eight, forty-four, and fifty storeys respectively – which together form the tallest residential development in Malaysia.

The twisting geometry of the three towers evolved gradually through detailed modelling analysis, their forms being sculpted to respond to the surrounding buildings and to maximise the dramatic views of the Park, the Petronas Towers and the surrounding city. The unusual external structure consists of a number of slender concrete sheer walls, which support a series of stacked blocks that are able to rotate subtly to allow the primary living areas and balconies in each of the 230 apartments to focus on the best available view. The arrangement of the shear walls allows a wide variety of plan sizes, and the internal organisation of the apartments is kept fluid, to facilitate individual planning options. Many areas are self-shaded by the overhang of the apartment above, which provides shelter on the balconies. Sky bridges link the towers at level 24 to create a sky lobby with unrivalled views of the fast-changing skyline.

At ground level, a four-storey perimeter commercial building contains offices, shops and cafés and frames a landscaped courtyard. Entirely free from cars, the courtyard forms the heart of the development – a tranquil urban oasis. Residents enter through the courtyard via a grand entrance on Jalan Binjai Road, which leads to lift banks on individual floors that are shared by two apartments each. At roof level, the perimeter building provides a variety of recreational facilities for residents. Linked by shaded arcades, and accessible throughout the day, they add a further level of amenity to high-rise urban living.

1

1. The Troika towers seen from the Park.

2. Sketches by David Nelson showing the relationship between the podium, residential towers and green spaces.

3. Looking out from a sky bridge on level 24. Sky bridges link the three towers to create a continuous sky lobby.

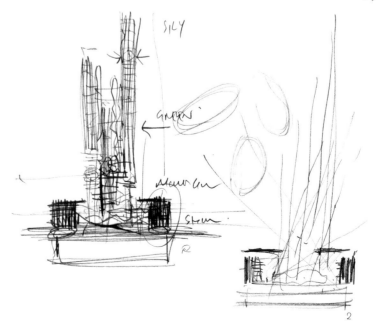

2

3

4

4. The approach to the entrance within the podium that connects the towers. The podium combines offices, shops and restaurants with the aim of creating a vertical city for living, working and leisure.

5, 6. The open-plan apartments have panoramic views over the city.

5   6

610 Lexington Avenue
New York, USA 2005 –

This 62-storey hotel and condominium tower at 610 Lexington Avenue continues the practice's investigations into the nature of the tall building in New York, exploring the dynamic between the city and its skyline. Located on the corner of Lexington and 53rd Street, it replaces the old YWCA building in Midtown Manhattan. Formally, it responds to the precedent set by two neighbouring twentieth-century Modernist icons – SOM's 21-storey Lever House of 1952 and Mies van der Rohe's 38-storey Seagram Building of 1958. In the spirit of Mies' philosophy of rationality, simplicity and clarity, the tower has a slender, minimalist geometric form, designed to complement these distinguished neighbours.

The entrance is recessed beneath a canopy that sits harmoniously alongside the entrance and pavilion of the Seagram Building. The entry sequence continues on a single plane from the street to reveal a glazed atrium that joins the tower to a smaller building on the right. The smaller building houses a bar and restaurant, hotel suites, conference facilities and a spa and swimming pool, while the tower contains lounge areas, hotel accommodation and condominiums on the higher levels. From the floor of the atrium, the tower rises like a soaring vertical blade, the view up creating a sense of drama and reinforcing the connection between the summit and the ground.

Some of the larger condominiums and the hotel's presidential suite occupy the entire floor area of the higher levels. The tower's slender form creates a narrow floor plate, allowing the interior spaces to be flooded with daylight and creating spectacular views across the city from every side. An innovative glazed skin wraps around the building, concealing the structural elements which are further masked beneath white shadow boxes. To preserve the smooth appearance of the facade, opening vents in the glazing flap discreetly inwards. The effect is a sheer envelope that shines a brilliant white in absolute contrast to the dark bronze of the Seagram building.

1

2

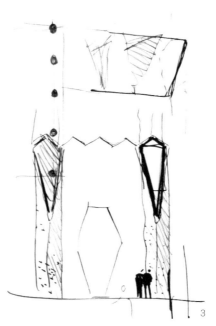

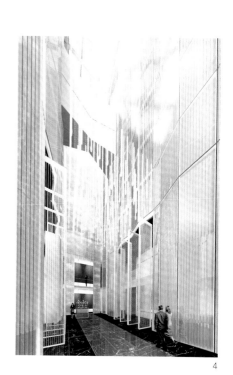

3

4

1, 2. Visualisations of the hotel reception and lounge.

3. Early sketch by Norman Foster illustrating the structural columns and buttresses within the hotel atrium.

4. Visualisation of the glazed hotel atrium, seen from the main entrance on 53rd Street.

5. Looking up at the building from the Citicorp Plaza on Lexington Avenue. Mies van der Rohe's Seagram building is visible behind the new tower.

5

Living Wall
Amman, Jordan 2006 –

Living Wall is a 150,000-square-metre mixed-use complex set on an excavated rock shelf at the base of a sheer cliff face in the centre of Amman. The place, its geology and history have been strong influences on the scheme's design. As well as occupying a strategic position in the city, it presents physical challenges that echo those faced at ancient Jordanian sites such as Petra, where the buildings were carved from the rock itself.

Six interconnected towers, with an average height of twelve floors, are grouped together on a seven-storey terraced podium of rough-hewn rock. The towers have sculpted forms with slender bases that seem to have been eroded, as if the rock around them had been scoured away by the wind. Within each tower, the functions are divided laterally, echoing the horizontal rock strata. Together they contain a boutique hotel, serviced apartments, a variety of residential units and offices, while the podium contains shopping and leisure activities. The solidity of the podium cladding forms a counterpoint to the transparency of the towers and blends the development into the surrounding landscape. The deep spaces between the towers house a variety of sheltered public spaces, including a sunken amphitheatre and a large sheltered piazza.

The towers are configured to minimise solar gain and maximise natural ventilation. They have double-skin facades with screens whose function is to provide shading and stimulate air circulation. This 'cloak' increases in density where the exposure to solar gain is greatest. Spaces behind the screens form sheltered balconies and terraces where people can socialise, rest and enjoy life out of doors, thus animating the facade as a 'living wall'. At both the higher levels and at the base of the towers there is an emphasis on transparency. Views across the city are unimpeded; there is a distinct sense of place and, with so much permeability and connectivity, both laterally and vertically, the scheme aims to create a strong spirit of community.

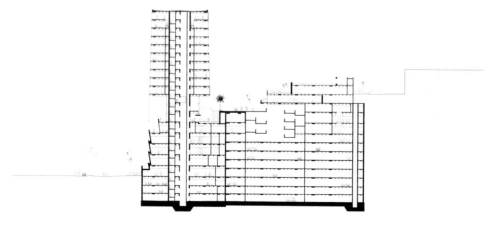

1

2

3

4. A visualisation of the overall development showing the six interconnected towers that rise above the terraced podium.

5. Model showing the massing of the six towers against the sheer cliff face.

4

1. Cross-section through one of the towers and the podium, which contains car parking, shops and leisure activities.

2. Looking across the rooftop of the hotel and residential tower showing the roof gardens and the view over Amman.

3. The public plaza at the base of the development.

5

U2 Tower
Dublin, Ireland 2007–

Located on the River Liffey, once the commercial life-blood of Dublin, the U2 Tower reflects the spirit of the docklands, past and present. The site was identified by the Irish authorities as a location for a landmark building that would celebrate the gateway from the sea into Dublin, and by extension into Ireland. With its dark, shimmering facade the tower draws on the original meaning of Dublin – the black pool – while its slender structure simultaneously evokes the tilting cranes that once lined the docks and the energy and dynamism that characterise the city today.

The development brings a mix of leisure uses to the former docklands, providing restaurants, shops and galleries at ground level, complemented by a five-star boutique hotel and a range of apartments above, with affordable housing at the base of the tower. The hotel café, with its roof garden, offers dramatic views towards the Irish Sea and the distant hills. It will become an exciting event space not only for the docklands, but for the city as a whole. Reinforcing a lively public realm on the dockside, a pavilion incorporates visitor information and bicycle hire, together with dedicated areas for people waiting for buses to the city centre or connections to a future light rail network and river buses, which will be introduced as the new activities of the docklands come into being.

Sustainability has been a key driver of the design. The project exploits a number of passive and active design strategies, which together make it one of the most energy efficient and environmentally advanced buildings in Ireland. These include the orientation of the facades to reduce solar gain and glare, and deeply recessed balconies on the south facade to provide shade. Other features comprise a combined heat and power plant, borehole cooling, and mirrored photovoltaic cells on the south-facing facade. An environmental centre at the apex of the building is animated by wind turbines that will glisten against the Dublin sky.

1

1. Night-time visualisation of the tower, which recalls the slender forms of the cranes that once lined the dockside.

2. Cross-section through the tower and the podium building. The tower contains restaurants, shops and galleries at ground level with a hotel and apartments above. The lower building provides affordable housing and has a sheltered roof garden.

Opposite: the tower's facades have reflective cladding that shimmers like fish scales.

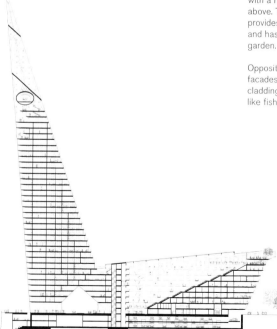

2

Florence High-Speed Railway Station

Florence, Italy 2003 –

Prompted by the creation of a new high-speed rail network, the Italian Government has instituted a major programme of new station building. This high-speed railway station in Florence will connect via a new tramline with the city's existing Santa Maria Novella station. Driven by a profound respect for the architecture of this magnificent city, and a quest for clarity of passenger movement, the scheme both celebrates the experience of entry into Florence and aims to reduce the complexities of modern travel.

Most of the Bologna-Florence high-speed line runs in tunnels. Correspondingly, platform level in the new station is 25 metres below ground. The station chamber consists of a single volume, 454 metres long and 52 metres wide, built using cut-and-cover techniques similar to those deployed at Canary Wharf. Arriving in this generous day-lit volume will give an immediate sense of space and light. Alighting, you will see the sky and sense the air of the city. Movement from the platforms to the street is via lifts or escalators. Between these two levels are two floors of shops, while a terrace at ground level offers a view of the trains coming and going below. The composition is capped by the arch of the glazed roof, which evokes the great railway structures of the nineteenth century.

The scheme is designed to ensure durability and ease of maintenance, and to minimise energy consumption and running costs. Daylight is a crucial part of this equation, so too is temperature control. The roof provides a system for effective temperature regulation by drawing warm air out through vents. It also incorporates photovoltaic cells to generate power. The walls and floors are lined with a palette of materials familiar throughout the city – including a figured green and white marble – which will patinate gracefully over time. Sensitive to its location, and forward looking in its use of energy and other resources, the station is offered as a model for contemporary rail travel.

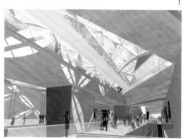

1-3. Visualisations of the station interior, showing the entry level, mezzanine level and escalators down to the platforms.

4. Cutaway axonometric showing the three interior levels and the 450-metre-long barrel-vaulted roof.

Opposite: a cutaway perspective rendering of the approach into the station, looking across the central platform.

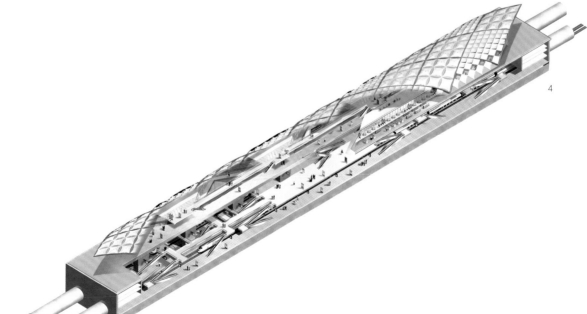

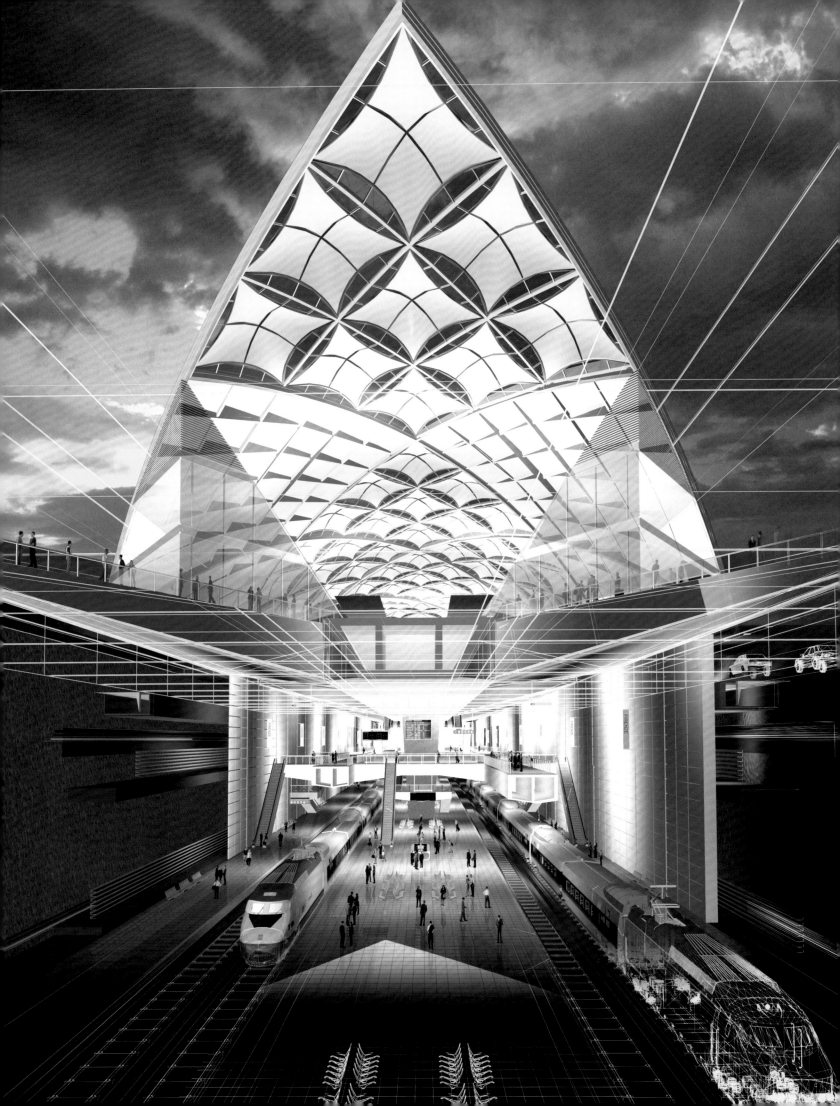

Queen Alia International Airport
Amman, Jordan 2005–

Queen Alia International Airport explores a vision of what the twenty-first century airport could be and offers a model for an ecologically responsible architecture. It is designed to evoke a distinctive sense of place, and to provide a greatly enhanced gateway to the region. The scheme allows the airport to grow by 6 per cent per annum for the next twenty-five years, increasing annual capacity from 3 million passengers to 12.8 million passengers by 2030. It will allow Amman to become the air hub for the Levant Region, and enable Jordan to host the 2014 Olympic Asian Games.

The project transforms the existing terminal buildings to provide separate arrivals and departures facilities and create a new entrance hall that establishes a legible progression for departing passengers from the set-down point right through to the departure lounge. Formally, the building draws from traditional Arabic architecture, with a variety of outdoor spaces and open-air gardens. In the courtyards, water pools reflect daylight into the building, provide passive air-cooling, and form a natural focus that directs passenger movement. Colonnades run around the gardens to soften distinctions between inside and outside. A broad canopy – its black external surface evocative of Bedouin tents – shelters the large external public area and evokes the excitement of a Middle Eastern bazaar.

The design embodies a comprehensive environmental strategy. Maximum use is made of natural light, split beams at the column junctions in the roof allowing daylight to flood deep into the building. The concrete roof structure acts as a thermal store to heat and cool the building; and black metal panels cover the domes to act as a heat shield, the heat being transfered to a network of pipes that pass through a passive heat exchange system to cool the terminal. The roof form also conserves water by collecting rainwater and night-time condensation. In addition, banks of photovoltaics will augment the mains electricity supply and reduce energy consumption.

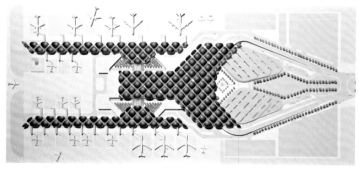

1

2

1. Plan view; the modular design allows the airport to grow incrementally over the next twenty-five years.

2. The approach to the departures area, sheltered beneath a broad canopy.

3. Visualisation of the boarding gate lounge; split roof beams allow daylight to penetrate deep into the building.

3

4

5

4. The check-in hall with its distinctive domed roof that draws from traditional Arabic architecture.

5. Aerial view of the airport complex showing the unifying black domed roof, evocative of Bedouin tents.

Spaceport America
New Mexico, USA 2007–

Located in the desert-like landscape of New Mexico, Spaceport will be the first building of its kind in the world. Its design aims to articulate the thrill of space travel for the first space tourists while making a minimal impact on the environment. Viewed from space, the terminal evokes Virgin Galactic's brand logo of the eye, and is suggestive of an elongated pupil, with the apron completing the iris. Approached from the historic El Camino Real trail, the terminal's organic form appears as a subtle rise in the landscape.

Organised into a highly efficient and rational plan, Spaceport has been designed to relate to the dimensions of the spacecraft. There is also a careful balance between accessibility and privacy. The astronauts' areas and visitor spaces are fully integrated with the rest of the building, while the more sensitive zones – such as the control room – are visible, but have limited access. Visitors and astronauts enter the building via a deep channel cut into the landscape. The retaining walls form an exhibition space that documents a history of space exploration alongside the story of the region and its settlers. The strong linear axis of the channel continues into the building on a galleried level to the super hangar – which houses the spacecraft and the simulation room – through to the terminal building. A glazed facade on to the runway establishes a platform within the terminal building for coveted views out to arriving and departing spacecraft.

With minimal embodied carbon and few additional energy requirements, the scheme has been designed to achieve the prestigious LEED Platinum accreditation. The low-lying form is dug into the landscape to exploit the thermal mass, which buffers the building from the extremes of the New Mexico climate as well as catching the westerly winds for ventilation; and maximum use is made of daylight via skylights. Intended to be built using local materials and regional construction techniques, it aims to be both sustainable and sensitive to its surroundings.

1

2

1. Visualisation of the visitors' walkway above the mission control room with its panoramic views over the apron.

2. Aerial view of the spaceport terminal. The building is conceived as a legible single volume with a strong linear axis that culminates in open views on to the apron and the spacecraft take-off.

3. Drawing showing the environmentally sustainable strategies employed in the terminal building to achieve a LEED Platinum accreditation.

Opposite: landscape plan of the spaceport which, when viewed from above, evokes Virgin Galactic's brand logo of the eye.

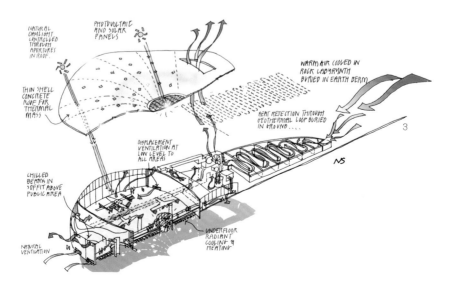

Heathrow East Terminal
London, England 2006–

If Stansted Airport can be seen as a reaction against the failings of the airport terminal as exemplified by Heathrow in the 1980s, then this new project brings that process full circle, replacing two obsolete Heathrow terminal buildings with a single integrated facility that expands on the Stansted model. The project is the result of a masterplan study, undertaken in 2004, which revealed the potential for redeveloping the existing Queen's Building and Terminal 2 once BA consolidated its operations in Terminal 5. This strategy will ensure that by 2012, when the new terminal is completed, 80 per cent of passengers travelling through Heathrow will enjoy a twenty-first-century airport experience.

Like Stansted, Heathrow East aims to restore some of the thrill and romance of travel by air, and to celebrate the act of arrival and departure, something that the earliest airport buildings evoked with great clarity. The form and orientation of the terminal, with its multifaceted, translucent roof, are designed to maximise natural light, which will flood the concourse on even the cloudiest days. The structure is conceived as a coherent, legible single volume so that, despite its size, way-finding is straightforward and the travel experience enhanced. The scheme also encourages the use of public transport through improved connections to the rail and bus infrastructure.

Driven by the constraints of building within a busy airport, this initial scheme continues the practice's investigations into modular construction. A study for BAA – the Pier Platform Strategy – which anticipated the requirement for modular systems by developing a generic aircraft pier, has also informed the design. Similarly, early projects such as the Sainsbury Centre, which explored the potential for wholly prefabricated structure and cladding, and Stansted, which took this a step further in the context of an airport, have each given clues. While the scale at Heathrow is vastly increased, the concept of low-cost, high-quality rapid construction, together with a commitment to an ambitious environmental programme, remains the same.

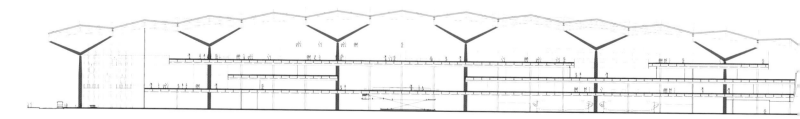

1. An impression of the lightweight roof canopy.

2. Aerial view of the terminal at dusk.

3. Cross-section from airside to landside; following the Stansted model, baggage handling and services are contained within an undercroft beneath the concourse.

2

4. The multifaceted translucent roof ensures that the concourse will be bathed in light on even the cloudiest days.

3

4

Walbrook Square

London, England 2004–

Located in the heart of the City, close to the Mansion House and the Bank of England, the 3.7-acre Bucklersbury House site is one of the largest redevelopment opportunities in London. This project – developed as a collaboration between Foster + Partners and Ateliers Jean Nouvel – aims to repair the damage done to the traditional urban grain of the area in the 1950s, creating new public routes and spaces, and introducing a mix of offices and shops, cafés, bars and restaurants. It has the potential both to create a vibrant urban quarter and to set new standards for the workplace.

The project comprises four buildings, each with their own distinctive character, which together define a new public space – Walbrook Square – which is accessed via new streets aligned with historic routes through the site. An important feature of the new square will be the foundations of the Roman Temple of Mithras, which were discovered on the site in 1954 during the construction of the existing Bucklersbury House. These archaeological remains are to be returned to their original location, at lower ground level, corresponding with the eastern bank of the ancient Walbrook river.

Individual buildings rise no higher than twenty storeys, which is significantly below the emerging cluster of tall buildings in the City, and they are designed to conform to St Paul's Heights and maintain strategic view corridors. The lower elements take the form of 'plinths', which respond to the heights of surrounding buildings and frame local views. Every facade will be different, tailored individually to its context, and the roofs will be landscaped to form green recreational spaces. The upper elements or 'clouds' will be seen from more distant views to float above the plinths. Their varying shapes, colouration and texture will catch the light differently and shimmer against the sky. They are also designed to work as solar collectors, making this a highly sustainable and energy efficient development.

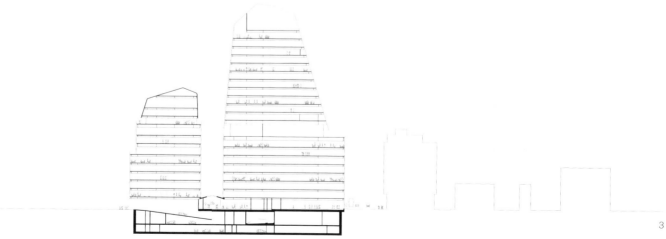

3

1

2

4

5

1. An aerial view of Walbrook Square with St Paul's Cathedral in the foreground.

2. View of the upper elements or 'clouds' of Walbrook Square on the City of London skyline.

3. A cross-section through the office buildings and central courtyard.

4. The development viewed from St Stephen's Row.

5. Looking into the new Walbrook Square.

200 Greenwich Street
New York, USA 2006–

A key component in the redevelopment of the World Trade Center site, this seventy-nine-storey building at 200 Greenwich Street continues the practice's investigations into the nature of the office tower. One of the most important urban planning and architectural challenges of recent times, the concept is driven by memory; but equally it is motivated by a sense of rebirth, its sparkling glazed crystalline form and diamond-shaped summit forming a bold new addition to the New York skyline.

The building occupies a pivotal position at the north-east corner of Memorial Park, and its profile reflects this role as a symbolic marker. Arranged around a central cruciform core, the shaft is articulated as four interconnected blocks with flexible, column-free office floors that rise to level sixty-four, whereupon the building is cut at an angle to address the Memorial below. Function rooms within the summit have spectacular views of the river, the park and the city. The core arrangement on the office floors allows for cross-corridor circulation, providing orientation and opening up views. The core culminates in flexible zones – places to locate staircases between floors or create double-height atria – which allows tenants to adapt the floors to suit their specific needs. Designed to meet the highest energy ratings, the project takes forward many of the ideas explored in the Hearst Tower and similarly aims to achieve the gold standard under the US Green Building Council's Leadership in Energy and Environmental Design Program (LEED).

Connections with the city at ground level are reinforced by glass walls, which create a visual relationship with the surrounding streets. At the Greenwich Street entrance, the triple-height lobby is connected to the city's subway system. The lobby rises in level along Vesey Street and includes a further connection with the transport network via escalators and a four-storey shopping area connecting with Fulton Street and spilling out on to the Wedge of Light plaza.

1

1. A cross-section through the tower and podium; the regular column-free office floors rise to level 64 where the building is cut at an angle to address the Memorial Park below.

2. Artist's impression showing the height relationship of the towers around Memorial Park.

Opposite: 200 Greenwich Street occupies a pivotal position in the World Trade Center redevelopment; its profile reflects its role as a symbolic marker.

Overleaf: Torre de Collserola, Barcelona (1988–1992); sketch by Norman Foster.

2

Works

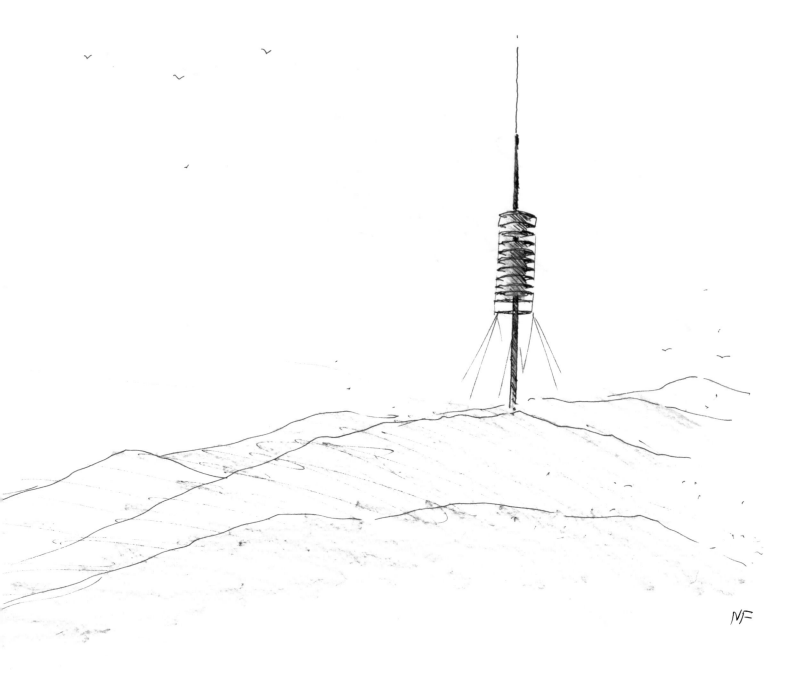

Sainsbury Centre for Visual Arts

Norwich, England 1974–1978 and 1988–1991

With the donation in 1973 of their collection of ethnographic and twentieth-century art to the University of East Anglia, together with an endowment for a new building, Sir Robert and Lady Sainsbury sought to establish the Sainsbury Centre as an academic and social focus within the campus. The Sainsburys shared a belief that the study of art should be an informal, pleasurable experience, one not bound by the traditional enclosure of object and viewer. As a result the Sainsbury Centre is much more than a conventional gallery, where the emphasis is on art in isolation. Instead, it integrates a number of related activities within a single, light-filled space.

The building itself brought a new level of refinement to the practice's early explorations into lightweight, flexible enclosures. Structural and service elements are contained within the double-layer walls and roof. Within this shell is a sequence of spaces that incorporates galleries, a conservatory reception area, the Faculty of Fine Art, senior common room and a restaurant. Full-height windows at each end open the space up to the surrounding landscape, while aluminium louvres line the interior to provide an infinitely flexible system for the control of natural and artificial light. Large enough to display the Sainsburys' extraordinary collection, yet designed to be intimate and inviting, the main gallery evokes the spirit of the collection's originally domestic setting.

A new gift from the Sainsburys in 1988 allowed the building to be extended to provide space for the display of the reserve collection, together with curatorial and conservation facilities and a space for exhibitions and conferences, giving the Centre far greater flexibility in its programming. The new wing extends the building below ground level, exploiting the contours of the site to emerge naturally in the form of a glazed crescent incised in the landscape. In 2004 a further programme of improvements was initiated to provide additional display space, an internal link between the main and Crescent Wing galleries, improved shop, café and other visitor facilities, and a new education centre.

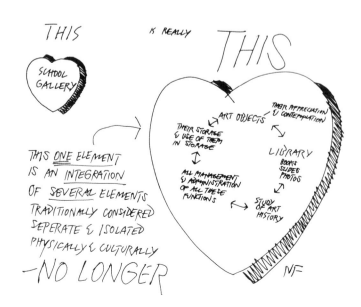

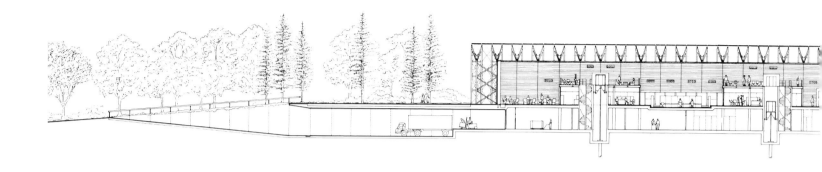

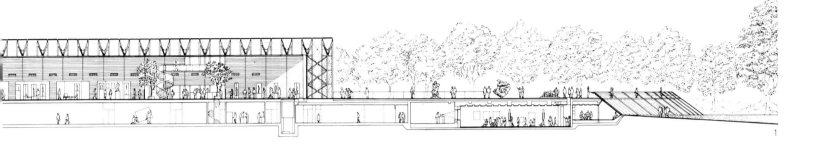

5   6   7

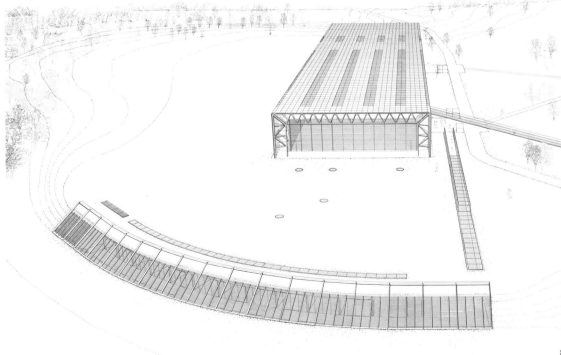

8

Previous pages, left: concept sketch by Norman Foster highlighting the advantages of a multi-faceted but integrated arts centre. Right: the Sainsbury Centre at dusk, seen from across the University's lake.

1. A long section through the Sainsbury Centre and Crescent Wing reveals how the extension forms a logical conclusion to the original undercroft level.

2. New entrance canopies were installed as part of the major refurbishment programme carried out in 2004.

3. A new lift and stair, installed in 2004, connect the main gallery level with the facilities of the Crescent Wing.

4. The open-plan gallery space with purpose-designed display cases and screens.

5, 6. The Reserve Collection in the Crescent Wing.

7. Looking along the circulation zone and the sweeping glass wall that define the perimeter of the Crescent Wing.

8. An aerial perspective of the Sainsbury Centre and Crescent Wing.

Overleaf: The Crescent Wing with the Sainsbury Centre behind, showing how the extension is dug into the natural slope of the site.

Carré d'Art
Nîmes, France 1984–1993

Médiathèques exist in most French towns and cities. Typically they embrace magazines, newspapers and books as well as music, video and cinema. Less common is the inclusion of a gallery for painting and sculpture. In Nîmes, the interaction within the same building of these two cultures – the visual arts and the world of information technology – held the promise of a richer totality. The urban context of Nîmes also acted as a powerful influence. The site faces the Maison Carrée, a perfectly preserved Roman temple. The challenge was to relate new to the old, but at the same time to create a building that represented its own age with integrity.

A singular modern building, yet one that references the courtyard and terraced vernacular of the region, the Carré d'Art is articulated as a nine-storey structure, half of which is sunk deep into the ground, keeping the building's profile low in sympathy with the scale of the surrounding buildings. The lower levels house archive storage and a cinema, while above, a roofed courtyard forms the heart of the building, exploiting the transparency and lightness of modern materials to allow natural light to permeate all floors. These upper levels are connected by a cascading staircase, linking the toplit galleries to the shaded roof-terrace café overlooking a new public square.

The creation of this urban space was an integral part of the project. Railings, advertising boards and parking spaces were removed and the square in front of the building was extended as a pedestrianised realm. The geometry of this piazza follows Nîmes' Roman grid in recreating tree-lined streets alongside the building and providing a new setting for the Maison Carrée. Lined with café tables and thronged with people, the new square has reinvigorated the social and cultural life of Nîmes. Together with these urban interventions, the Carré d'Art shows how a building project, backed by an enlightened political initiative, can not only encourage a dialogue between ancient and modern architectures but can also provide a powerful catalyst for reinvigorating the social and physical fabric of a city.

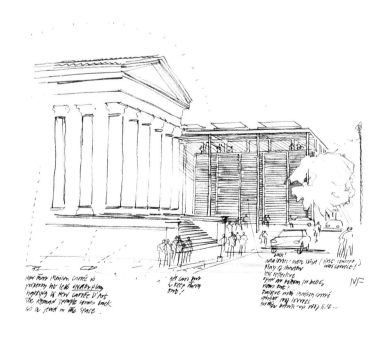

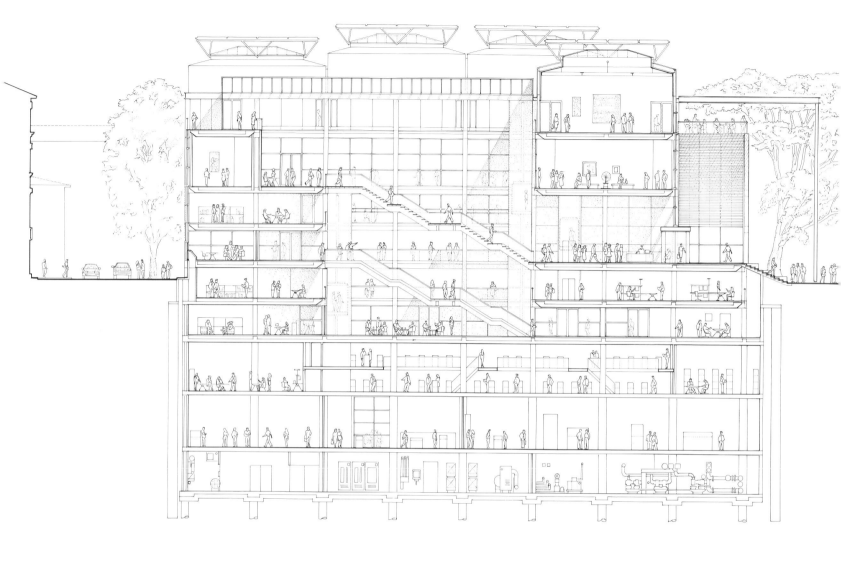

Previous pages, left: sketch
by Norman Foster outlining
what would become the
defining view of the Carré
d'Art, from the steps of
the Roman Maison Carrée.
Right: detail of the front
of the building.

1. Cross-section through
the building. In order to
respect the roof-line of the
surrounding city, five of the
building's floors are sunk
below ground and daylit
via the central atrium.

2. The revitalised urban
square in front of the Carré
d'Art, renamed Place de
la Maison Carrée.

2

3

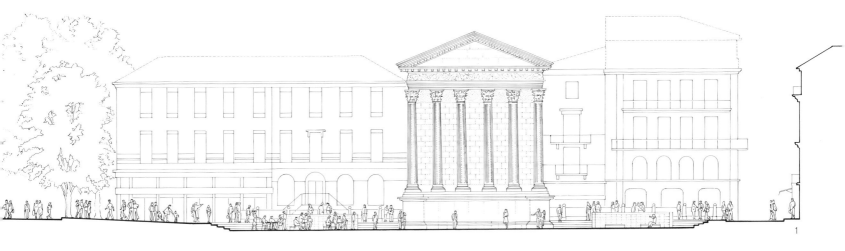

3. View out towards the Maison Carrée from the café terrace.

4. The triple-height volume of the adult library.

5. Rising six storeys through the heart of the building, the atrium staircase links all the main public areas.

6. One of the galleries on the upper level.

Overleaf: The loggias of the old Maison Carrée and the new Carré d'Art face each other across the square.

Sackler Galleries, Royal Academy of Arts
London, England 1985–1991

The commission for the Sackler Galleries at the Royal Academy of Arts provided the practice with its first opportunity to work within the context of a historic building. Although perceived by the visitor as a single entity, the Royal Academy in fact consists of two buildings: the original Palladian house, converted by Lord Burlington in the eighteenth century, and a Victorian gallery block behind, linked by a grand central staircase. The project brief required the replacement of the undistinguished nineteenth-century Diploma Galleries at the top of Burlington House and the improvement of access routes throughout the building.

The key to unlocking the design solution was the rediscovery of the light-well between Burlington House and the Victorian galleries, into which a new lift and staircase were inserted. In the process redundant historical accretions were peeled away, revealing the garden facade of Burlington House for the first time in over a century. Cleaned and repaired, it contrasts strikingly with the Victorian structure and the free-standing new insertions. The new work is demonstrably of its own time, using modern materials for modern ends, but it also enables a rediscovery of the potential of Burlington House and the Victorian galleries, much of which had become inaccessible over time.

In addition to this historical reclamation, the Sackler Galleries achieved new environmental standards, allowing the Royal Academy to meet the exacting criteria set by international exhibitions. These include a glazed reception area, which incorporates the parapet of the Victorian galleries, now recast as a display space for sculpture from the Academy's permanent collection. Notable along this simultaneously modern and antique route is Michelangelo's tondo of the Virgin and Child with the Infant St John. The Royal Academy was the first in a line of projects to demonstrate a clear philosophy about how contemporary interventions can be made in historical structures – a theme subsequently explored in the Reichstag in Berlin and the Great Court at the British Museum.

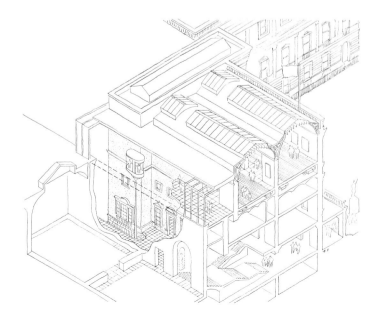

Previous pages, left: a cutaway drawing by Norman Foster of the final scheme. Right: view of the new glass lift with the newly revealed garden facade of Burlington House behind.

1-3. Details of the glass staircase that rises up to the Sackler Galleries.

4. A cross-section through the Sackler Galleries, taking in the Royal Academy's courtyard and entrance hall.

5-7. Studies of the sculpture promenade by artist Ben Johnson: Classical figures and busts are displayed on the existing parapet.

8. A view of the south gallery.

9. The main entrance to the galleries, along the sculpture promenade.

10. The galleries are naturally lit from above. Adjustable louvres are used to control lighting levels.

1

2

3

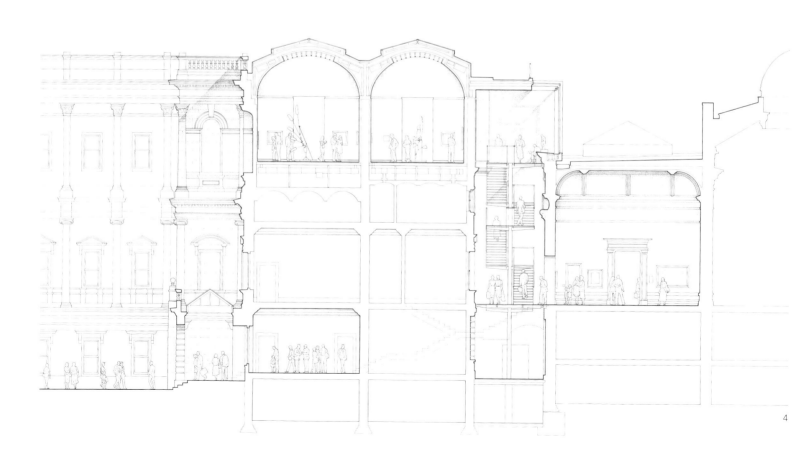

4

5

6

7

8

9

10

American Air Museum, Duxford
Duxford, England 1987–1997

Duxford airfield in Cambridgeshire was a Battle of Britain fighter station. Later, as one of a hundred US Airforce bases in Britain, it was the headquarters of the 78th Fighter Group. Now maintained by the Imperial War Museum, it has the finest collection of American aircraft outside the United States. Nineteen of its thirty-eight aircraft are airworthy and it attracts over 350,000 people each year to its summer air displays. The centrepiece of the collection is also the largest – a B-52 bomber.

The brief for the Air Museum was to provide a permanent home for the B-52 and twenty other aircraft dating from the First World War to the Gulf War and to commemorate the role of the American Air Force in the Second World War and the thousands of airmen who lost their lives. There was also a desire for the museum to highlight the take-offs and landings during air shows and create a window on to the runway.

The dimensions of the B-52 (a 61-metre wingspan and 16-metre-high tail fin) established the building's height and width, and provided the principal axis through which the museum is entered. The building's drama comes from the powerful arc of the roof – engineered to support suspended aircraft – and the sweep of the glazed wall overlooking the runway. A continuous strip of glazing around the base of the vault washes the interior in daylight. The result is a light and open space, despite the fact that the structure is partly dug into the ground, a formal device that has been compared to the air force's 'blister hangars', which were designed to be invisible from the air. In 1998 the Air Museum won the Stirling Prize RIBA Building of the Year Award. The jury wrote: 'The success of this project lies in the resonance between the elegant engineered form of the building and the technically driven shapes of the aeroplanes. The building itself sustains the fascination of these objects.'

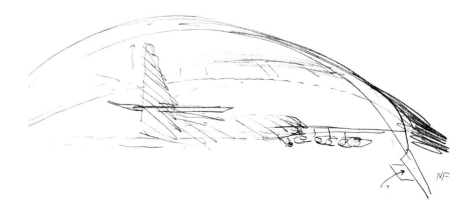

1 2

Previous pages, left: Norman Foster's concept sketch emphasises the B-52 as generator of the building's section. Right: looking through the glazed end wall out on to the runway.

1. Lining the curving approach to the entrance is a sequence of etched glass panels by the artist Renato Niemis, which forms a memorial to the American airmen killed during the Second World War. Each panel depicts in silhouette individual aircraft lost in action by the fighter and bomber groups.

2. The building's entrance, a discreet doorway that gives little indication of the space beyond.

3. The airfield seen on one of Duxford's popular summer air-display days.

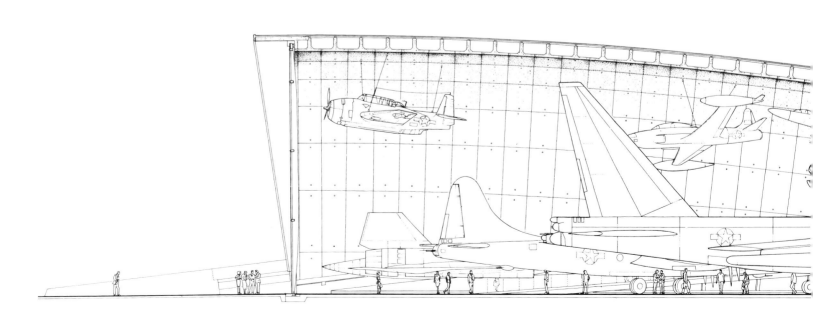

3

4

5

6

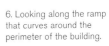

4. Visitors to the museum find themselves nose to nose – quite literally – with the aircraft on display.

5. The panorama of the runway as seen through the museum's full-height glass end wall.

6. Looking along the ramp that curves around the perimeter of the building.

7, 8. The museum has the largest collection of USAAF aircraft outside the United States, spanning a historical spectrum from the First World War to the first Gulf War. Many of the aircraft are still airworthy.

9. Cross-section through the building; visitors enter at a raised level, corresponding with the cockpit of the B-52.

7

8

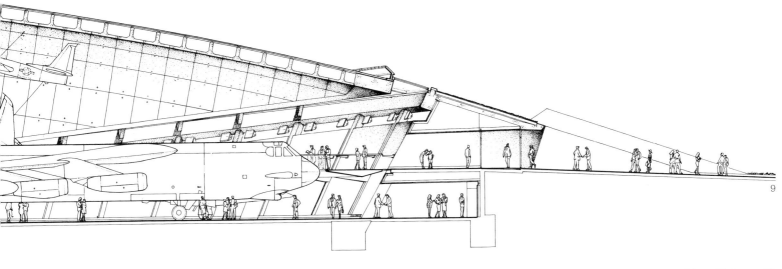

9

Musée de Préhistoire des Gorges du Verdon

Quinson, France 1992 – 2001

This museum, located in the medieval village of Quinson in Haute Provence, preserves and illustrates the rich traces of Stone Age life uncovered within the exceptional archaeological site of the nearby Gorges du Verdon. The architecture of Quinson is characterised by traditional stone buildings and drystone walls and the new building responds to this context by combining modern construction techniques with local materials used in their simplest, most expressive form.

The museum is one of a family of buildings that are partially buried or cut into their sites in order to reduce their apparent scale. Here, the sloping ground was used to advantage, allowing the museum to be folded into the landscape in section. The 'dug-in' edge of the lenticular plan – a form reminiscent of a *calisson*, a Provençal delicacy – is defined by a long drystone retaining wall. This wall continues the line of an existing village wall and flows into the building to guide visitors into the double-height foyer. This space is designed to be cool and refreshing on a hot summer's day – reminiscent of a wine cellar, or one of the caves that the museum celebrates.

The building is multi-functional, including areas for academic study alongside a reference library and research laboratories. On the ground level, accessed from the foyer, a children's teaching area reinforces the building's social and educational programme, while its auditorium, capable of seating 100 people for lectures, can be used independently for village events. From the foyer, a curved ramp leads up to the first floor to begin the circular route around the museum display. Ambient light levels within the galleries are kept to a minimum and light is focused on the objects rather than the space. Dioramas show scenes of hunting, fishing and other aspects of Stone Age life. The centrepiece of the exhibition is a reconstruction of one of the caves in the Gorges du Verdon, which are otherwise inaccessible.

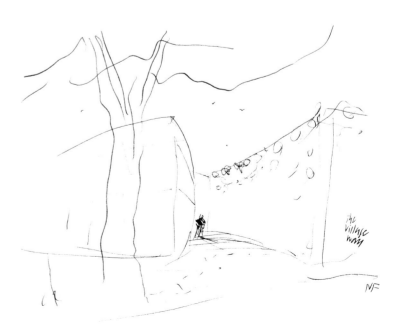

1

2

Previous pages, left: Norman Foster's sketch study shows how an existing village drystone wall is continued and folded into the museum, forming the link between old and new. Right: an aerial view of the museum looking south over the Gorges du Verdon.

1. The village of Quinson is characterised by traditional stone buildings and drystone walls.

2. The in-situ concrete facade uses an aggregate matched to the colour of the local stone.

3. A detail of the entrance with its oversailing canopy.

4. Norman Foster's sketches explore the detailing of the 'prow' of the museum's concrete facade.

5. From the entrance hall, a ramp arcs up to the first floor to begin the route through the exhibition.

6, 7. In the display areas ambient light levels are kept to a minimum; light is focused on the objects rather than the space.

8. Visitors line the ramp leading up to the exhibition spaces.

9. A cross-section through the entrance hall, first floor exhibition spaces, and the museum's centrepiece – a reconstructed cave from the Gorges du Verdon.

3

4

5

6
7

8

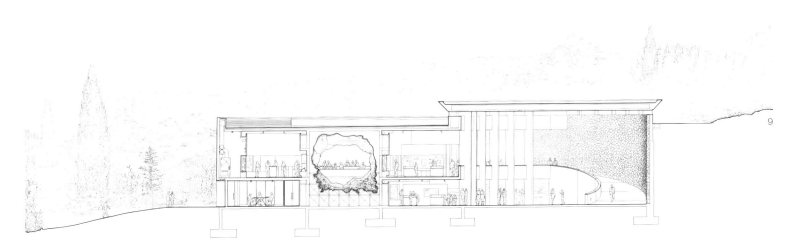

9

The Great Court at the British Museum
London, England 1994–2000

The courtyard at the centre of the British Museum was one of London's long-lost spaces. Originally a garden, soon after its completion in the mid-nineteenth century it was filled by the round Reading Room and its associated bookstacks. Without this space the Museum was like a city without a park. This project is about its reinvention.

With over five million visitors annually, the British Museum is as popular as the Louvre or the Metropolitan Museum of Art. However, in the absence of a centralised circulation system it was congested and difficult to navigate, which created a frustrating experience for the visitor. The departure of the British Library provided the catalyst for removing the bookstacks and recapturing the courtyard as a new public focus. The Great Court is entered from the Museum's principal level and connects all the surrounding galleries. Within the space there are information points, a bookshop and a café. At its heart is the magnificent volume of the Reading Room, now an information centre and library of world cultures, which for the first time in its history is open to all. Broad staircases encircling the Reading Room lead up to a temporary exhibitions gallery and a restaurant terrace. Below the courtyard are the Sainsbury African Galleries, an education centre, and facilities for schoolchildren.

The glazed canopy that makes all this possible is a fusion of state-of-the-art engineering and economy of form. Its unique geometry is designed to span the irregular gap between the drum of the Reading Room and the courtyard facades, and forms both the primary structure and the framing for the glazing, which is designed to maximise daylight and reduce solar gain. As a cultural square, the Court also resonates beyond the confines of the Museum, forming a new link in the pedestrian route from the British Library to Covent Garden and the river. To complement this artery, the Museum's forecourt has been restored to form a new civic space. Together with the Great Court, it is a major new amenity for London.

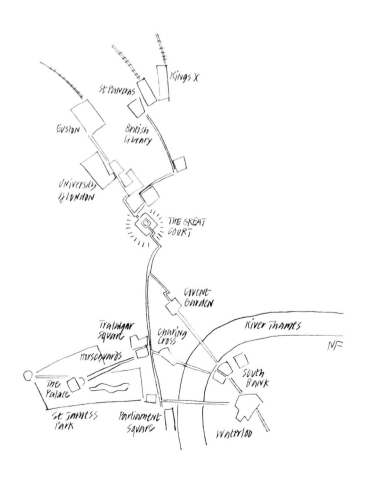

1

2

Previous pages, left: sketch by Norman Foster highlighting the pivotal position occupied by the Great Court on the pedestrian route between Bloomsbury, the South Bank and Westminster. Right: looking up at the newly clad drum of the Reading Room.

1. The restaurant terrace, with its fabric awning.

2. Early design sketch by Norman Foster.

3. Although it is covered, the Great Court retains the feel of an outside space.

4-6. An urban experience in microcosm, the Great Court encourages exploration and recreation in equal measure.

7. The new Sainsbury African Galleries, located below the Great Court.

8. The restored Reading Room plays a central role as the main information centre within the Museum, housing the Paul Hamlyn Library.

9. A cross-section along the north-south axis of the Museum, from the forecourt and front hall, through the Great Court to the north entrance.

Overleaf: looking into the Great Court from the Museum's front hall.

3

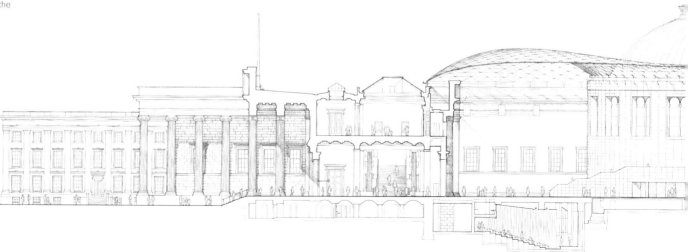

4

5

6

7

8

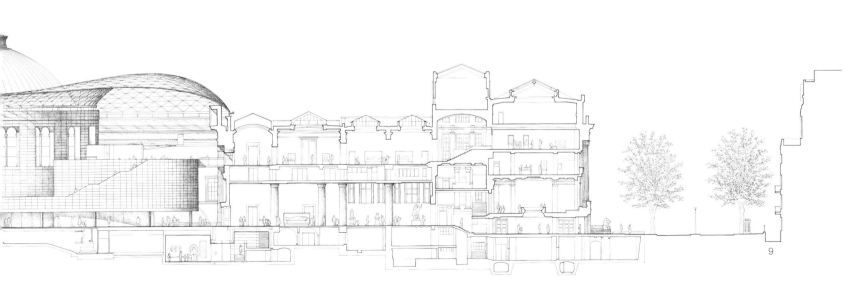

9

The Sage Gateshead

Gateshead, England 1997–2004

The Sage Gateshead is a regional music centre of international standing, with approximately half a million visitors each year. It fills a 'gap on the map' for music venues in the North-East and has helped to consolidate Tyneside's position as an arts destination. The building forms the heart of an exciting project to regenerate Gateshead's river frontage. It lies alongside the Baltic Centre for Contemporary Art and the Tyne Bridge with its great arch, which is echoed in the form of the Sage's roof.

The Sage provides three auditoria and accommodation for the Regional Music School and also acts as a base for the Northern Sinfonia and Folkworks, which promotes folk, jazz and blues performances. The largest of the three main performance spaces is an acoustically state-of-the-art concert hall that seats up to 1,650 people. The second hall can be arranged to suit folk, jazz and chamber performances and seats up to 400 people. The third space is both a rehearsal hall for the Northern Sinfonia and the focus of the Music School. The school is accessible to children, schools and people of all ages, raising the profile of the region as an innovative provider of musical education.

Each auditorium was conceived as a separate enclosure but the windswept nature of the site suggested a concourse to link them along the riverfront. As a result the entire complex is sheltered beneath a roof that is 'shrink-wrapped' around the buildings. Containing cafés, bars, shops and box office, the concourse acts as a foyer for the auditoria and as a common room for the Music School, which is located beneath it. Back-of-house hospitality areas have been kept to a minimum to encourage performers to interact with students during the day and to mix with their audiences in the bars in the evenings. With its informal atmosphere and unrivalled views out across the Tyne, this has become one of the city's great social spaces.

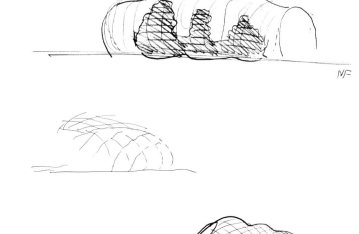

2

3

1

4

Previous pages, left: concept sketches by Norman Foster exploring the form of the roof over the Sage's three auditoria. Right: night-time view, looking across the River Tyne.

1. The central stage of Hall Two.

2. The rehearsal space in the Northern Rock Foundation Hall.

3. Children practising in the Education Centre.

4. The main stage of the largest of the auditoria, Hall One, as seen from the first tier of seating.

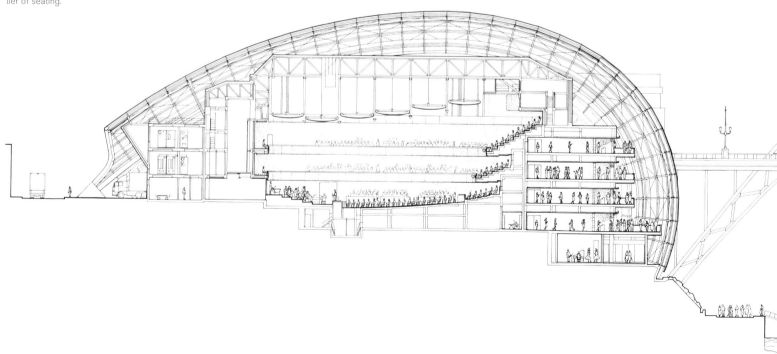

5

6

5-7. The foyers wrap around the auditoria and enjoy spectacular views out across the Tyne.

8. Cross-section through Hall One looking towards the Tyne Bridge.

Overleaf: The silvery form of the Sage seen across the roofscape of nineteenth-century Newcastle.

7

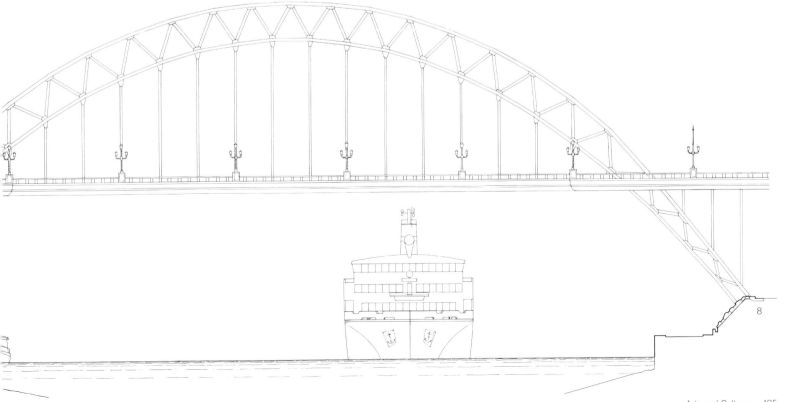

8

Smithsonian Institution Courtyard
Washington DC, USA 2004–2007

The Smithsonian Institution occupies the former United States Patent Building, once described by the poet Walt Whitman as 'the noblest of Washington buildings'. Built between 1836 and 1867, the Patent Building is the finest example of Greek Revival architecture in the United States and a celebrated part of the capital's urban fabric. Now designated as a National Historic Landmark, the building was rescued from impending demolition in 1958 by President Eisenhower, who transferred it to the Smithsonian Institution for use as the National Portrait Gallery and the Smithsonian American Art Museum. The enclosure of the building's grand central courtyard was prompted by a desire to transform the public's experience of the Smithsonian's galleries and provide the Institution with one of the largest event spaces in Washington.

The enclosed courtyard forms the centrepiece of the building's long-term renovation programme, which also included the redesign of the galleries with contemporary interactive displays, the addition of a conservation laboratory, an auditorium and greatly increased exhibition space. Visitors can enter the surrounding galleries from the courtyard, and out of museum hours the space regularly hosts a variety of social events, including concerts and public performances. Designed to do 'the most with the least', the fluid-form, fully glazed roof canopy develops structural and environmental themes first explored in the design of the roof of the Great Court at the British Museum, bathing the courtyard with natural light.

Structurally, the roof is composed of three interconnected vaults that flow into one another through softly curved valleys. The double-glazed panels are set within a diagrid of fins, clad in acoustic material, which together form a rigid shell that needs to be supported by only eight columns. Visually, the roof is raised above the walls of the existing building, clearly articulating the new from the old. Seen illuminated at night, this canopy appears to float above the Patent Building, symbolising the cultural importance of the Smithsonian Institution and giving new life to a popular Washington landmark.

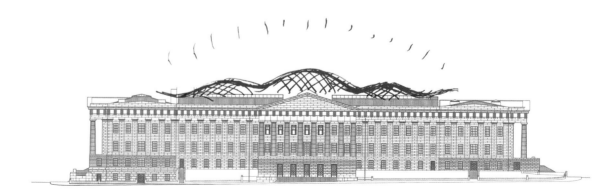

1

2

Previous pages, left: Norman Foster's competition concept sketch, showing the canopy 'floating' above the old Patent Building. Right: looking towards the G Street entrance, with the café to the right. The enclosure encompasses a landscaped courtyard, with mature trees, planting and a water feature, seen in the foreground.

1. A detail of the roof structure, seen from inside, showing the form of the softly curved 'valleys'.

2. Exterior roof detail; geometric patterns are created by the flat glass panels set within the curving roof form.

3. An elevated view of the Smithsonian and the courtyard roof seen from the corner of 7th and S Street.

4. The courtyard is Washington's largest event space and can be used for a variety of performances, as seen here on the public opening day.

5. Children playing on the scrim of water that runs the entire length of the courtyard.

6. The courtyard has given the Smithsonian a new visitor focus and provides access to the surrounding galleries.

7. A view of the café in the north-east corner of the courtyard.

8. Long section looking north; the galleries that line the courtyard look out into the space.

3

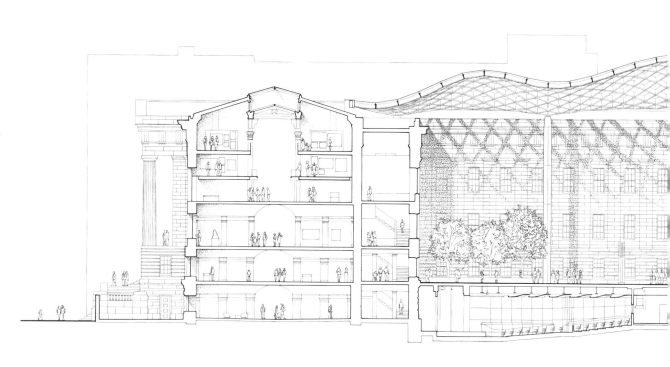

4

5

6

7

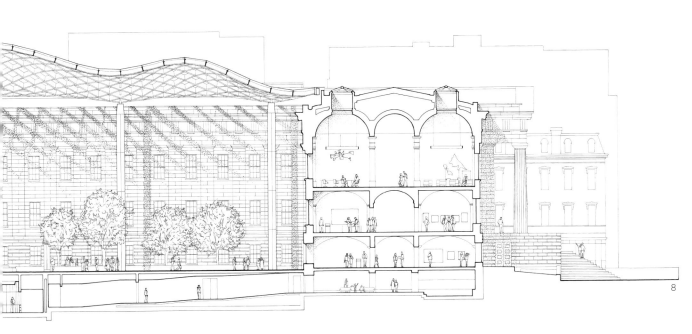

8

Duisburg Masterplans
Duisburg, Germany 1988–

The practice's work in Duisburg began in the late 1980s with the Microelectronic Park, which integrated buildings for new-technology companies and created a new linear park within a dense residential district. The first of many German projects to be realised, it explored fresh approaches towards energy and ecology; and given the trend towards clean, quiet industries, demonstrated the potential to create attractive, mixed-use neighbourhoods that combine places to live and work.

The underlying themes of that project were reinforced by a masterplan for the physical and economic regeneration of the Inner Harbour – the final piece of which is Eurogate – which has combined new construction with selective refurbishment to connect the waterfront with the centre of Duisburg, and establish a new urban quarter with all the amenities of a modern city for pleasurable urban living. The design team engaged with the community over a long period of time to create a scheme that emphasises the quality of infrastructure over grand-statement design. The first steps involved creating new arteries – green avenues, parks and canals – to provide the settings for housing and other buildings. Other initiatives sought to bring the waterfront to life by introducing leisure and river traffic. The success of these wide-reaching improvements is in no small part due to the imagination and determination of the Duisburg Inner Harbour Development Company, with whom the practice has a close working relationship.

Most recently, a masterplan for the centre of Duisburg inner city aims to continue the transformation of the city into an even more sustainable urban community. It seeks to revitalise the city centre, to strengthen the city's identity by improving its civic spaces, and to promote higher-density development, with a rich mix of culture, leisure, commerce and housing at its heart. Collectively, these projects have become a paradigm for the practice, embodying a number of themes and concerns that are central to the search for sustainable solutions to life in the twenty-first-century city.

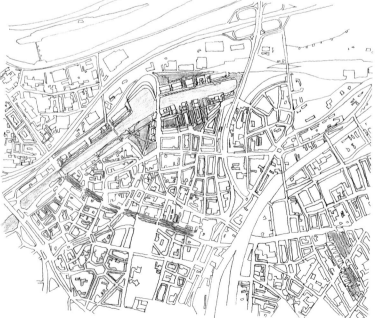

Previous pages, left: drawing of the city by Norman Foster, highlighting the areas for renewal. Right: photomontage of Duisburg Inner Harbour looking east with the curve of Eurogate on the northern bank and new housing blocks in the foreground.

1. A masterplan model of the Microelectronic Park showing the integration of new technology companies and the creation of a new public garden within an established residential district.

2. View north-east towards the Microelectronic Centre, looking across the park.

3. Concept sketch of the Microelectronic Centre by Norman Foster.

4. Looking up at the glazed roof of the atrium in the Telematic Centre.

5. The curved triple-glazed facade of the Business Promotion Centre.

6. Model of the Inner Harbour Masterplan area. The masterplan offers a framework for development that will be implemented gradually over several years.

7. The Steiger Schwanentor – an embarkation point for Rhine pleasure cruises.

8. Many of the existing harbour buildings have been restored and put to new uses.

9. New 'canals' form armatures for residential development, by a variety of architects.

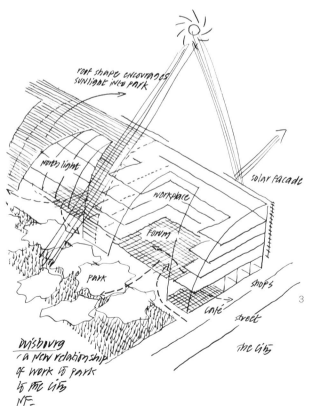

6

10. A five-storey housing development by the Foster studio, which overlooks a secluded garden.

11. Norman Foster's sketch illustrates the relationship between the new housing and the existing harbour buildings.

7

8

9

10

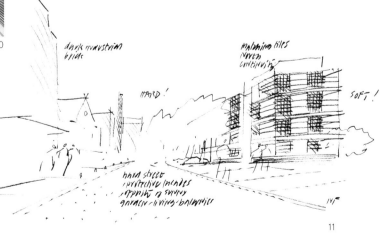

11

World Squares for All Masterplan
London, England 1996–2002

The 'World Squares for All' masterplan area of Central London is familiar the world over. It contains a World Heritage Site – the Palace of Westminster and Westminster Abbey – and such national emblems as Nelson's Column and the Cenotaph. Yet when this exercise began, its two major civic spaces, Trafalgar Square and Parliament Square, were effectively reduced to traffic gyratories and the area as a whole was largely hostile to pedestrians. The aim was to improve visitor facilities and pedestrian access while enhancing the settings of the buildings, monuments and spaces.

Cities such as Amsterdam, Barcelona and Paris have shown how the containment of traffic can contribute to the economic and cultural vitality of city centres. However, a project of this kind is a balancing act, which must promote genuinely integrated solutions, something that holds true for any historic urban environment attempting to sustain contemporary activities. The first step, therefore, was an extensive programme of research, which involved detailed studies of traffic and pedestrian movement and consultations with 180 public bodies and thousands of individuals. One of the main tools utilised was a plan model of London developed by Space Syntax at University College, London, which demonstrated the potential for pedestrian access and connectivity. This research led to the development of two possible approaches, which were presented at a public exhibition in Whitehall in November 1997. The response was overwhelming support for change.

The first phase of the masterplan to be implemented focused on Trafalgar Square. As part of a comprehensive programme of detailed improvements, the northern side of the square in front of the National Gallery was closed to traffic and a wide pedestrian plaza created, which connects via a flight of steps to the central part of the square. Although in architectural terms it is a fairly discreet intervention, its effect has been radical, transforming the experience of the square for visitors and with none of the traffic chaos predicted by the critics.

1

1. An aerial view of the World Squares for All Masterplan area, which runs from Trafalgar Square in the north through to Parliament Square and Great Peter Street in the south.

2. Norman Foster's sketch map of the same area, highlighting its landmarks and thoroughfares.

3, 4. The masterplan proposals followed a long period of research and public consultation, from a space-use analysis by Space Syntax to observational data collected in the field.

5, 6. Before and after views of Trafalgar Square, looking towards the National Gallery.

7, 8. Before and after images of Trafalgar Square looking towards St Martin-in-the-Fields. Instead of being isolated by traffic, the National Gallery and the square now form part of a unified spatial sequence.

9, 10. Parliament Square as it appears today, and a visualisation of how it might be transformed under the masterplan proposals. The southern side of the square, closest to Westminster Abbey, would be closed to traffic.

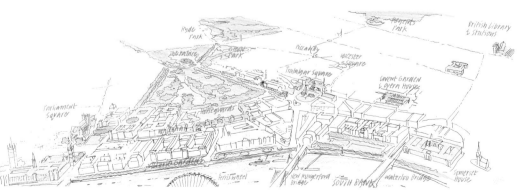

2

3

4

5

6

7

8

9

10

Trafalgar Square
London, England 1999–2003

The transformation of Trafalgar Square represents the first phase of the practice's 'World Squares for All' masterplan – the culmination of many years' work to improve the urban environment in the heart of London. It is the result of a careful balancing act between the needs of traffic and pedestrians, the ceremonial and the everyday, the old and the new.

Trafalgar Square was laid out in the 1840s by Charles Barry. Dominated by Nelson's Column, it is lined by fine buildings, including the Church of St Martin-in-the-Fields and South Africa House to the east, Canada House to the west, and the National Gallery to the north. Yet, despite its grandeur, by the mid-1990s the square had become choked by traffic, the central area visited only by those willing to risk their safety. There was an obvious need and support for change. Proposals were developed after consultations involving 180 separate institutions and thousands of individuals. The most significant move was the closure of the north side of the Square to traffic and the creation of a broad new terrace, which forms an appropriate setting for the National Gallery and links it via a flight of steps to the body of the square. Below the terrace, a new café with outdoor seating provides a much-needed visitor amenity.

Detailed improvements in the square and the adjacent streets include new seating, improved lighting and traffic signage and a paving strategy that utilises visual and textural contrasts. The contemporary interventions continue the boldness of Barry's original design, using traditional materials – York stone, granite, and bronze – in addition to salvaged granite bollards and slabs, which originally formed part of the north terrace retaining wall. Every aspect of the redesign improves universal access, including two new platform lifts and disabled lavatories. The cumulative effect has been to transform the life of the square. A once hostile urban environment has been restored as a truly civic space.

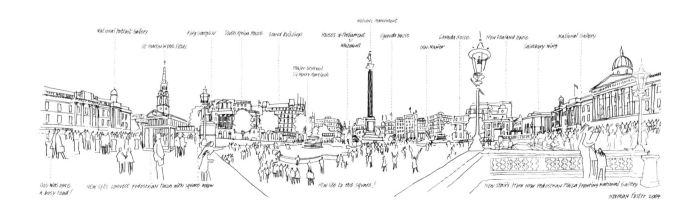

1

AS IT WAS BEFORE
PEDESTRIANS forced around the edge
ROADS on all four sides

2

3 4 5

Previous pages, left:
Norman Foster's sketch of
the transformed Trafalgar
Square. Right: the newly
completed square, opened
up and immediately
enlivened as a publicly
accessible space.

1. Looking north towards
the portico of the National
Gallery. The broad flight of
steps that now connects the
square with the new terrace
in front of the gallery has
become a popular vantage
point – a place to sit and
enjoy the view.

2. Sketch by Norman Foster
of the square as it was
before – hemmed in on
all four sides by traffic.

3-5. A series of mid-summer
views of the new grand
staircase leading down
into the square.

6. Taken from the balcony
of Canada House, on the
western side of the square,
this panorama shows how
Trafalgar Square has been
reinvented as a public
space, freed from the traffic
congestion that once made it
inhospitable.

6

City Hall and More London Masterplan
London, England 1998 – 2008

City Hall houses the chamber for the London Assembly and the offices
of the mayor and staff of the Greater London Authority. It forms the focal
point of the More London development – a new working community
on the south bank of the Thames between London and Tower Bridges.
Occupying a strategic position on the cultural route from Tate Modern, the
Globe Theatre and Southwark Cathedral to HMS Belfast and the Design
Museum, More London has played a key role in the social and economic
regeneration of the borough of Southwark.

One of the capital's most symbolically important new projects, City Hall
advances themes explored in the Reichstag, expressing the transparency
and accessibility of the democratic process and demonstrating the
potential for a sustainable, virtually non-polluting public building. Designed
using advanced computer-modelling techniques the building represents a
radical rethink of architectural form. Its shape achieves optimum energy
performance by minimising the surface area exposed to direct sunlight
and maximising shading. Offices are naturally ventilated, photovoltaics
provide power and the building's cooling systems utilise ground water
pumped up via boreholes. Overall, City Hall uses only a quarter of the
energy consumed by a typical air-conditioned London office building.

Home to a workforce of some 15,000 people, More London integrates
a broad mix of uses within a new network of streets and public spaces.
A strong diagonal boulevard, which follows the ideal pedestrian route from
London Bridge Station to Tower Bridge, is intersected by smaller routes
and alleyways that forge links between the activity of the waterfront and
the residential community of Bermondsey. The landscaping in the streets
and piazzas includes tree planting and water features and extends to the
design of paving and street furniture. Alongside the offices, there are
shops, restaurants and cafés, and the development includes the Unicorn
Children's Theatre, a hotel, supermarket and fitness club. Together they
help to create a lively and congenial social environment on the riverside.

Previous pages, left: early sketches of City Hall by Norman Foster. Right: looking up through the public ramp that spirals past the chamber of the London Assembly to reach a public reception space on the top floor, known as 'London's Living Room'.

1. Looking down on to the roof of City Hall, with its array of photovoltaic panels, fitted in 2007.

2. Cross-section through City Hall, showing the assembly chamber and the spiralling ramp that forms the main public route through the building.

3, 4. Views of the ramp as it winds up around the foyer and the assembly chamber.

5. Looking out from the balcony of 'London's Living Room' towards Tower Bridge.

6, 7. Two views of the diagonal boulevard that links Tooley Street with the riverside. More London has established an entirely new city quarter with offices, a hotel, supermarket, health club, shops, cafés, bars and restaurants and a new home for the Unicorn Children's Theatre.

1

2

3

4

5

6

7

8

8. An aerial view of City Hall and More London, with Tower Place in the foreground.

9, 10. More than half the site is given over to open public space. 'The Scoop', a sunken amphitheatre adjacent to City Hall, hosts public events including an open-air music festival.

9

10

Torre de Collserola

Barcelona, Spain 1988–1992

In anticipation of the communications requirements of the 1992 Olympic Games, Barcelona was facing an explosion of transmission masts on the neighbouring Tibidabo mountainside. Sensing the environmental impact this would have, Mayor Pasqual Maragall decided that the communications and broadcasting infrastructure for the entire region should be coordinated. He convinced the three primary players – national and Catalan television and Telefonica – to build a shared telecommunications tower. The competition brief posed the problem as a balancing act between operational requirements and the desire for a monumental technological symbol. The solution reinvents the telecommunications tower from first principles.

A conventional reinforced-concrete tower would have required a shaft with a 25-metre-diameter base in order to achieve the 288-metre height required. Following an analysis of precedents, including suspension bridges and shipbuilding techniques, an entirely new structural concept emerged: a hybrid concrete and steel-braced tube, with a base diameter of only 4.5 metres, which dramatically minimises the tower's impact on the mountainside. In order to meet a construction programme of just twenty-four months the construction of shaft, mast and equipment decks was overlapped. As the shaft was poured, the steel-framed decks and public viewing platform were assembled on the ground ready to be jacked, inch by inch, into position. In a final flourish, the steel radio mast was telescoped inside the hollow shaft.

The equipment decks are suspended from the shaft by three primary trusses and braced by Kevlar cables, which are transparent to broadcasting signals. Equipment is installed or removed by lift, and a crane at the top of the mast hoists antennae into place. Inherent flexibility ensures that the tower will be able to respond to a rapidly evolving telecommunications future.

The concept

- The only constant is change
- A new symbol
- Not a conversion
- The New age – The future.
- max freedom here!

NF

1

2

3

8

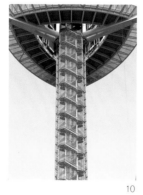

9

10

11

4   5   6   7

Previous pages, left: Norman Foster's concept sketch emphasises how the structure should touch the ground lightly. Right: view of the tower from below. The triangulated decks maximise space and optimise stability and aerodynamic efficiency.

1. A sketch by Norman Foster, indicating the tower's symbolic importance as a landmark on the Barcelona skyline.

2-7. As this sequence suggests, the tower's distinctive profile is visible from all across the city.

8. The 288-metre tower seen across the wooded slopes of Collserola.

9-11. Not only is the tower a focal point, it is also a vantage point. This sequence follows the public route up the tower, which culminates in a public viewing gallery.

12, 13. An elevation and cross-section, showing how the twelve floors of accommodation are supported on the central stayed mast. Two servicing levels are buried into the hillside at the foot of the tower.

12

13

Millennium Bridge
London, England 1996–2000

The Millennium Bridge springs from a creative collaboration between architecture, art and engineering. Developed with sculptor Anthony Caro and engineers Arup, the commission resulted from an international competition. London's only pedestrian bridge and the first new crossing on this part of the Thames in more than a century, it links the City and St Paul's Cathedral to the north with the Globe Theatre and Tate Modern on Bankside. A key element in London's pedestrian infrastructure, it has created new routes into Southwark and encouraged new life on the embankment alongside St Paul's.

Structurally, the bridge pushes the boundaries of technology. Spanning 320 metres, it is a very shallow suspension bridge. Two Y-shaped armatures support eight cables that run along the sides of the 4-metre-wide deck, while steel transverse arms clamp on to the cables at 8-metre intervals to support the deck itself. This groundbreaking structure means that the cables never rise more than 2.3 metres above the deck, allowing those crossing the bridge to enjoy uninterrupted panoramic views and preserving sight lines from the surrounding buildings. As a result, the bridge has a uniquely thin profile, forming a slender arc across the water. A thin ribbon of steel by day, it is illuminated to form a glowing blade of light at night.

The bridge opened in June 2000 and an astonishing 100,000 people crossed it during the first weekend. However, under this heavy traffic the bridge exhibited greater than expected lateral movement, and as a result it was temporarily closed. Extensive research and testing revealed that this movement was caused by synchronised pedestrian footfall – a phenomenon of which little was previously known in the engineering world. The solution was to fit dampers discreetly beneath the deck to mitigate movement. This proved highly successful and the research undertaken by the engineers has resulted in changes to the codes for bridge building worldwide.

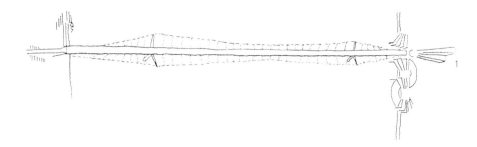

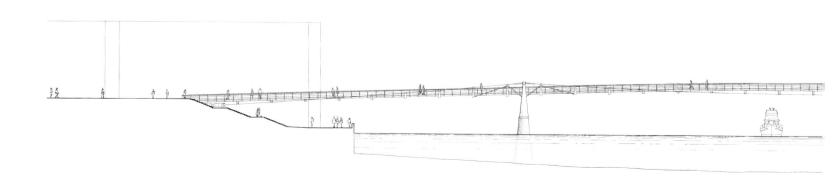

3

4

5

COLLECTION 2002

6

Previous pages, left: Norman Foster's early concept sketch for the bridge drew upon the importance of its axial relationship with St Paul's Cathedral. Right: looking north across the bridge towards St Paul's and the distant towers of the Barbican.

1. In this plan study of the bridge by Norman Foster, the design of the southern end of the bridge is still being explored.

2-6. As the only dedicated pedestrian crossing on this section of the Thames, the Millennium Bridge is thronged with people throughout the day. Not only has it brought increasing numbers of visitors to St Paul's Cathedral and Tate Modern, it has transformed the economic fortunes of Bankside and a wider swathe of Southwark.

7. An elevation of the bridge running from north (left) to south. A very shallow suspension structure, it spans 320 metres from bank to bank.

Overleaf. The bridge's low-slung cables and arms allow people to enjoy uninterrupted views in both directions.

7

Millau Viaduct

Gorges du Tarn, France 1993–2005

Bridges are often considered to belong to the realm of the engineer rather than that of the architect. But the architecture of infrastructure has a powerful impact on the environment and the Millau Viaduct, designed in close collaboration with structural engineers, illustrates how the architect can play an integral role in the design of bridges. It follows the Millennium Bridge over the River Thames in expressing a fascination with the relationships between function, technology and aesthetics in a graceful structural form.

Located in southern France, the bridge connects the motorway networks of France and Spain, opening up a direct route from Paris to Barcelona. The bridge crosses the River Tarn, which runs through a spectacular gorge between two high plateaux. Interestingly, alternative readings of the topography suggested two possible structural approaches: to celebrate the act of crossing the river or to articulate the challenge of spanning the 2.46 kilometres from one plateau to the other in the most economical manner. Although historically the river was the geological generator of the landscape, it is very narrow at this point, and so it was the second reading that suggested the most appropriate structural solution.

A cable-stayed, masted structure, the bridge is delicate, transparent, and has the optimum span between columns. Each of its sections spans 342 metres and its columns range in height from 75 metres to 245 metres (equivalent to the height of the Eiffel Tower), with the masts rising a further 90 metres above the road deck. To accommodate the expansion and contraction of the concrete deck, each column splits into two thinner, more flexible columns below the roadway, forming an A-frame above deck level. The tapered form of the columns both expresses their structural loads and minimises their profile in elevation. Not only does this give the bridge a dramatic silhouette, but crucially, it also makes the minimum intervention in the landscape.

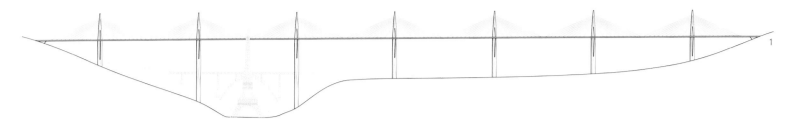

2

3

Previous pages, left: Concept sketches by Norman Foster arguing for a visually light structure, and emphasising how the viaduct should be thought of as spanning the whole valley rather than simply the river. Right: view looking west downstream along the Tarn and up towards the highest of the viaduct's seven masts.

1. Scale comparison, showing the Eiffel Tower and Eiffel's Pont du Garabit – two structural engineering icons of the nineteenth century – in relation to the road deck, which at its highest point is 235 metres above ground level.

2. The road deck hovers dramatically above the cloud line in the Tarn valley.

3. A detail of the viaduct's aerodynamic edge screen.

4. A dramatic aerial view of the viaduct. The wide angle lens used in this shot makes the structure looked curved, though in reality it crosses the Tarn Gorge in a straight line to establish a direct motorway connection between Paris and Barcelona.

4

Lycée Albert Camus

Fréjus, France 1991–1993

The Lycée Albert Camus is located in the rapidly expanding town of Fréjus on the Cöte d'Azur, and as part of the French lycée polyvalent system it offers a semi-vocational education to young people in their last three years of schooling. Like the Cranfield Library completed a year earlier, the school's design challenges the heaviness of the established educational building standard with a flexible and open structure.

Developed in response to its site and to a low-energy concept for the Mediterranean climate, the school's linear plan was designed to keep active building services to a minimum. Interestingly, the most effective ecological diagram was also the natural social diagram, with a linear 'street' forming the heart of the school both as a natural air movement system and a central circulation route. Bisected by an entrance hall, the street, at this point, forms a 'village square', with its own café and casual seating, acting as a focal point for the students. Fresh air is pulled through the street, the solar chimney effect allowing warm air to rise through ventilation louvres in the linear skylight. The layering of the roof, with a light metal shield protecting the concrete vaults from the sun, also encourages a cooling flow of air – a technique found in the vernacular architecture in the region – whilst brises-soleil along the southern elevation provide a broad band of dappled shade.

The school provides two floors of classrooms alongside double-height reception spaces, and is oriented to separate a public entrance on the north side from a more private, shaded southern edge. Materials were chosen in response to the climate and to exploit local construction expertise, notably the exposed concrete frame, which continues the French tradition of high-quality in-situ concrete. Its high thermal mass allows this structure to act as a 'heat sink', slowing the rate of temperature change within the building and enabling it to be cooled naturally without mechanical refrigeration.

1

2

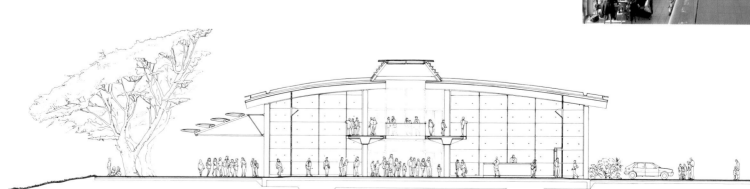

3

4

1-3. A sequence through the school's interior showing the central 'street', a typical barrel-vaulted classroom, and the double-height entrance space and café.

4. A cross-section through the entrance hall and central street.

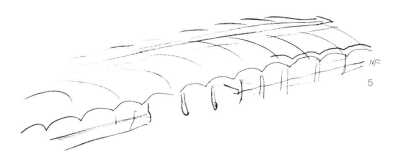

5. Concept sketch by Norman Foster showing the repeating pattern of the school's vaulted roof.

6. Looking along the school's southern facade, shaded by brises-soleil and mature cypress trees.

Academies

Peterborough and Folkestone, England 2003–2007

The concept of a visionary, light-filled school that would be open, democratic and flexible, can be traced to the practice's proposals for Newport School in 1967. Newport anticipated trends that today form the basis of the Academies Programme, a radical enterprise funded jointly by the DfES and private sponsors. The Thomas Deacon Academy and Folkestone Academy follow those in Bexley and Brent as the second generation of such schools to open. Conceived as inspirational and state-of-the-art places of learning, they are designed to create exciting new opportunities for pupils and to play a key role in the regeneration of local communities by establishing after-school social and educational facilities.

The Thomas Deacon Academy is the largest of the practice's new schools. The building comprises two ribbons of classrooms that enclose a central concourse sheltered beneath a dramatic, light transmitting roof. This central space is the academic and social heart of the school and accommodates a lecture theatre at ground level and a library above. The curves of the perimeter classrooms create six distinct three-storey colleges, each containing teaching areas and communal spaces. This arrangement breaks down the scale of the building, both physically and socially, and by increasing the external edge it also maximises the potential to draw natural light and ventilation inside.

As a response to the school's pastoral teaching system, Folkestone Academy provides eight distinct 'house' spaces, each contained within a 14-metre diameter three-storey drum. Clad in timber, punctuated with glass strips, the houses offer a degree of privacy while still allowing in natural light. The entire building sits beneath a diagonal steel lattice, with circular light-wells that allow daylight to filter down into the interior. Flexibility and the creation of social spaces have been important factors. Perimeter classrooms are designed to be rearranged to suit different teaching styles, while two triple-height internal courtyards provide informal gathering areas for use in school time and after hours.

1

2

3

4

Previous pages, left: sketch by Darron Haylock of the main entrance to the Thomas Deacon Academy, which is located at the westerly edge of the building. Right: looking down towards the library of the Thomas Deacon Academy.

1, 2. Views of the 'network study areas' at the Thomas Deacon Academy; these are dedicated spaces for social interaction and collective or flexible study.

3. A curving staircase leads to the upper floor at Thomas Deacon Academy.

4. Looking down into the library; the rooflights create a dynamic play of light across the space.

5. Cross-section through the concourse and auditorium of the Thomas Deacon Academy.

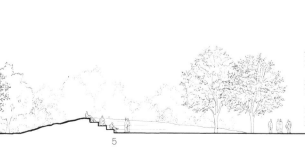

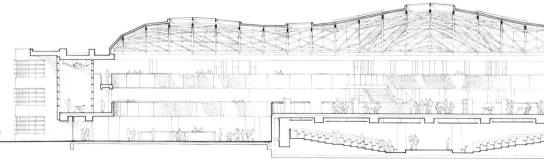

5

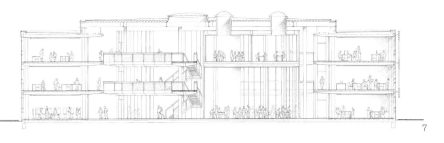

6. The roof of the Folkestone Academy extends over the public entrance to create a striking angular canopy.

7. Cross-section through of the communal courtyard and perimeter classrooms of the Folkestone Academy.

8. The triple-height communal courtyard, with views into one of the eight 'houses', which are contained within a 14-metre diameter drum.

9. Students enter from the south from one of two openings to the courtyard which leads directly to the houses.

10. Folkestone Academy's roof forms a diagonal lattice into which solid or translucent panels are inserted.

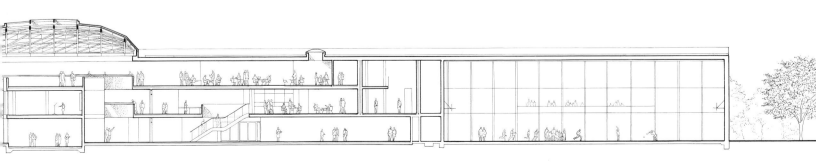

University of Cambridge, Faculty of Law
Cambridge, England 1990–1995

Cambridge University has the largest law school in Britain, with 800 undergraduates and 200 postgraduate students. Combining its own sense of tradition with a forward-looking commitment to change, the Faculty of Law required a new building that would provide state-of-the-art facilities for teaching and research, comprising the Squire Law Library, five auditoria, seminar rooms, common rooms and administrative offices.

Located at the heart of the University's Sidgwick Site, the focus of humanities education at Cambridge, the building is surrounded by lawns and mature trees. This low density, green garden context is the essence of Cambridge. The challenge was to preserve this natural setting and to minimise the building's apparent size. The response was to create a rectangular plan cut on the diagonal to follow the geometry of the neighbouring History Faculty and pedestrian routes across the site. The building has a relatively small footprint, yet provides 8,500 square metres of accommodation without exceeding four storeys. This was achieved by digging the auditoria below ground, while the curving glass of the north facade helps the building to recede visually.

The Faculty of Law building has also set new standards for energy efficiency on the Cambridge campus, deploying a number of passive and active strategies. Natural lighting is used to dramatic effect, especially in the library, which occupies the upper three terraced floors and enjoys uninterrupted views of the gardens, while the full-height atrium that forms the focus of the building draws daylight into the lower levels. The building's partially buried structure and exposed concrete frame combine to give it high thermal mass, making it slow to respond to outside temperature changes. Together with high insulation values, this allows the use of mechanically assisted natural ventilation throughout – only the lecture theatres require seasonal cooling. A lighting management system reduces energy consumption, while heat recovery coils, linked to the air extract, reclaim waste heat. Interestingly, the building's environmental performance was put to the test during its first summer, one of the hottest on record. Happily, it performed very well.

1

2

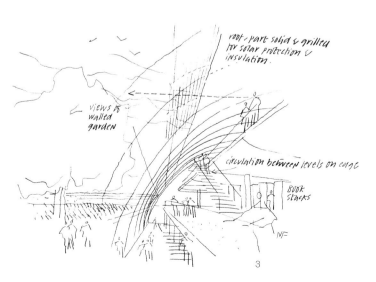

3

1. Staircases cascade down through the triple-height atrium space.

2. The library occupies four terraced floors and has uninterrupted views over the gardens.

3. Sketch by Norman Foster exploring movement and views through the library.

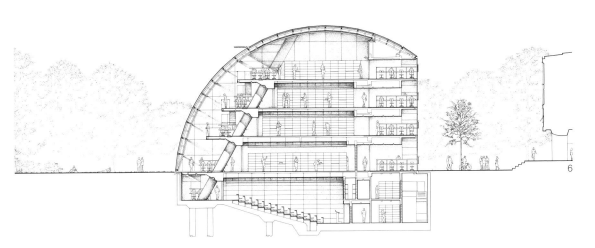

4. An aerial view of the building highlights its place within the garden setting of the Sidgwick Site.

5. Night-time view of the curving north facade, which is designed to minimise the building's impact in the landscape.

6. Cross-section through the auditorium and terraced library floors.

Imperial College Buildings
London, England 1994–2004

Imperial College of Science, Technology and Medicine is an independent constituent part of the University of London. Located in London's scientific and cultural heartland in South Kensington, it occupies a campus whose comprehensive redevelopment after the Second World War left a legacy of poorly coordinated building stock and impoverished public spaces. The practice's masterplan for the campus's renewal identifies key sites for redevelopment and environmental improvement. To date, four new buildings have been completed: the Sir Alexander Fleming Building, the Flowers Multi-Disciplinary Research Building, the Faculty Building and the Tanaka Business School.

The Sir Alexander Fleming Building represents a major advance in medical research facilities. Designed for long-term flexibility in response to rapid changes in microbiological research, it encourages social and intellectual interaction to an unprecedented degree. A central research forum structures internal circulation and allows researchers to interact across disciplines. Laboratories are wrapped around the forum, as are teaching spaces and offices. Fully glazed at its northern end, the forum looks out on to Queen's Lawn and Queen's Tower, one of the last vestiges of the Edwardian campus. The smaller Flowers Building is similarly designed for flexibility, although its laboratories have more specialised requirements.

The Faculty Building brings together all the College's administrative staff in a building designed to facilitate communication. It forms a new edge to Dalby Court and its vivid blue cladding is in striking contrast to the utilitarian 1960s architecture that surrounds it. The Tanaka Business School is located strategically as the 'front door' into the campus and links with the refurbished Royal School of Mines to give the College a unified facade on to Exhibition Road. Circular lecture theatres, based on the interactive Harvard Business School model, are contained within a six-storey, stainless-steel drum. The drum stands at the heart of a space that serves as a new 'entrance hall' for the campus and provides exhibition space to showcase the College's achievements in the fields of science, technology and medicine.

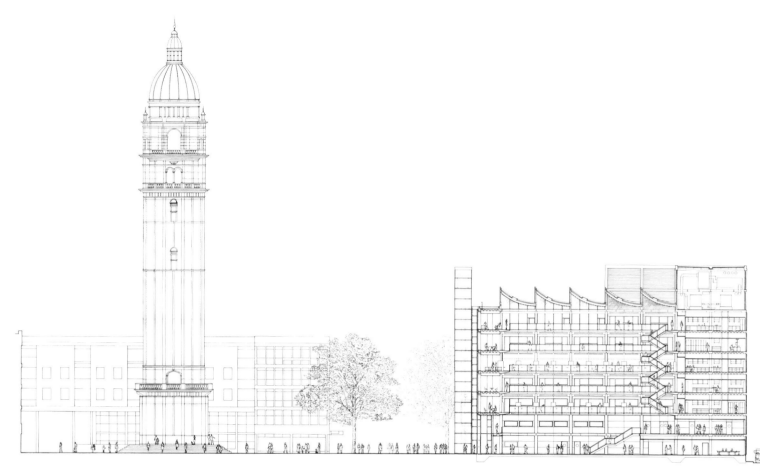

Previous pages, left: sketch by Norman Foster. Right: the five floors of the research forum in the Sir Alexander Fleming Building.

1. Cross-section through the Sir Alexander Fleming Building, with the Queen's Tower to the north.

2. View of the upper floors and curving roof profile of the research forum.

3, 4. Day- and night-time images of the building's glass facade.

5, 6. Exterior and interior of the Faculty Building.

7, 8. The main circulation stair and facade of the Flowers Building.

9. The Tanaka Business School as seen from Exhibition Road.

10. Detail of the six-storey drum containing the Business School's circular lecture theatres.

11, 12. Staircase detail and café space in the atrium of the Business School.

5

6

7

8

9

10

11

12

Center for Clinical Sciences Research, Stanford University
Stanford, USA 1995–2000

Stanford University has long been recognised as a centre for clinical excellence. The Center for Clinical Sciences Research (CCSR) provides the School of Medicine with state-of-the-art modular laboratory and office space for its programme of research into cancer and other diseases. Its design responds to emerging trends for interdisciplinary biomedical research, encouraging intercommunication and providing flexible, light-filled working spaces in which research teams can expand and contract with ease.

The brief called for close proximity between laboratories, core support areas and offices. Two symmetrical wings frame a shaded courtyard, which provides a comfortable environment for social interaction and has become both the social heart of the building and a popular route through the campus. Offices overlook the courtyard and a stand of bamboo provides occupants with a degree of privacy. Environmental systems take advantage of Palo Alto's climate, which is among the most benign in the United States. Offices are naturally ventilated for most of the year, with mechanical assistance only on extremely hot days; and the laboratory and office spaces are predominantly naturally lit. Seismic performance was a key concern: the campus lies close to the San Andreas Fault and the laboratories contain highly sensitive equipment. In response, the building employs a concrete shear-wall structural system and bridges spanning the courtyard rely on friction pendulum bearings to allow for seismic movement between the wings.

Over the years Stanford University has pioneered new approaches to clinical and scientific research. Most recently it has spearheaded a sea change that embraces an interdisciplinary approach. The CCSR established the first wave of change at Stanford, which was consolidated by the Clark Center. Together, these two buildings have had a significant impact on the architecture of research facilities around the world. Not only have they set new international technical standards, they represent an exciting new research environment in which interaction between disciplines and individuals is encouraged as an essential part of working life.

An interior, community alive with shadows + sparkle of light.

private world looking out...

1

2

Previous pages, left: design sketch by Norman Foster. Right: looking into the central courtyard – a space animated by the play of light.

1. Looking up at the glazed roof of the courtyard.

2. Shadow patterns on the courtyard floor.

3. The building seen through the trees of the Stanford campus, with the Santa Cruz mountains in the distance.

4-7. A series of interior views of the conference room, laboratory modules, and the interconnecting bridges, linking laboratory spaces to the central courtyard.

8. View into the café area of the central courtyard – the social hub of the building.

9. Cross-section through the building showing the close connection between laboratory, office and support spaces.

3

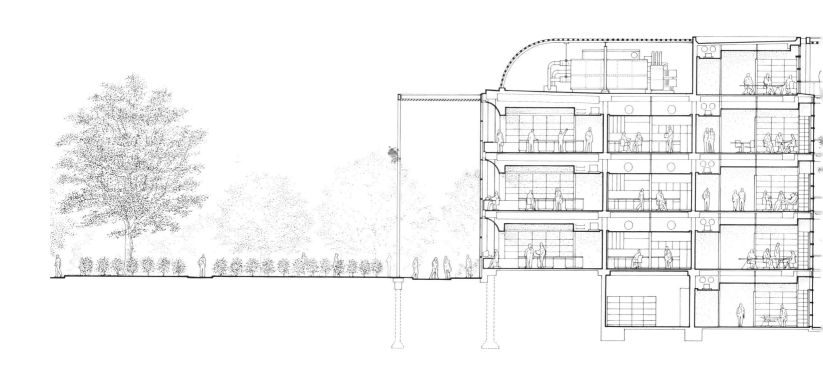

4

5

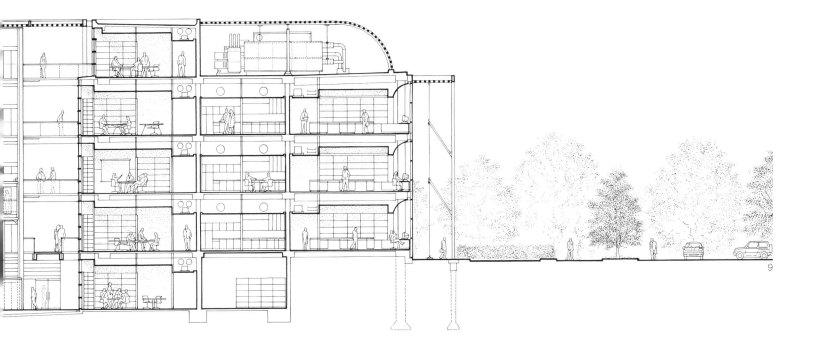

6

7

8

9

James H Clark Center, Stanford University
Stanford, USA 1999–2003

The Clark Center continues the practice's investigations into the physical nature of the research environment, which began at Stanford with the Centre for Clinical Sciences Research (CCSR). The CCSR reflected changes then taking root in research methodology and was designed to facilitate an inter-disciplinary approach and promote interaction between scientists. The Clark Center takes this formula a stage further, driven by the pioneering Bio-X programme, which has remodelled the landscape of science and technological research at Stanford. It is a building in which social encounters and impromptu conversations are regarded as integral to scientific endeavour.

Providing laboratory, office and social spaces for 700 academics from the Schools of Humanities and Sciences, Engineering and Medicine, the Clark Center is strategically located on the campus between the core science and engineering buildings and the medical centre. It acts as a social magnet for the University, encouraging students, lecturers and researchers from diverse disciplines to mix. In contrast to the traditional laboratory facility with its closed rooms and corridors, the Clark Center is open and flexible: external balconies replace internal corridors and laboratory layouts can be reconfigured at will. All benches and desks are on wheels and can be moved to allow ad-hoc team formation that can respond easily to fast-evolving research needs. This versatility is further enhanced by workstations that plug into an overhead system of exposed services with flexible connections.

Externally, the building takes the form of three wings of laboratories that frame an open courtyard. Overlooked by balconies, the forum at the heart of the courtyard is used for exhibitions, concerts and other events, while the busy restaurant on the ground floor has become a social focus for the entire campus. A coffee bar on the third floor of the building is located to encourage people to pass by the laboratory spaces, to bump into colleagues and exchange ideas along the way.

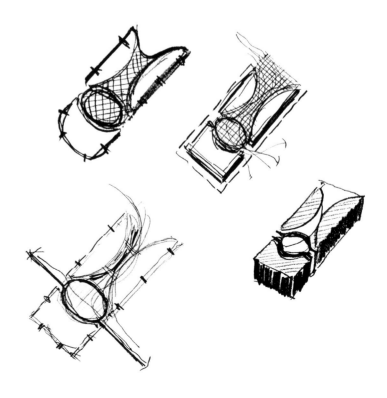

1

2

3

Previous pages, left: design sketches by David Nelson. Right: looking down the central courtyard; balconies and inter-connecting bridges replace internal corridors.

1-4. A series of interior views of the laboratory modules: any bench and desk configuration can be plugged into the flexible overhead services.

5. A cross-section through the courtyard, showing the two wings of laboratory space and the subterranean low-vibration physics laboratory.

6. The entrance to the building lies on a main pedestrian route through the campus.

7. Looking up at the bridges that link the two wings.

8, 9. A view across the building's central forum, as seen during the opening ceremony in October 2003, and (below) the forum space on a typical term-time day.

4

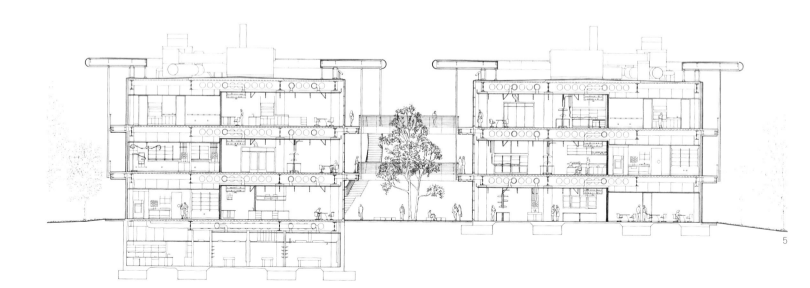

5

6 7 8

9

Petronas University of Technology
Tronoh, Malaysia 1998 – 2004

Petronas University of Technology was founded in 1997 and when completed, will be the region's largest academic centre for the study of civil, mechanical, chemical and electrical engineering. Fully funded by the oil company Petronas, it aims to blend the best academic training with hands-on industrial experience to produce a new generation of graduates who can contribute to Malaysia's industrial development.

Located within the dramatic landscape at Seri Iskandar, 300 kilometres north of Kuala Lumpur, the 450-hectare site is characterised by steep hills and lakes formed by flooded disued tin mines. The design responds to the physical landscape of the site and to the weather patterns particular to this part of the world. While it can be intensely hot in the sun, in the monsoon season the skies open every afternoon to bring torrential rain, creating a cycle in which the ground is alternately scorched and soaked. To allow students to move around the campus while shaded from the sun or protected from downpours, crescent-shaped canopies protect the pedestrian paths that wind around the site. Held aloft by slender columns, these canopies intersect to encircle a landscaped park. Where possible, the planting and terrain have been left in a natural state, although some marshy land has been flooded to form a natural water installation.

Arranged around the edge of the park are buildings for teaching and research, contained in four-storey blocks that tuck beneath the edges of the canopies. Cafés and other communal student facilities are located at the canopy intersections, which also correspond to the entrances to the housing blocks. Marking the main entrance to the University is the drum-like form of the resource centre. Containing a library and multi-purpose theatre, it is the chief social hub of the campus. Future expansion will see the completion of a sports stadium and a mosque – amenities that will be shared with the residents of a new town planned adjacent to the University.

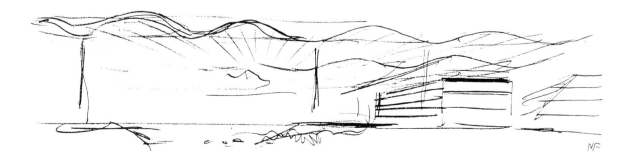

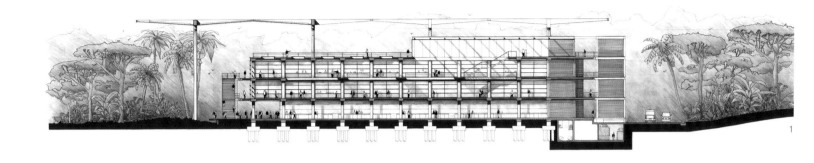

Previous pages, left: concept sketch by Norman Foster illustrating the idea of a flowing roof canopy. Right: looking across the park towards a section of one of the campus' crescent roofs.

1, 2. A section and elevation (right) through one of the academic departments showing the clear separation between roof canopy and building blocks below.

3. An aerial view of the completed campus.

4-6. Views in and around one of the sun protected 'pocket' spaces at the intersection of the roof canopies.

7. Interior view from within the Chancellor Complex looking across the public plaza from the library to the convocation hall.

8, 9. Laboratory spaces inside the academic block.

10. The interior of the main campus library.

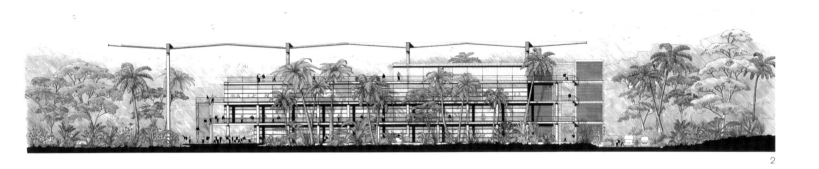

2

7

8   9   10

Free University of Berlin
Berlin, Germany 1997–2005

The foundation of the Free University in 1945 marked the rebirth of liberal education in Berlin after the war; since then it has occupied a central role in the intellectual life of the city. Today, with more than 39,000 students, it is the largest of Berlin's three universities. This redevelopment scheme includes the restoration of its Modernist buildings and the creation of a new library.

The University's mat-like campus was designed by Candilis Josic Woods Schiedhelm, and when the first phase was completed in 1973 it was hailed as a milestone in university design. The facade was designed by Jean Prouvé, following Le Corbusier's 'Modulor' proportional system. It was fabricated from Cor-Ten steel, which has self-protecting corrosive characteristics. The rusty appearance of these buildings led to the nickname of 'die Rostlaube' – the 'rust-bucket'. However, in the slender sections used by Prouvé the steel was prone to decay, which by the late 1990s had become extensive. As part of a comprehensive process of renewal the old cladding has been replaced with a new system detailed in bronze, which as it patinates over time emulates the colour tones of the original.

The new library for the Faculty of Philology occupies a site created by uniting six of the University's courtyards. Its four floors are contained within a naturally ventilated, bubble-like enclosure, which is clad in aluminium and glazed panels and supported on steel frames with a radial geometry. A translucent inner membrane filters daylight and creates an atmosphere of concentration, while occasional transparent openings allow glimpses of sunlight. The bookstacks are located at the centre of each floor, with reading desks arranged around the perimeter. The serpentine profile of the floors creates a pattern in which each floor swells or recedes with respect to the one above or below it, generating a sequence of generous, light-filled spaces in which to work. Amusingly, the library's cranial form has earned it a nickname of its own – 'The Berlin Brain'.

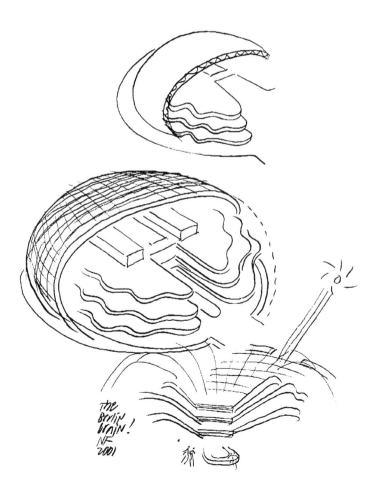

Previous pages, left: a sketch by Norman Foster of the Free University library – the 'Berlin Brain'. Right: glazed panels in the outer shell allow daylight to flood in, filtered by a translucent inner membrane.

1, 2. Before and after details of the Free University's cladding; the original system, designed in collaboration with Jean Prouvé, was detailed in Cor-Ten steel, which deteriorated badly over time. The new cladding echoes the detailing of the original, but is executed in naturally patinated bronze, an extremely durable material.

3. An aerial view of the mat-like Free University campus, punctuated by the silvery form of the library.

4. Standing on an upper floor of the library looking down towards the entrance.

5. The main entrance to the library, from one of the 'streets' that form the main circulation routes through the original University building.

6. Reading desks line the perimeter of each floor. The library's floors follow serpentine curves, each floor swelling and receding in relation to the one above and below it to create a series of double-height spaces in which to work.

7. An informal seating area on the upper floor of the library.

1

2

3

4

5

8. Sketch by Norman Foster of the serpentine library floors, exploring the way in which they create double-height space and open up views.

9. Cross-section, showing how the library 'plugs in' to the network of streets within the existing University building.

Overleaf: The library at dusk.

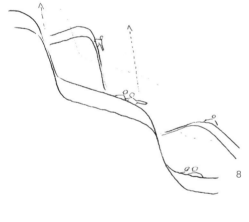

7

8

6

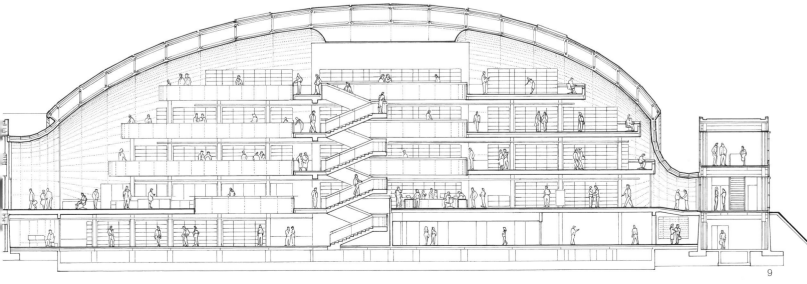

9

Her Majesty's Treasury

London, England 1996–2003

Most office buildings dating from the early part of the last century are not naturally suited to modern working practices. However, many of them add to the architectural wealth of our cities and can be restructured to fit contemporary needs. Her Majesty's Treasury is such a building. Situated between Parliament Square and Horse Guards Parade, it was completed in 1917 and is Grade II listed. In refurbishing the building, the challenge was to transform a labyrinthine and frequently under-utilised set of spaces into an efficient and enjoyable working environment.

The existing building has a roughly symmetrical plan, with two parts linked by a drum-like courtyard. Each half of the building is punctuated by smaller courtyards and light-wells, which were hitherto unused. In an echo of the strategy deployed in the Great Court at the British Museum, some of the courtyards have been capped with translucent roofs to create five-storey spaces that variously house a library, a café, training rooms and an entrance atrium. External courtyards have been landscaped with planting and pools to form recreation spaces for staff, while the central drum, hitherto used for parking, has been opened up as a new public space. Internally, more than 7 miles of partitions were removed to create open-plan offices. This radical reorganisation has enabled the entire Treasury staff to be accommodated comfortably in the western half of the building, allowing the remainder to be occupied by other government departments.

Significantly, the refurbished building has set new environmental standards in Whitehall. The reconfigured light-wells help to ventilate the building naturally, forming thermal chimneys through which air from the office spaces is exhausted by vents at roof level. Fresh air is drawn into the building through the windows, which have also been upgraded to provide improved security. This natural ventilation cycle is assisted by 'windcatchers' mounted on the roof. Heating, lighting and communication systems have been similarly modernised, so that the building combines a sense of history with a contemporary working environment.

1

2

3

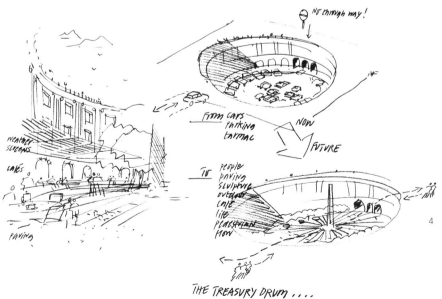

4

THE TREASURY DRUM . . . .

5 6 7

1, 2. The large courtyards within the Treasury building have been landscaped to provide a major new staff amenity.

3. An aerial view of the Treasury building, with Parliament Square in the foreground and St James' Park beyond.

4. Norman Foster's sketches describe the transformation of the central drum-shaped courtyard, which is to be reopened as a public route.

5-7. The smaller light-wells that punctuate the building have been roofed over to create a library, a café and a range of other facilities. The roofs are formed from clear polycarbonate 'pillows'.

8. Looking into the staff café, created during the first phase of the Treasury's redevelopment. The hanging banners are by Danish artist Per Arnoldi.

8

New German Parliament, Reichstag
Berlin, Germany 1992–1999

The transformation of the Reichstag is rooted in four related issues: the Bundestag's significance as a democratic forum, an understanding of history, a commitment to public accessibility and a vigorous environmental agenda. As found, the Reichstag was mutilated by war and insensitive rebuilding. The reconstruction takes cues from the original fabric; the layers of history were peeled away to reveal striking imprints of the past – stonemason's marks and Russian graffiti – scars that have been preserved as a 'living museum'. But in other respects it is a radical departure; within its heavy shell it is light and transparent, its activities on view.

Public and politicians enter the building together and the public realm continues on the roof in the terrace restaurant and in the cupola, where ramps lead to an observation platform, allowing the people to ascend symbolically above the heads of their elected representatives in the chamber. The cupola is now an established Berlin landmark. Symbolic of rebirth, it is also fundamental to the building's natural lighting and ventilation strategies. At its core is a 'light sculptor' that reflects horizon light down into the chamber, while a motorised sun-shield tracks the path of the sun to block solar gain and glare. As night falls, this process is reversed. The cupola then becomes a beacon on the skyline, signalling the strength and vigour of the German democratic process.

The building provides a model for the future by burning renewable biofuel – refined vegetable oil – in a cogenerator to produce electricity, a system that is far cleaner than burning fossil fuels. The result is a 94 per cent reduction in carbon dioxide emissions. Surplus heat is stored as hot water in an aquifer deep below ground and can be pumped up to heat the building or to drive an absorption cooling plant to produce chilled water. Significantly, the building's energy requirements are so modest that it produces more energy than it uses, allowing it to perform as a mini power station in the new government quarter: it is an object lesson in sustainability.

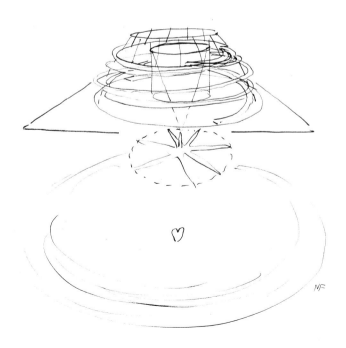

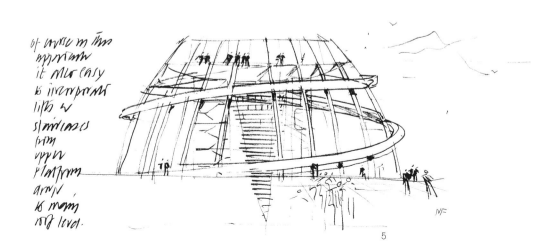

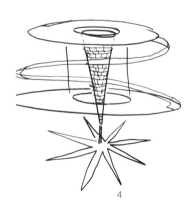

9   10

Previous pages, left: concept sketch by Norman Foster. Right: Gerhard Richter's 'Flag' seen through the Reichstag's portico.

1. At night, the Reichstag's cupola becomes a beacon, visible across the city.

2. Design sketch of the cupola by Norman Foster.

3. The west front of the Reichstag.

4, 5. Early design studies by Norman Foster.

6, 7. The Reichstag has redefined notions of public space and in the process has become one of Berlin's leading visitor attractions.

8. The restaurant terrace.

9. Looking into the chamber towards the seat of the President of the Bundestag.

10. A suspended steel bridge in the north corridor.

11. North-south cross-section through the parliamentary chamber.

Overleaf: inside the cupola.

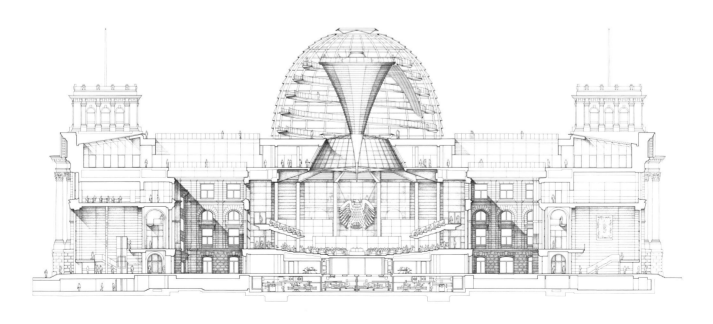

11

Supreme Court

Singapore 2000–2006

Singapore's Supreme Court is a major new judicial centre conceived in response to the city's rapidly growing population and the limited facilities of the old Supreme Court building, which it stands alongside. Located within the Colonial District, on the north bank of the Singapore River, the building takes its cue from the scale of the neighbouring civic buildings, offering a modern reinterpretation of their colonial vernacular to convey an image of dignity, transparency and openness.

The building houses twelve civil courts, eight criminal courts and three appeal courts, together with facilities for the Singapore Academy of Law, and is organised to reflect the hierarchies of the judicial system. Formally, it is articulated as a series of blocks, cut through with arcades, designed to knit the building into the city fabric. The civil courts are located on the lower floors, with the criminal courts above. The court of appeal, the highest court, is raised symbolically in a disc-like form at the top of the building – a contemporary iteration of the old courthouse's dome. Like the Reichstag's cupola, it incorporates a viewing platform that offers a dramatic panorama across the city. The blocks containing the courts are punctuated by a broad central atrium, which forms the processional circulation route through the building, and brings daylight down through the public spaces. Flanking the courts are administrative blocks, which step back at ground level to create a covered arcade along the street.

The building is designed for long-term flexibility, including future changes in the size and configuration of the courtrooms and advances in information technology. It employs a palette of high-quality materials including glazed stone – a laminate of glass and stone – which appears solid, but by day allows light to filter through it, and by night emits a warm glow. Environmentally, it incorporates a range of passive climate-control devices, including solar shading to the offices, and the roofs are planted with trees, creating a blanket of greenery that shelters a public promenade.

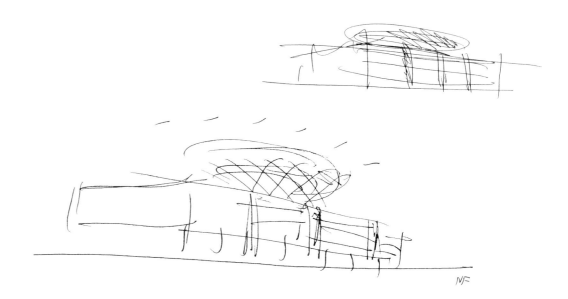

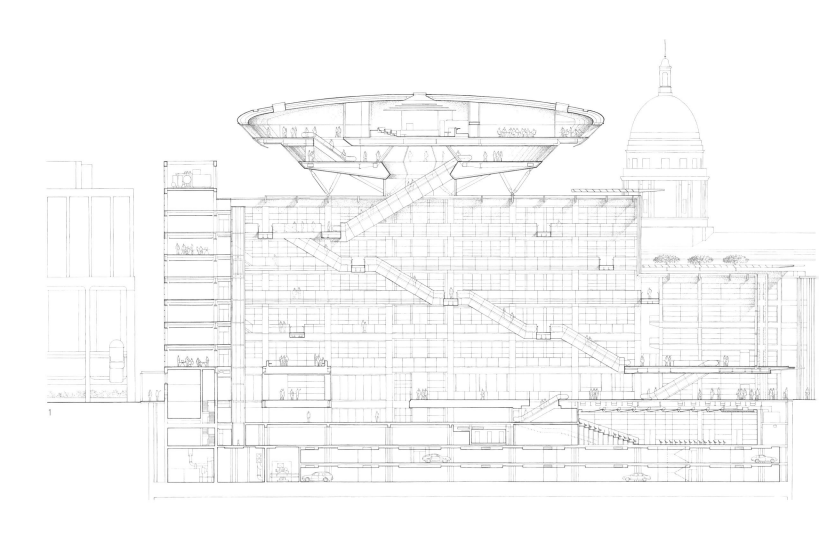

1

4

Previous pages, left: a sketch by Norman Foster exploring the design of the disc-like court chamber at the top of the building. Right: looking down into the atrium.

1. Cross-section through the atrium and the court of appeal at the top of the building.

2. Banks of glazed lift shafts in the atrium.

3. The central atrium space with its glazed roof.

4. The building at night; the dome of the old Supreme Court is seen in the background.

5. Looking out through the glazed facade of the atrium towards the central business district.

6. Escalators provide the main circulation link between levels, the long escalator in the centre rising to the appeals court on the uppermost floor.

Palace of Peace and Reconciliation
Astana, Kazakhstan 2004–2006

In September 2003, Kazakhstan – the largest of the former Soviet Republics – hosted the inaugural Congress of Leaders of World and Traditional Religions in the capital, Astana. Spurred by the Congress' success, the President of Kazakhstan decided to make it a triennial event. The Palace of Peace was conceived as a permanent venue for the Congress and a global centre for religious understanding, the renunciation of violence and the promotion of faith and human equality.

In addition to representing the world's religious faiths, the Palace houses a 1,500-seat opera house, educational facilities, and a national centre for Kazakhstan's various ethnic and geographical groups. This programmatic diversity is unified within the pure form of a pyramid, 62 metres high with a 62 x 62-metre base. Clad in stone, with glazed inserts that allude to the various internal functions, the pyramid has an apex of stained glass by the artist Brian Clarke. Spatially, it is organised around a soaring central atrium, which is animated by shifting coloured light patterns. A glass lens in the floor of the atrium casts light down into the auditorium and creates a sense of vertical continuity from the lowest level of the building to the very peak. The assembly chamber is raised at the top of the building, supported on four inclined pillars – 'the hands of peace'. Lifts take delegates to a garden-like reception space from where they ascend to the chamber via a winding ramp.

The Astanian climate posed a significant challenge, with a temperature range from 40°C in summer to -40°C in winter. The construction schedule also had to be extraordinarily rapid, the Palace needing to be complete in time for the second Congress in 2006. Together, these demands led the design team to develop a structural solution that utilises prefabricated components, which could be manufactured off-site during the winter months and erected during the summer. Remarkably, the entire process from briefing to opening was completed in just twenty-one months.

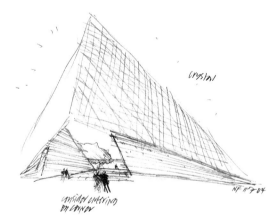

Previous pages, left: sketches by Norman Foster. Right: night-time view from the surrounding park.

1. The building illuminated for the opening ceremony, seen against a burst of fireworks.

2. Cross-section showing the pure form of the pyramid above ground and the 1,500-seat opera house below ground. A glass lens in the floor of the atrium creates a sense of vertical continuity from the lowest level to the apex of the pyramid.

3. The entrance at night, seen from the ceremonial axis that runs through Astana.

4. Early sketch by Norman Foster; the building is seen as a sculptural form set in a park landscape.

5. A processional ramp winds up through the winter garden to reach the assembly chamber.

6. View of the cradle, or 'the hands of peace', that supports the assembly chamber. The stained glass window in the apex, by artist Brian Clarke, animates the space with shifting light patterns.

1

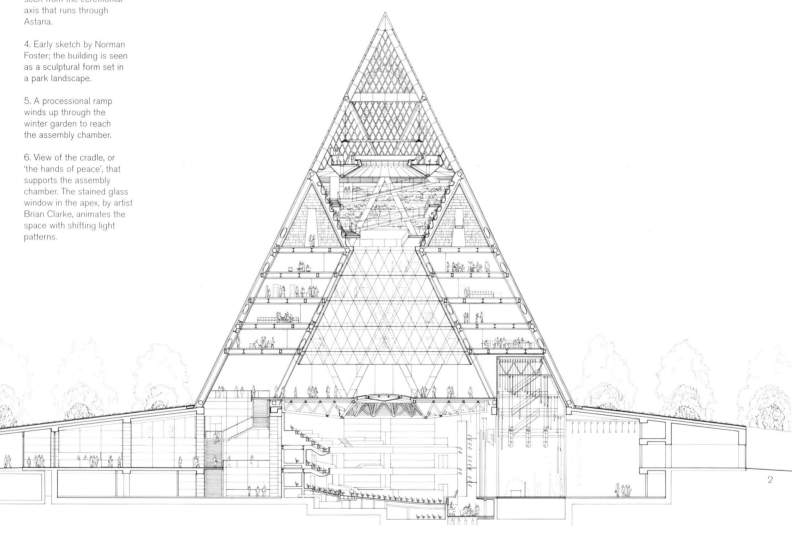

2

3

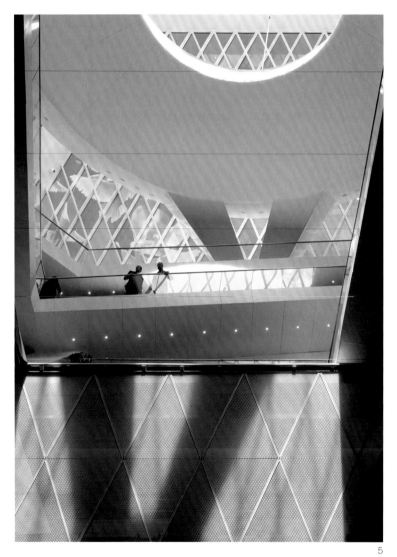

5

6

7. People gather in the main foyer before a performance in the opera house.

8. Attendees at the inaugural Congress of Leaders of World and Traditional Religions. The Palace was conceived as a permanent venue for the Congress and a global centre for religious understanding.

7

8

Motor Yacht *Izanami*
1991–1993

The design of most sea-going vessels – from 'gin palaces' to cross-Channel ferries – tends to split responsibilities, with a naval architect working on the hull, while the superstructure and interior are completed by a designer. The results are often top-heavy, with cabins that are the reverse of shipshape. In contrast, the development of this 58.5-metre private yacht saw architects and engineers working closely together, just as they would on a building. Inspired by naval vessels, in which functional efficiency takes precedence over styling, *Izanami* is as sleek as a patrol boat, but with decks and interiors evocative of a traditional yacht.

Fabricated entirely from aluminium, the hull and superstructure together form a semi-monocoque construction of welded skin, frames and longitudinal stiffeners. The superstructure is articulated as three elements – suggesting the head, thorax and abdomen of an insect – which define the owner's cabin, the crew's quarters and the wheelhouse, respectively. The structure is formed from large plates, some of which rise through two decks. These plates were rolled to create a slight convex curve, which not only increased their rigidity, but also – like entasis on a Classical entablature – helped to avoid the concave appearance sometimes encountered when flat planes meet at an angle. Picture windows in these planes maximise views from the main cabin and upper-deck spaces, while the interiors focus on a restrained palette of materials, with equally comfortable accommodation provided for passengers and crew.

Izanami has transatlantic and worldwide cruising capabilities and is built to German Lloyd's certification and ABS standards. It is powered by two MTU diesel engines rated at 4,800 horsepower and has a design speed of 30 knots, although 34 knots was achieved during sea trials. That is equivalent to the speed of sleek transatlantic liners of the past, and almost twice that possible using a conventional displacement hull of the same size. In Norman Foster's phrase, *Izanami* is 'a Ferrari of the water'.

1

2

1, 2. Two views of the owner's suite – looking in from the main deck, and a corner of the saloon.

3. Starboard elevation showing *Izanami*'s full 58.5 metre length.

4. *Izanami* photographed during sea trials in the North Sea. The vessel is immediately distinguished by its planar wheelhouse and sleek, almost military appearance.

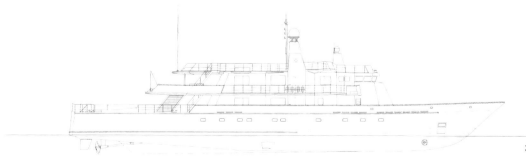

3

Nomos Table and Desking System
1985–1987

Office furniture, like the office itself, must be adaptable to changing work patterns. The Nomos concept is rooted in an earlier foray into furniture design. In 1981, when the practice expanded into a new studio, no existing furniture system could provide tables that were adjustable for meetings, draughting or display. The outcome was a custom-designed table (modified versions of which were used in the Renault Centre in Swindon), made in a small production run by a sympathetic workshop. When the Italian furniture manufacturer Tecno subsequently commissioned the practice to develop the design, they required a system that could optimise floor space, accommodate cabling and be easily reconfigured.

The concept of Nomos (a Greek word meaning 'fair distribution') is based on the relationship between the users and the space they occupy. At the heart of the design is a flexible kit of precision-engineered components that can be combined to create bespoke working environments for individuals or groups. The starting point is the spine, to which are added legs, feet, supports, work surfaces and superstructures, while a vertebra-like conduit carries cabling. With its characteristic splayed feet the desk is evocative of the lunar landing module, or a grasshopper with its thin body and slim legs. Utilising this highly stable frame, the system can accommodate shelves, storage, screens, lighting and signage – an assembly governed by the ergonomics of the human form, seated or standing.

In 1999 Tecno commissioned a new table to mark the millennium. The rectangular and circular-topped tables are long-established favourites, but in the quest for another classic shape, smooth curves were investigated to encourage better eye contact across the table's length. In tune with this more informal approach, the primary frame is also expressed in a vivid palette – red, yellow or blue – with other elements in bright chrome, while a more classical option has a chrome frame with the secondary elements in black.

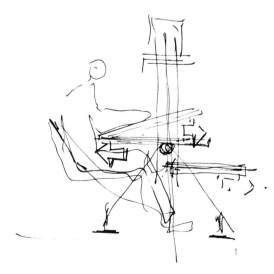

1

2

1. Norman Foster's concept sketch for Nomos, conceived as a flexible office desking system.

2. The Nomos desking system and Kite! chair used together.

3-6. Like a bicycle, the Nomos table's frame can be specified in a variety of colour options.

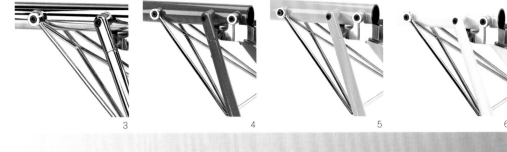

3   4   5   6

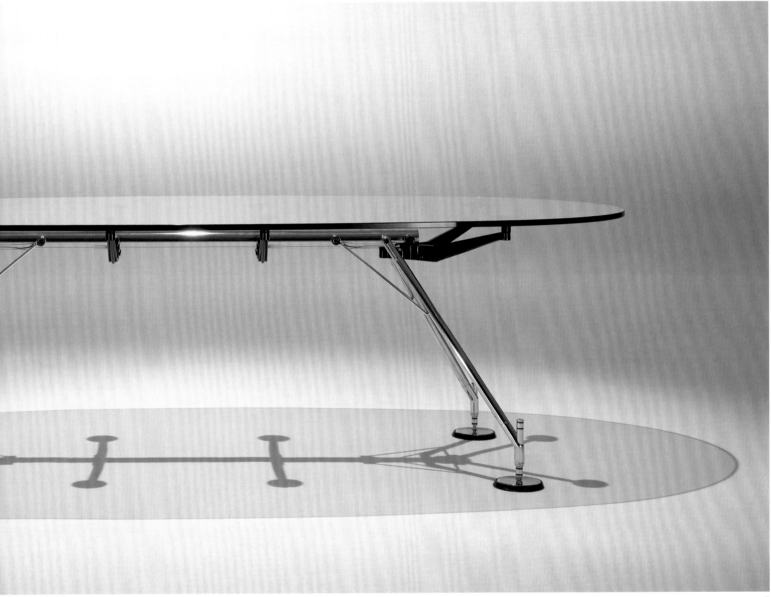

7

7. Commissioned to celebrate the Millennium, the Nomos 2000 table has a distinctive oval top, which encourages better eye contact across its length and makes it ideal for use as a dining or boardroom table.

8. A plan view of the assembled Nomos table frame.

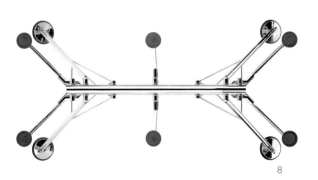

8

Product Design

The smallest details of daily life, from the shape of a door handle to the finish of a breakfast tray, are often taken for granted, but it is with these small elements that we have the most direct contact. These objects are like architecture in miniature: they must be functional but also pleasing to use, possessing good ergonomic, aesthetic and tactile qualities. The practice has an established team of industrial designers, working on items ranging from tableware to electronic goods, both for specific building projects and for manufacture.

Bathroom suites normally consist only of 'ceramic' items, requiring people to match taps, accessories and other elements as best they can. The practice has a holistic approach to design and believes this separation to be artificial. It has collaborated with two German companies – Duravit and Hoesch – to design a bathroom suite with a fully complementary range of sanitaryware, furniture, taps and accessories, which provides cohesive interiors for domestic and commercial bathrooms. The Place kitchen, designed for Dada, is similarly integrated, with adaptable features including worktops that can be raised or lowered to suit the activity, whether preparing food or eating.

At a smaller scale, the NF 95 Door Handle for Fusital was partly inspired by the bird-shaped form of a medieval door handle in Magdeburg Cathedral, and by the design of penknives, in which the mechanism is sandwiched between grips in a variety of materials. The handle consists of a metal plate held between grips contoured to the shape of the hand. This investigation continued in door handles developed with Trapex. Further collaborations have included the Diplomat Pen for Helit, which complements a range of desktop accessories, and products for lighting manufacturers, such as Artemide, iGuzzini and Louis Poulsen. Originally conceived for the Posthaus restaurant in St Moritz, the Ilium light concept has now been extended to a family of lights for Italian lighting manufacturer Nemo.

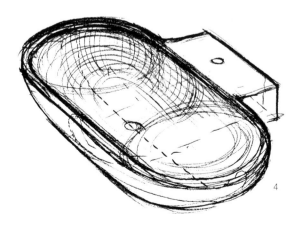

2

3

1

4

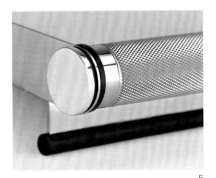

5

6

1. The Diplomat pen complements the range of Helit Foster Series Desk Accessories (2008).

2. Ilium light for Italian manufacturer Nemo, originally conceived for the interior design of the Posthaus restaurant, St Moritz (2007).

3. A bidet and toilet from the Bathroom Foster series (2001).

4. Norman Foster's design study for a washbasin – another component in the Bathroom Foster series.

5. Detail of the laser-cut aluminium breakfast tray designed for Alessi (1998).

6. A Trapex FT door handle, with a black rubber grip (2005).

7. The Place range of kitchen furniture was the result of a year-long collaboration with the Italian company Dada (2004).

8, 9. The NF 95 door handle shown in its family of related objects and an early design sketch by Norman Foster (1995).

7

8

9

wood

leather
plastic

metal
dull/shiny
glass

rubber
plastic

Furniture

From its earliest days the practice has designed furniture and fixtures in order to bring greater cohesion to particular building projects. Often proprietary products have been neither suitable nor flexible enough for a defined need, and so new designs have been developed. The design of furniture has also developed as a discipline within the Foster studio and products are commissioned by major manufacturers. A recent example, the Foster 500 series armchair, produced by Walter Knoll, is based on a dimensional module that can be configured to create a variety of spatial arrangements.

An example of a product evolving through first-hand experience of architectural design challenges, the Airline seating for Vitra is a flexible product range that relates directly to the practice's work at Stansted and Chek Lap Kok airports. Based on a limited 'kit-of-parts', the Airline range offers differing levels of comfort, dimensions, materials and configurations, ease of transportation, installation and servicing and can be tuned to suit individual requirements while still maintaining a very competitive cost per seat. Similarly marrying flexibility with manufacturing discipline, the Kite! chair – which was originally commissioned by Tecno to accompany the Nomos desk – reflects a shift towards greater informality in working patterns and more flexibility for personal expression in the office environment. Like a kite, it comprises an efficiently engineered frame over which soft fabrics can be stretched.

As with larger scale architectural commissions, the principles of sustainability underpin the studio's approach to furniture design. The 20-06 chair was designed for Emeco, the manufacturers of the classic 10-06 Navy® Chair originally made for submarines in World War II. Its sleek aluminium silhouette is deceptively tough but lightweight, using less aluminium than the original Navy chair; and 80 per cent of the material used is recycled. The ergonomically shaped aluminium seat and back are hand-welded, giving it a minimal, seamless appearance as well as an estimated 150-year lifespan.

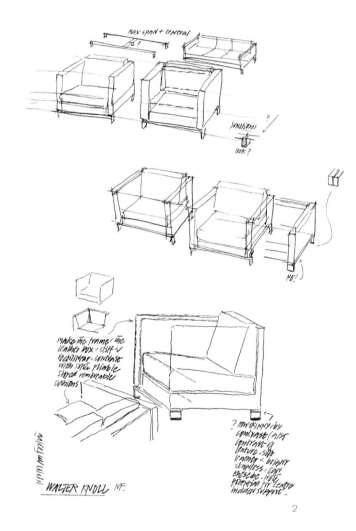

2

1

3

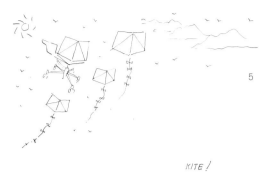

5

1. The 503 sofa series for Walter Knoll; the sofa complements the 500 series chair, but has a thicker arm profile and higher back (2005).

2, 3. The 500 series chair for Walter Knoll, with design sketches by Norman Foster (2002).

6

7

8

4. Kite! is a flexible seating system designed to complement the Nomos table and desk (1997).

5. An early sketch for Kite! by Norman Foster.

6. The Airline seating system for Vitra (1997).

7. A Thonet A900 Series chair (1997).

8. The aluminium Emeco 20-06 chair (2006); its ergonomically shaped seat and back are hand-welded.

Great Glasshouse, National Botanic Garden of Wales
Llanarthne, Wales 1994–2000

Set in rolling hills overlooking the Tywi Valley in Carmarthenshire, the Great Glasshouse forms the centrepiece of the 230-hectare National Botanic Garden of Wales. The largest single-span glasshouse in the world, containing more than a thousand Mediterranean plant species, it reinvents the glasshouse for the twenty-first century, offering a model for sustainable development.

Elliptical in plan the building swells from the ground like a glassy hillock, echoing the undulations of the surrounding landscape. The aluminium glazing system and its tubular-steel supporting structure are designed to minimise materials and maximise light transmission. The toroidal roof measures 99 by 55 metres, and rests on twenty-four arches, which spring from a concrete ring beam and rise to 15 metres at the apex of the dome. Because the roof curves in two directions, only the central arches rise perpendicular to the base, the outer arches leaning inwards at progressively steep angles. The building's concrete substructure is banked to the north to provide protection from cold northerly winds and is concealed by a covering of turf so that the three entrances appear to be cut discreetly into the hillside. Within this base are a public concourse, a café, educational spaces and service installations.

To optimise energy usage, conditions inside and outside are monitored by a computer-controlled system. This adjusts the supply of heat and opens glazing panels in the roof to achieve desired levels of temperature, humidity and air movement. The principal heat source is a biomass boiler, located in the park's Energy Centre, which burns timber trimmings. This method is remarkably clean when compared with fossil fuels, and because the plants absorb as much carbon dioxide during their lifetime as they release during combustion, the carbon cycle is broadly neutral. Rainwater collected from the roof supplies 'grey water' for irrigation and flushing lavatories while waste from the lavatories is treated in reed beds before release into a watercourse.

Previous pages, left: Norman Foster's sketch, showing how the Glasshouse nestles in the landscape. Right: looking up through the overarching glass roof.

1. A long-section through the Glasshouse; its gently curving form echoes the undulating profile of the Carmarthenshire hills.

2-4. The glass roof allows maximum light to reach the plants but overheating is avoided through the use of computer-controlled panels in the glazing, which open automatically to ventilate the building.

5, 6. The Glasshouse in the landscape.

2

3

4

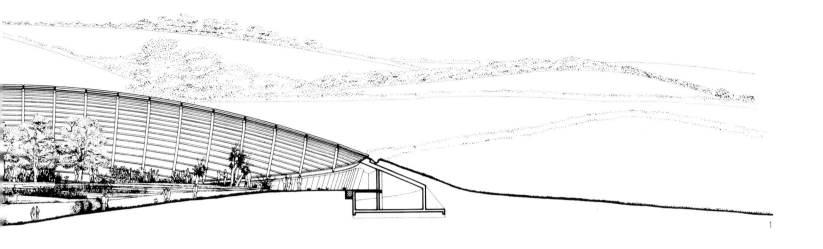

1

5

6

Wembley Stadium
London, England 1996–2007

Originally built for the British Empire Exhibition of 1924, and in turn the site of the Olympic Games in 1948 and the football World Cup Final in 1966, the old Wembley Stadium was the most important sports and entertainment venue in Britain. The challenge in reinventing it for a new century was to build on that heritage and yet create a venue that would be memorable and magical in its own right. With 90,000 seats, standing almost four times the height and covering twice the area of the original, the new stadium is the largest covered arena in the world.

Facilities are designed to maximise spectator enjoyment; seats are larger than the old ones, with more leg-room; the highest tiers are easily accessed via escalators; and the concourse that wraps around the building provides catering for up to 40,000 spectators at any one time. One of the things that make the stadium special is the retractable roof, which ensures that the spectator experience is comfortable in all weathers. When the roof is open it enables the turf to get sufficient sunlight and air to maintain perfect condition, while in poor weather it can be closed to cover the entire seating bowl. The roof is supported structurally by a spectacular 133-metre-high arch that soars over the stadium, providing an iconic replacement for the old building's twin towers; conceived as a triumphal gateway, floodlit at night it is a strong symbol for the new Wembley and a new London landmark.

The stadium is designed to be ideal for football. Its geometry and steeply raked seating tiers ensure that everyone has an unobstructed view. To recreate the intimate atmosphere and the distinctive 'Wembley roar' for which the old stadium was famous, the seats are located as close to the pitch as possible. Yet the building has also been consciously 'future proofed', with the ability to host a variety of events, including international track and field events to Olympic standard if required.

reflective during the day - a symbol day & night.

glistening at night on the skyline - a jewel - a tiara!

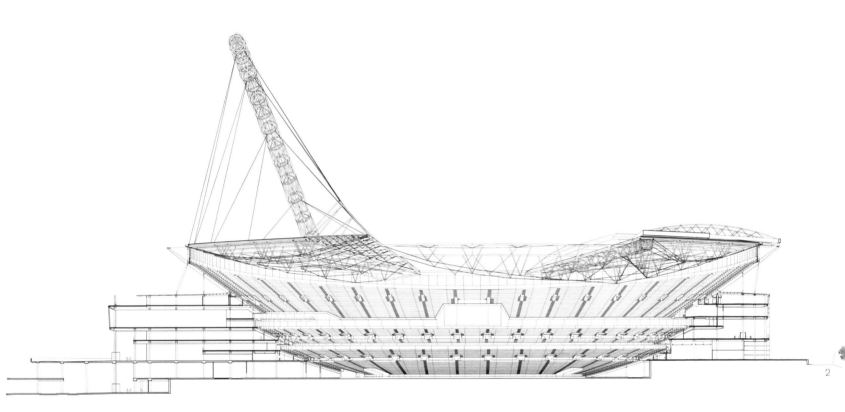

Previous pages, left:
sketches by Norman Foster
exploring the Wembley
arch's role as a landmark on
the London skyline. Right:
the stadium illuminated to
celebrate the FA Cup Final,
seen across the waters of
Brent Reservoir.

1. Looking south along
Olympic Way, the main public
approach to the stadium.

2. North-south cross-section
through the stadium bowl.

3, 4. Aerial views of the
stadium from the north-east
and east respectively; the
roof is seen fully open.

5　　　　　　6

7

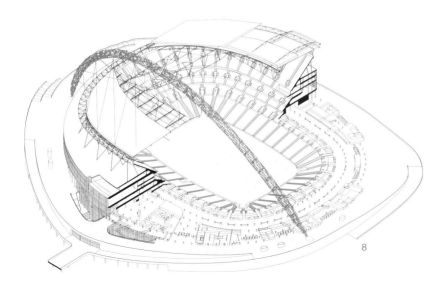

8

5, 6. The atrium on the
north side provides access
to the hospitality areas and
also acts as a pre-function
gathering space.

7. The stadium viewed from
the west.

8. Cutaway drawing showing
how hospitality areas are
arranged in a 'drum' that
wraps around the seating
bowl.

Overleaf: The Red Arrows
soar overhead before the
kick-off of the 2007 FA Cup
Final – the first to be held in
the new stadium.

Elephant House
Copenhagen, Denmark 2002–2008

Set within a historic royal park, adjacent to the Frederiksberg Palace, Copenhagen Zoo is the largest cultural institution in Denmark, attracting over 1.2 million visitors a year. Among the Zoo's more than 3,000 animals, its group of Indian elephants is perhaps its most popular attraction. Replacing a structure dating from 1914, this new Elephant House seeks to restore the visual relationship between the zoo and the park and to provide these magnificent animals with a stimulating environment, with easily accessible spaces from which to enjoy them.

Research into the social patterns of elephants, together with a desire to bring a sense of light and openness to a building type traditionally characterised as closed, even fortified, provided powerful starting points. The tendency for bull elephants in the wild to roam away from the main herd suggested a plan form organised around two separate enclosures, which are dug into the site, both to minimise the building's impact in the landscape and to optimise its passive thermal performance. Covered with lightweight, glazed domes, these spaces maintain a strong visual connection with the sky and changing patterns of daylight. The elephants can congregate here, or out in the adjacent paddocks. Broad public viewing terraces run around the domes externally, while a ramped promenade leads down into an educational space, looking into the enclosures along the way. Barriers between the animals and visitors are discreet, and the paddock walls are concealed in an elongated pool of water so that the approaching visitor encounters the elephants as another 'surprise' in the Romantic landscape of the park.

Significantly, in terms of the elephants' well-being, the building sets new zoological standards. For example, the main herd enclosure will for the first time enable elephants in captivity to sleep together, as they would in the wild, while the floors are heated to keep them dry and thus maintain the health of the elephants' feet. Other key aspects of the design are the result of research into the elephants' natural habitat. The paddocks recreate a section of dry riverbed as found at the edge of the rainforest – a favourite haunt of Asian elephants. With mud holes, scattered pools of water and shading objects, it will be a place where the animals can play and interact freely.

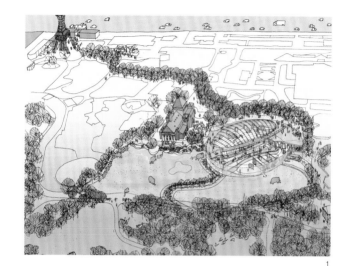

1

1. Drawing showing the Elephant House's location within Copenhagen Zoo.

2. Sketches by Norman Foster, exploring the double-dome structure.

3, 4. The roof glazing has a leaf pattern 'frit' to provide shading; opening vents allow natural ventilation.

5. A bull elephant newly arrived in its enclosure.

6. Cross-section through the two elephant enclosures and the ramped promenade that leads down to the educational space.

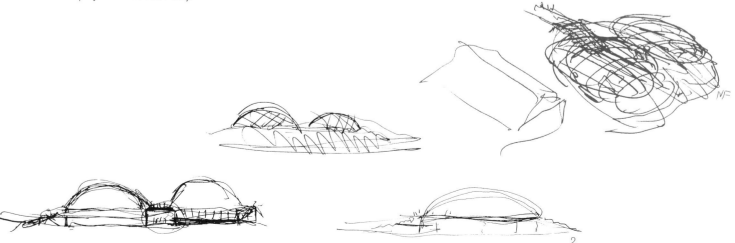

2

3

4

5

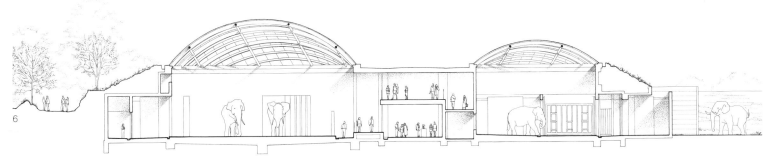

6

La Voile
St Jean Cap Ferrat, France 1999–2002

The stretch of Mediterranean coastline around St Jean Cap Ferrat boasts some of the twentieth century's most celebrated houses – by architects including Le Corbusier, Eileen Gray and Oscar Niemeyer – the best of them fusing Modernist principles with vernacular tradition. La Voile continues this pattern, integrating a tightly planned family house within a steeply sloping site and exploiting passive methods of environmental control.

The physical fabric of the house is a complex interweaving of old and new. It was originally built in the mid-1950s as a simple masonry structure. However, over the years it had undergone major alterations that had undermined its vernacular Mediterranean character. The starting point for this project, therefore, was to strip away the clutter that had accumulated around the house and to adapt the three-storey masonry shell to form the container for a new sequence of spaces designed to celebrate the view and the changing quality of natural light. The spatial and social focus of the house is a double-height living space that looks out to sea through a winter garden whose glazed walls slide back in fine weather to admit sunlight and fresh air.

A swimming pool has been inserted at the rear of the house in a compact structure, which also houses a garage. All the new elements are designed to complement the rugged nature of the original architecture, so that it nestles into the surrounding rough landscape – the garrigue – of hardy indigenous shrubs. The 'lightness' of these new elements contrasts deliberately with the 'heaviness' of the old. Interestingly, the most dramatic of the new interventions is also the least visible. Building on the local tradition of the pergola, two large steel arches spring from the rear of the swimming pool and vault over the house. The arches carry the canvas 'sails' that provide natural shade from the intense Mediterranean sun and support a fine net of vines designed to conceal the house beneath a camouflaging 'green veil'.

1   2

3

Previous pages, left: an early
sketch by Norman Foster
explaining how a lightweight
green canopy is placed
over the heavy base of the
house. Right: a detail of
the stretched fabric panels
that provide sun shading to
the terraces and the south
facade.

1, 2. The living space
occupies a three-storey
volume created by scooping
out the intermediate floors of
the original house.

3. Looking out to sea across
the swimming pool on the
upper terrace level.

4. East-west cross-section
showing how the bedrooms
and other spaces wrap
around the main volume
of the living room.

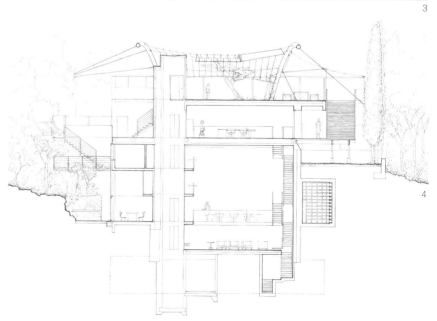

4

5, 6. The southern wall of the living space is fully glazed and can be slid aside to open the space up to sunlight and sea air.

7. North-south cross-section through the house showing its relationship with the sea below.

8. The house at night, with the lights of the Corniche in the distance.

5

6

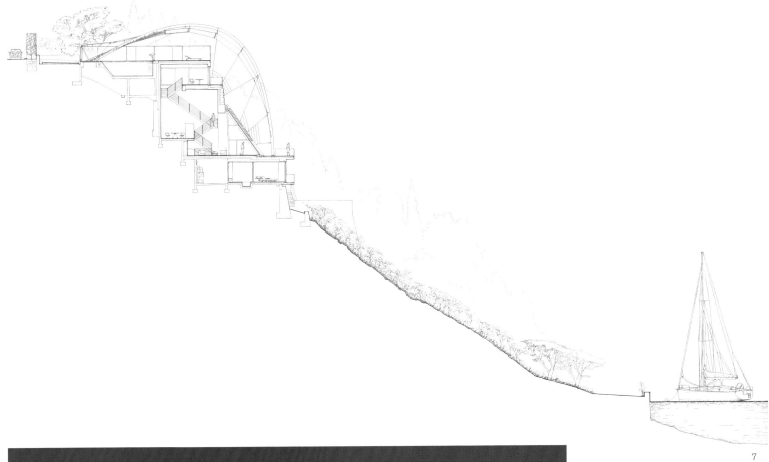

7

8

House in Kamakura
Kamakura, Japan 2000 – 2004

Designed for a Japanese collector of modern and Buddhist art, this house was conceived as a contemporary retreat with traditional influences. The house occupies a site rich with historical associations, including a Shinto shrine and man-made caves that once formed part of a workshop for crafting samurai swords. The house is one of three buildings originally planned for the site, those yet to be built comprising an art gallery and function space, with specialised storage. The overall composition is intended to tie these buildings together in a harmonious arrangement, informed by the Japanese belief that nature is at its most beautiful when considered in relation to the man-made.

A series of parallel structural walls organises the interior spaces of all three buildings, and these are further articulated by perpendicular infill walls that carry the service functions. The house is planned around the rugged landscape and focuses on a mature cherry tree. Circulation is organised so as to capture a sequence of carefully framed landscape views, the route through the house progressing from darkened to fully lit rooms, revealing and framing en route items from the client's extensive art collection. A comprehensive integrated lighting system, which includes fibre-optic installations, dedicated spotlights, and naturally backlit glass blocks, further emphasises major individual art works. Special attention has been paid to the subtle use of colour, with muted tones and dark grey ceilings that add a degree of intimacy.

The design team developed a number of specialised materials for the project. The primary walls are clad with a custom-manufactured reconstructed stone, while glass blocks made from recycled television tubes provide diffused daylight. The floors are covered in part with antique Chinese tiles, and the indoor pool is finished in glazed volcanic stone. Throughout the house, the play of light and shade, created through a combination of materials and finishes, artificial and natural light, is intended to evoke the quietude of traditional Japanese architecture.

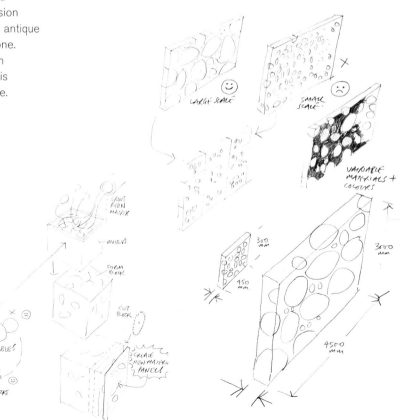

Previous pages, left: sketches by David Nelson illustrating the stage-by-stage construction of the custom-made cast-stone blocks that were used to construct the house. Right: looking towards the glass-block wall that terminates the hallway at its living room end. The spots of light in the wall are formed by fibre-optically lit glass 'nuggets' cast within the wall panels.

3

4

2

5

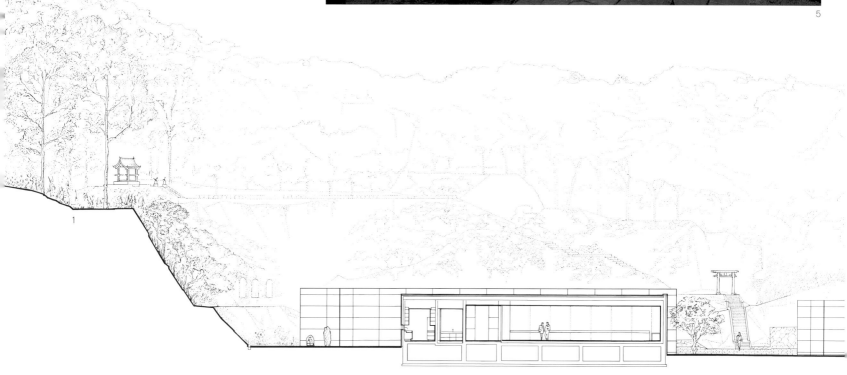

1

1. East-west cross-section, from the Shinto shrine to the left, down through the guest pavilion and main house.

2. Looking down across the roof of the house, with Kamakura and the coast in the far distance.

3. A view of the Shinto shrine, which occupies an elevated position at the rear of the house.

6

7

8

4. A view out from the al-fresco dining table on the first-floor terrace.

5. The pool and bedroom areas of the main house seen from the terraced garden.

6. Antique Chinese paving stones cover the floor in the hallway.

7. Looking into the living room from the hallway.

8. A small vernacular dwelling is incorporated within the heart of the house, forming a space for prayer and meditation.

Albion Riverside

London, England 1999–2003

The development of Albion Riverside reinforces a growing new community on the south bank of the Thames, alongside the Foster studio between Battersea and Albert Bridges. A mixed-use development, its ingredients are designed to promote a lively urban quarter where people can live, work and enjoy life in the heart of the city. The scheme comprises three separate buildings linked by new public spaces and routes. Shops, business spaces, cafés and leisure facilities are grouped at ground level, with parking below and residences, including low-cost housing, above.

The principal building on the waterfront is eleven storeys high. Its massing is designed to respect the heights of neighbouring buildings and to frame the view of the river from the opposite bank. Arcing back from the water's edge, the building forms an asymmetrical crescent to create a public space alongside the river walk. The facades are principally of glass, creating elevations that vary in appearance and sparkle according to prevailing light conditions and changing viewpoints. On the river facade, curved balconies with clear glass balustrades are accessed through full-height sliding glazed panels, which allow the apartments to open out on to the water. The strong horizontal line of the balconies reinforces a sense of visual order, allowing the clutter of inhabitation to proliferate but not dominate. The southern facade, in contrast, is veiled, clad in a fine net of aluminium rods, and pierced by recessed balconies and windows. The roof continues the building's curving form, wrapping over and around in a single sweep.

A typical floor in this building contains twenty-six apartments, arranged around four service cores. In total there are 183 apartments, ranging from one to four bedrooms, and twelve duplex penthouses. Informing all of the apartment layouts is a sense of flexibility – sliding partitions allow spaces to be opened up or divided for different uses, while balconies offer an extension of living spaces and are deep enough to encourage outdoor dining.

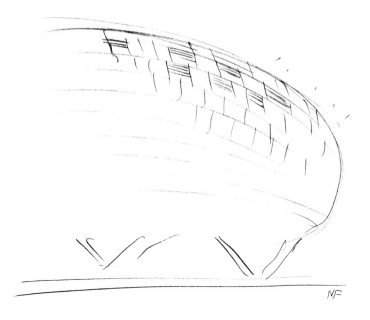

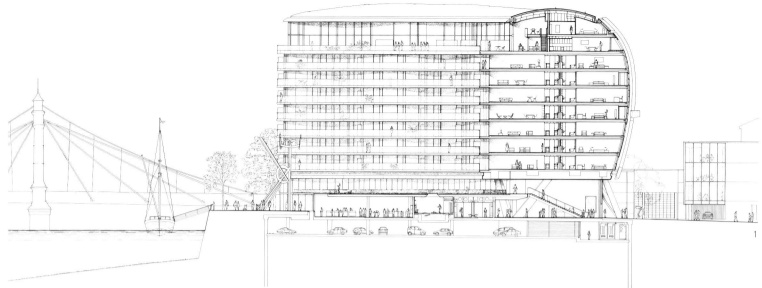

1

Previous pages, left: design
sketch by Norman Foster.
Right: the building seen at
low tide from Albert Bridge.
The snaking balconies catch
the light and optimise views.

1. Cross-section through
the building from the
riverside walk and Albert
Bridge on the left, to
Hester Road on the right.
Nine apartment floors are
arranged above galleries
and commercial spaces
at street level.

2. Looking up at the fluid
form of the northern facade.
Balconies with glazed
balustrades run continuously
along the river frontage.

3. A small private garden
for residents is laid out on
the roof of the commercial
accommodation – a detail
reminiscent of the Willis
Faber building.

4. Looking east along
the landscaped riverside
walkway – one of the few
publicly-accessible riverside
spaces in the capital.

4

2
3

Chesa Futura
St Moritz, Switzerland 2000 – 2004

Chesa Futura (literally, 'house of the future') fuses state-of-the-art computer design tools with centuries-old construction techniques to create an environmentally sensitive apartment building. Although its form is novel, it is framed and clad in timber – one of the oldest and most sustainable building materials. In Switzerland, building in timber is particularly appropriate in that it follows indigenous architectural traditions, developed and refined over centuries. The building's larch shingles will respond naturally to exposure to the elements, changing colour over time to a silver-grey, and will last for a hundred years without the need for maintenance.

The building consists of three storeys of apartments and an underground level for car parking, plant and storage. Although small, the site is spectacularly located on the edge of a steep slope, looking down across the town of St Moritz towards the lake. Responding to this location and to weather patterns in the Engadin Valley, the building's bubble-like form allows windows and balconies on the southern side to open up to sunlight and panoramic views, while the colder, north facade is more closed, punctuated with deep window openings in the Engadin tradition. In Switzerland, where snow lies on the ground for many months of the year, there is a long tradition of elevating buildings to avoid the danger of wood decaying due to prolonged exposure to moisture. That tradition is reinterpreted here by raising the building on pilotis and allowing the ground plane to continue unbroken beneath it – a move that has the added advantage of allowing the lower level apartments to enjoy views that would otherwise be denied.

Taken overall, Chesa Futura might be regarded as a mini manifesto for architecture, not just in Engadin but in other parts of the world too. Contrary to the pattern of sprawl that disfigures the edges of so many expanding communities, it shows how new buildings can be inserted into the existing grain at increased densities, while sustaining indigenous building techniques and preserving the natural environment.

lightly touching down ....perched on the slope ...

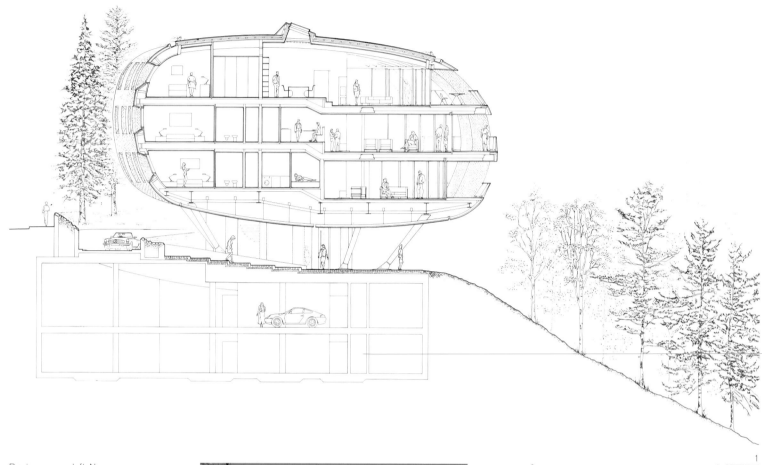

Previous pages, left: Norman Foster's sketch emphasises how the building 'touches down lightly'. Right: detail of the southern facade with its recessed balconies.

1. Cross-section through the apartments. The building is elevated above two levels of subterranean parking.

2. The building seen from the west.

3. Seen from higher up the mountain, the building nestles into the dense fabric of St Moritz.

4. Looking out across St Moritz from one of the deeply recessed balconies.

5, 6. Extracts from a series of sketches by Norman Foster depicting the building in its context.

Overleaf: The building takes its place within St Moritz.

4

CONTEXT   THE TOWN SQUARE - ST MORITZ
High density · urban - everything
within walking distance.

5

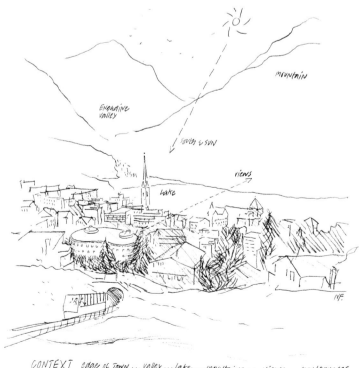

CONTEXT edge of town ... valley ... lake ... mountains ... views ... sun terraces

6

Millennium Tower
Tokyo, Japan 1989

Tokyo is among the 'megacities' forecast to exceed populations of fifteen million by 2020. The Millennium Tower challenges assumptions about such future cities and presents a solution to the social challenges of urban expansion on this scale and the particular problems of Tokyo, with its acute land shortages. Commissioned by the Obayashi Corporation, it provides one million square metres of commercial development, stands 170 storeys high and is the world's tallest projected building.

Rising out of Tokyo Bay, 2 kilometres offshore, the tower is capable of housing a community of up to 60,000 people, generating its own energy and processing its own waste. A vertical city quarter, it would be self-sustaining and virtually self-sufficient. The lower levels accommodate offices and 'clean' industries such as consumer electronics. Above are apartments, while the uppermost section houses communications systems and wind generators. A high-speed 'metro' system – with cars designed to carry 160 people – tracks both vertically and horizontally, moving through the building at twice the rate of conventional express lifts. Cars stop at intermediate 'sky centres' at every thirtieth floor; from there, individual journeys may be completed via lifts or escalators. This continuous cycle reduces travel times – an important factor in a vertical city, no less than a horizontal one. The five-storey sky centres have different principal functions – one might include a hotel, another a department store. Each is articulated with mezzanines, terraces and gardens to encourage a sense of place.

Developed in response to the hurricane-strength wind forces and earthquakes for which the region is notorious, the tower's conical structure, with its helical steel cage, is inherently stable. It provides decreasing wind resistance towards the top – where it is completely open – and increasing width and strength towards the base to provide earthquake resistance. The project demonstrates that high-density or high-rise living does not mean overcrowding or hardship; it can lead to an improved quality of life, where housing, work and leisure facilities are all close at hand.

1. Extracts from Norman Foster's concept sketches.

2. Cross-section through the tower. Punctuated at regular intervals by five-storey sky centres, the tower can absorb a wide variety of deep and shallow plan accommodation, from new technology industrial spaces to restaurants, hotels and apartments. Communications and energy infrastructure occupies the upper levels.

Opposite: Visualisation showing the 170-storey tower located 2 kilometres offshore in Tokyo Bay.

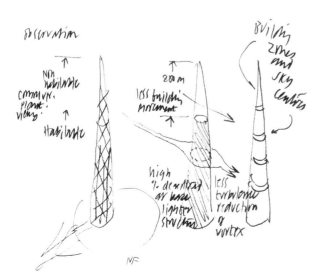

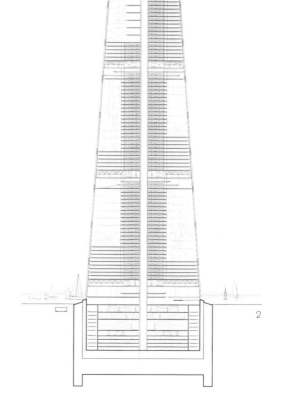

2

Stansted Airport
Stansted, England 1981–1991

Stansted Airport challenged all the rules of airport terminal design. It went back to the roots of modern air travel and literally stood conventional wisdom on its head. The earliest airport buildings were very simple: on one side there was a road and on the other a field where aircraft landed into the wind. The route from landside to airside involved a walk from your car through the terminal and out to your plane, which was always in view. Stansted attempted to recapture the clarity of those early airfields, together with some of the lost romance of air travel.

From the traveller's point of view, movement through the completed building is straightforward and direct – there are none of the level changes and orientation problems that characterise most airports. Passengers progress in a fluid movement from the set-down point through to the check-in area, passport control and departure lounges, where they can see the planes. From there, an automated tracked transit system takes them to satellite buildings to board their aircraft. This degree of clarity was achieved by turning the building 'upside down', banishing the heavy environmental services usually found at roof level to an undercroft that runs beneath the concourse floor. The undercroft also contains baggage handling and was able to accommodate a mainline railway station, which was integrated into the building late in the design process.

Service distribution systems are contained within the 'trunks' of the structural 'trees' that rise up from the undercroft through the concourse floor. These trees support a lightweight roof that is freed simply to keep out the rain and let in light. Entirely daylit on all but the most overcast of days, the constantly changing play of light gives the concourse a poetic dimension and also has significant energy and economic advantages, leading to running costs half those of any other British terminal. Energy efficient, environmentally discreet within its rural setting, technologically advanced yet simple to use and experience, Stansted has become a model for airport planners and designers worldwide.

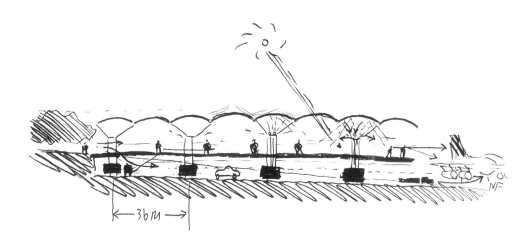

Previous pages, left:
Norman Foster's sketch of
the environmental concept.
Right: a lightweight roof,
freed from services, allows
natural light to flood the
concourse.

1. Norman Foster's sketch
shows the simplicity of
passenger flow through
the airport on a single level.

2. From the landside of the
terminal, aeroplanes landing
and taxiing across the
runway are clearly visible.

3. Shops and concession
stands are integrated
within flexible, free-standing
enclosures.

4. View across the baggage
hall; the main concourse
is naturally lit on all but
the most overcast of days.

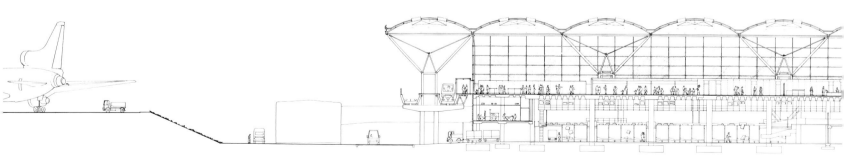

5

6

8

7

5, 6. Approaches to the terminal from the car park and bus station.

7. The terminal's roof extends by one structural bay to form a canopy over the set-down point.

8. The train station housed in the building's undercroft provides a direct link to central London.

9. A cross-section from airside to landside. Passenger movement through the terminal building is clear and direct. Baggage handling and services are contained within an undercroft beneath the concourse.

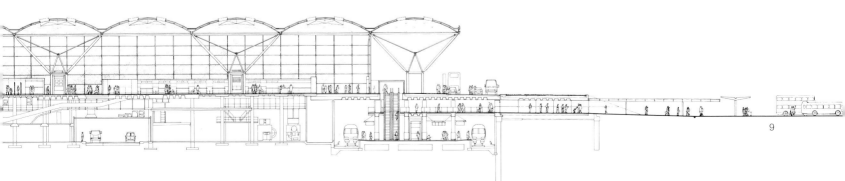

9

Hong Kong International Airport, Chek Lap Kok
Hong Kong 1992–1998

Lying at the hub of a global region reaching across Asia and Australasia, Chek Lap Kok is one of the world's largest and most advanced airports. Completed in 1998 as Hong Kong's sole air terminal, by 2040 it will handle eighty million passengers per annum – the equivalent of London's Heathrow and New York's JFK airports combined. Among the most ambitious construction projects of modern times, the land on which the airport stands was once a mountainous island. In a major reclamation programme, its 100-metre peak was reduced to 7 metres above sea level and the island was expanded to four times its original area – equal to the size of the Kowloon peninsula.

The terminal building extends a concept the practice pioneered at Stansted Airport – a model since adopted by airport planners worldwide. It is characterised by a lightweight roof, free of service installations; natural lighting; and the integration beneath the main concourse of baggage handling, environmental services and transportation. With its soaring spaces, bathed in light, it forms a spectacular gateway to the city. Routes are legible and orientation is simple: you are aware of the land on one side and the water on the other and you can see the aircraft. Similarly, the vaulted roof provides a constant reference point as you move to or from your plane. Departing passengers pass through the East Hall, the largest airport retail space in the world; if an airport on this scale can be thought of as a 'city in microcosm' then this is its market square.

Travellers reach the airport from Hong Kong via either mainland road or rail links, which cross two new suspension bridges and a causeway to Lantau to the south. Those arriving by train alight at the Ground Transportation Centre, which is integrated at the eastern end of the terminal. Remarkably, the entire journey between city and airport can be completed in just twenty minutes.

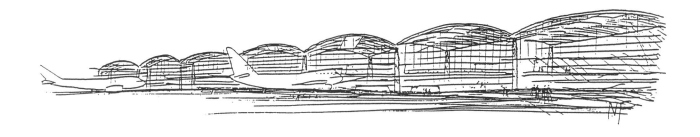

Previous pages, left: sketch by Norman Foster illustrating the airport's undulating roof. Right: view of the passenger set-down area, with Lantau Island in the background.

1. Cross-section through the airport's East Hall with an elevation of the twin, vaulted wings behind.

2. An aerial view of the terminal building, with its distinctive Y-shaped plan.

3. Norman Foster's concept sketch defining the directional roof vaulting.

4. View of the 'meeters and greeters' area in the arrivals hall.

2

The roof is developed out of one simple vault module. The height and width varies according to needs. The structure orders and lights the spaces.

a

b

3

c

The grain and angle of the structure provides instant orientation both inside the building and also from the outside.

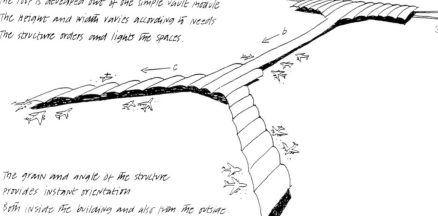

4

5

6

7

5, 6. Views of the check-in area at the eastern end of the terminal and the double-height arrivals atrium.

7. Detail of the daylight reflectors that run along the underside of the concourse roof.

Overleaf: Looking out from the check-in area towards the aircraft and the backdrop of Lantau Island.

Beijing International Airport, Terminal 3

Beijing, China 2003 – 2008

Beijing's new international terminal is the world's largest and most advanced airport building — not only technologically, but also in terms of passenger experience, operational efficiency and sustainability. Completed as the gateway to the city for athletes participating in the twenty-ninth Olympiad, it is designed to be welcoming and uplifting. A symbol of place, its soaring aerodynamic roof and dragon-like form celebrate the thrill and poetry of flight and evoke traditional Chinese colours and symbols.

Located between the existing eastern runway and the future third runway, the terminal building and Ground Transportation Centre (GTC) enclose a floor area of 1.3 million square metres and will accommodate an estimated 50 million passengers per annum by 2020. Although conceived on an unprecedented scale, the building's design expands on the new airport paradigm created by Stansted and Chek Lap Kok. Designed for maximum flexibility to cope with the unpredictable nature of the aviation industry, like its predecessors, it aims to resolve the complexities of modern air travel, combining spatial clarity with high service standards. Public transport connections are fully integrated, walking distances for passengers are short, with few level changes, and transfer times between flights are minimised. Like Chek Lap Kok, the terminal is open to views to the outside and planned under a single unifying roof canopy, whose linear skylights are both an aid to orientation and sources of daylight — the colour cast changing from red to yellow as passengers progress through the building.

The terminal building is one of the world's most sustainable, incorporating a range of passive environmental design concepts, such as the south-east orientated skylights, which maximise heat gain from the early morning sun, and an integrated environment-control system that minimises energy consumption. In construction terms, its design optimised the performance of materials selected on the basis of local availability, functionality, application of local skills, and low cost procurement. Remarkably, it was designed and built in just four years.

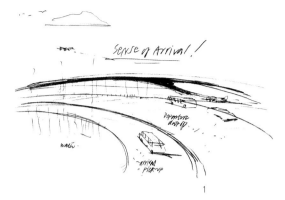

1

2

Previous pages, left: competition sketch by Norman Foster. Right: detail of the triangular rooflights showing the integration of structure, lighting and ceiling systems.

1. Sketch by Norman Foster demonstrating the 'sense of arrival'.

2. View from the Ground Transportation Centre platform level.

3. Exterior view of one of the gates, showing the raked glazing.

4. Aerial view revealing the compact plan form.

5. Sketch by Norman Foster defining the building's form; the curves increase the perimeter to accommodate more aircraft.

6. View of the 'meeters and greeters' area in T3A.

7. Looking down into the automated people mover (APM) station which connects T3A and T3B.

8. Cross-section through the centre of terminal T3A showing the direct relationship between the Ground Transportation Centre and check-in hall.

Overleaf: The view on arrival at terminal T3B.

6

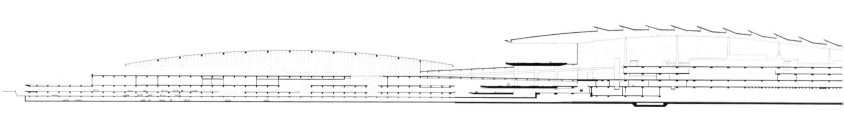

3

4

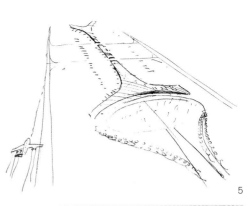

5

7

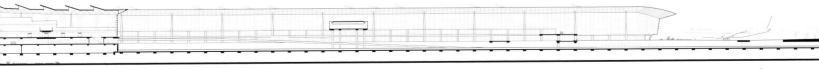

8

新机场 新国门 喜迎四海宾朋

Repsol Service Stations

Spain 1997

When the Spanish oil company Repsol commissioned a new service station system, the challenge was to update its roadside identity while delivering an innovative yet highly flexible solution capable of being easily constructed at 200 sites planned across Spain.

The result is a modular canopy system in the Repsol signature colours of red, white and orange. Clusters of these structures form a series of overlapping 'umbrellas' that shelter the station forecourt. The canopy head is an inverted pyramid, its crisp edges balanced by the less emphatic lines of the cladding. The umbrellas vary in number, height and in the degree of overlap between them, according to the specifics of each site. Alongside and underneath these canopies, the associated shop unit, car wash, petrol pumps and signage elements belong to a related family of pure, box-like forms. Together they provide maximum flexibility in planning and accommodate numerous variations in site configuration. All these elements are factory made and easily transported and installed on site, providing cost benefits while ensuring high quality standards and rapid delivery.

The canopies themselves are arranged in a predetermined sequence which ensures that a red one is always the tallest. This brightly coloured combination creates a strong three-dimensional image and clearly breaks the mould of the established service station forecourt. Even from the air Repsol's identity is announced unmistakably. On the road, the stations are clearly identifiable from a distance and vivid and inviting when approached.

1

3

1. Norman Foster's sketch study explores the visual impact of the new service station system from the perspective of a passing motorist.

2, 3. A typical station forecourt seen at night. The 'umbrellas' are finished in Repsol's signature colours of red, orange and white.

Metro System

Bilbao, Spain 1988–1995 and 1997–2004

A metro system is an excellent demonstration of how the built environment influences the quality of our lives. The building of tunnels for trains is usually seen in isolation from the provision of spaces for people – even though they are part of a continuous experience for the traveller, starting and ending at street level. Designed and constructed in two phases to create a pair of interconnecting lines along the banks of the River Nervión, the Bilbao Metro is unusual in that it was conceived as a totality: architectural, engineering and construction skills were integrated within a shared vision.

The great majority of subway systems today are uniformly difficult to negotiate, relying on elaborate signage systems to tell you where to go. In Bilbao, in contrast, the architecture itself is legible. Routes in and out, via escalators or glass lifts, lead directly to cavernous stations, which are high enough to accommodate stainless steel mezzanines and staircases above the trains. The experience of moving through a single grand volume is dramatic, and the concept offers flexibility for change. The curved forms of these spaces are expressive of the enormous forces they are designed to withstand, while their construction reflects Bilbao's strong engineering tradition. Most of the elements were made locally and Spanish engineers who had pioneered mobile gantries for the aerospace industry exploited this technology to erect the prefabricated concrete panels that line the stations.

The glassy structures – or 'Fosteritos' – that announce the inner-city Line 1 stations at street level are as unique to Bilbao as the Art Nouveau Metro entrances are to Paris, their shape evocative of inclined movement and generated by the profile of the tunnels themselves. The canopies admit natural light by day, and are illuminated at night, forming welcoming beacons in the streetscape. On Line 2, where deep-cut stations made it impossible to use escalators, banks of lifts create iconic and easily recognisable entrance points.

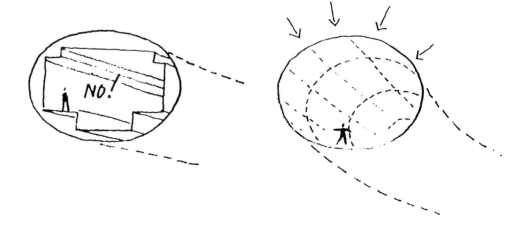

1   2   3

Previous pages, left: concept sketches by Norman Foster arguing for the direct expression of structure in the stations. Right: passengers enter and exit through the Metro's distinctive glass canopies – known popularly in Bilbao as 'Fosteritos'.

1-4. 'Fosteritos' in the streetscape.

5. Axonometric drawing of a typical station showing the direct route from platform to street.

6-8. The sequence from the station mezzanine, via escalators up towards the light of the street. Routes are simple and clearly defined; the need for signage is minimised.

9. Looking along the cavern of Abando station – a typical subterranean Line 1 station. The precast concrete shell expresses the form of the tunnel and contrasts with the lighter filigree of steel stairs and mezzanines.

4

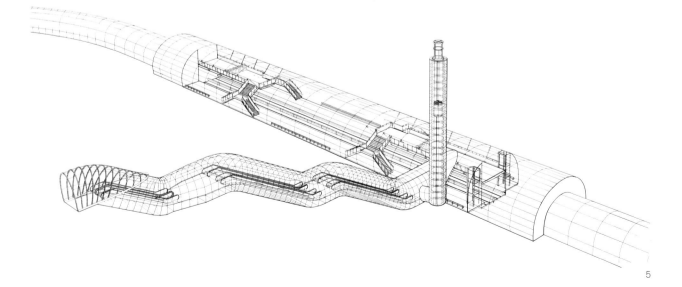

5

6

7

8

9

10

11

10. Some of the Line 1 stations, such as Sarriko, seen here, are located closer to ground level and were constructed using cut-and-cover techniques.

11. Similarly, Ansio station on Line 2 lies close to street level. Daylight floods down on to the platforms.

Canary Wharf Underground Station
London, England 1991–1999

The Jubilee Line extension is one of the greatest acts of British architectural patronage of recent years, comprising eleven new stations by as many architects. The practice's station at Canary Wharf is by far the largest of these – when the development of the area is complete, it will be used by more people at peak times than Oxford Circus, currently London's busiest Underground destination.

The station is built within the hollow of the former West India Dock using cut-and-cover construction techniques, and at 300 metres in length is as long as Canary Wharf Tower is tall. At ground level, the entire roof of the station is laid out as a landscaped park, creating Canary Wharf's principal public recreation space; the only visible station elements are the arcing glass canopies that cover its three entrances and draw daylight deep into the station concourse. By concentrating natural light dramatically at these points, orientation is enhanced, minimising the need for directional signage. Twenty banks of escalators transport passengers in and out of the station, while administrative offices, kiosks and other amenities are sited along the flanks of the ticket hall, leaving the main concourse free and creating a sense of clarity and calm.

Due to the high volume of station traffic, the guiding principles in the design were durability and ease of maintenance. The result is a simple palette of hard-wearing materials: fair-faced concrete, stainless steel and glass. This robust aesthetic is most pronounced at platform level where the concrete tunnel walls are left exposed. In contrast to the simplicity of its materials, the station introduces many complex security and technological innovations: glazed lifts enhance passenger comfort and deter vandalism; access to the tracks is blocked by platform-edge screens, which open in alignment with the doors of the trains. Servicing is also enhanced: cabling runs beneath platforms or behind walls, with access via maintenance gangways, allowing the station to be maintained entirely from behind the scenes.

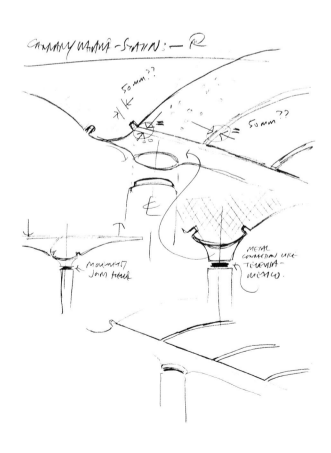

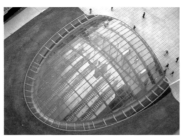

1

2

3

Previous pages, left: design sketches by David Nelson exploring the detailing of the junction between the columns and the concrete roof vault. Right: looking up the bank of escalators that lead to the western entrance.

1-3. Seen from above or from street level, the station entrance canopies convey a sense of transparency and lightness.

4. Escalators rise dramatically from the concourse towards the light. The glazed canopies concentrate natural light at the exit points, thereby aiding orientation within the station.

4

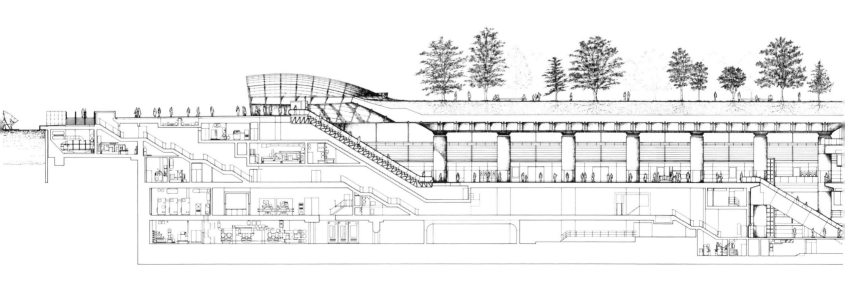

5

6

7

5. The station interior relies on a simple palette of hard-wearing materials: fair-faced concrete, stainless steel and glass.

6. The station's robust aesthetic is most pronounced at platform level where the concrete diaphragm tunnel walls are left exposed.

7. The station concourse during the early evening rush hour.

8. A long section through the station. At 300 metres in length, it is as long as Canary Wharf Tower is tall. Twenty banks of escalators move passengers in and out of the station.

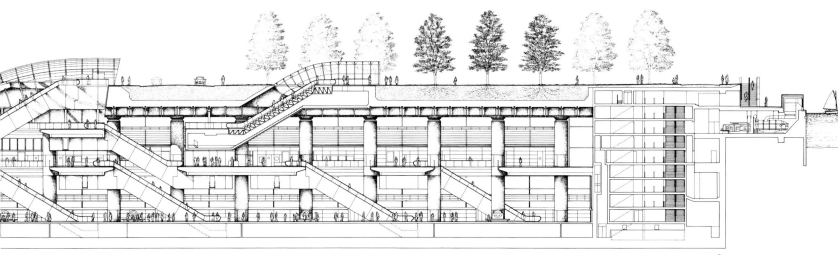

8

Expo Station
Singapore 1997–2001

Railway stations, like airports, are often the first buildings that people experience when arriving in a city and they therefore have an important symbolic role as urban gateways. Singapore's Expo Station is the first mass rapid transport station that visitors to the city encounter when travelling along the new Changi Airport Line. Built to serve the new Singapore Expo Centre, its design is both a celebration of arrival and a response to one of the warmest climates in the world.

The station is announced externally by two highly sculptural roof elements, which overlap to dynamic visual effect and appear to hover weightlessly above the heavy concrete base. A 40 metre-diameter disc, clad in stainless steel, shelters the ticket hall and marks the station entrance, while a 130 metre-long, blade-like form, sheathed in titanium, covers the platforms, its reflective soffit constantly animated with the reflections of passengers and passing trains. The station is used by very large numbers of people at peak times and so creating clear sight-lines and a strong sense of orientation were fundamental to its design. At ground level, the concourse is open, with views on one side to the street, and on the other side to a lush tropical garden created between the station and the Expo Centre. The elevated platforms are reached from the concourse and ticket office at street level by lift or escalators. Enclosure is kept to a minimum and passengers can look up through a long cut in the floor structure to glimpse the trains coming and going overhead.

Environmentally, the station's open form has other benefits, encouraging a cooling flow of air through the building. The choice of roof materials also has an environmental significance. Internally, the polished metal surface reflects daylight down through the building, minimising the need for artificial lighting, while externally, the cladding deflects the sun's rays, thus helping to create a microclimate on the platforms that is refreshingly up to four degrees cooler than the outside temperature.

1

2

1, 2. Two views of the station at street level. A stainless-steel disc marks the entrance and ticket hall, while a titanium-clad, blade-like form roofs the platforms.

3. Long-section through the station showing the distinctive profiles of the two different roof forms.

Opposite: view along the platform; reflective panels in the roof canopy direct daylight down through the station.

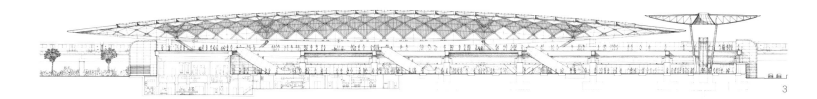

3

EXIT ↘

West
Platform 2

West

Dresden Station
Dresden, Germany 1997–2006

Completed in 1898, Dresden's main railway terminus is one the most impressive late-nineteenth-century railway stations in Europe. Linking Dresden with Berlin and Prague, the railway played a significant role in the city's industrial and economic growth. However, during the Second World War, along with much of the old city, the station was severely damaged in Allied bombing raids. Insensitive repair work after the war was compounded by poor maintenance, the building finally reaching a state where remedial conservation was required.

The starting point was to strip away additions and alterations made to the building over the last sixty years in order to restore the integrity of the original design. Circulation within and through the station has been rationalised. This includes pulling back the central tracks to create an open space at the heart of the building which can be used as a market place, or for cultural events. Externally, the most striking new element is the glass dome above the main circulation crossing. The approach followed here is similar to that explored at the Reichstag. Original surfaces have been exposed wherever possible, but there has been no attempt to recreate old forms or replace lost ornament: new and old are clearly articulated.

By far the largest new element is the 30,000-square-metre covering to the roof of the train shed. Originally the roof was partially glazed, but after the war it was boarded over. The station's elaborate wrought iron structure has now been restored and sheathed in a translucent skin of Teflon-coated glass fibre. If required, this canopy can be extended to provide cover for international high-speed trains (ICE), which are twice the length of the old platforms. The new roof transmits 13 per cent of daylight, which significantly reduces the need for artificial lighting. At night, light is reflected off the underside of the canopy, creating an even wash throughout the station, while from outside the whole structure radiates an ethereal silvery glow.

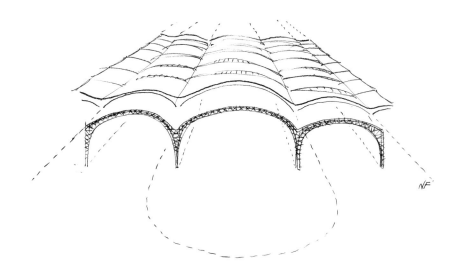

1

Previous pages, left: sketch by Norman Foster showing how a new lightweight fabric canopy wraps the existing station roof structure. Right: the nineteenth-century wrought-iron structure has been restored, but the old heavy roof covering has been stripped away, replaced by a translucent fabric canopy that floods the concourse with natural light.

1. An aerial view of the station from the north-east, looking across Wienerplatz. The building was originally designed to serve both domestic and international trains, the former terminating in the central 'nave' and the latter passing through on elevated tracks contained within the two side 'aisles'.

2. View along the platforms in the central nave towards the station head building.

3. Looking up through the glazed cupola that replaces the station's lost nineteenth-century dome.

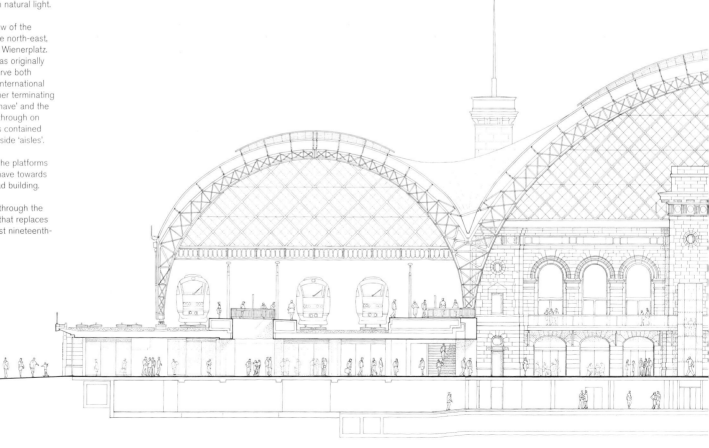

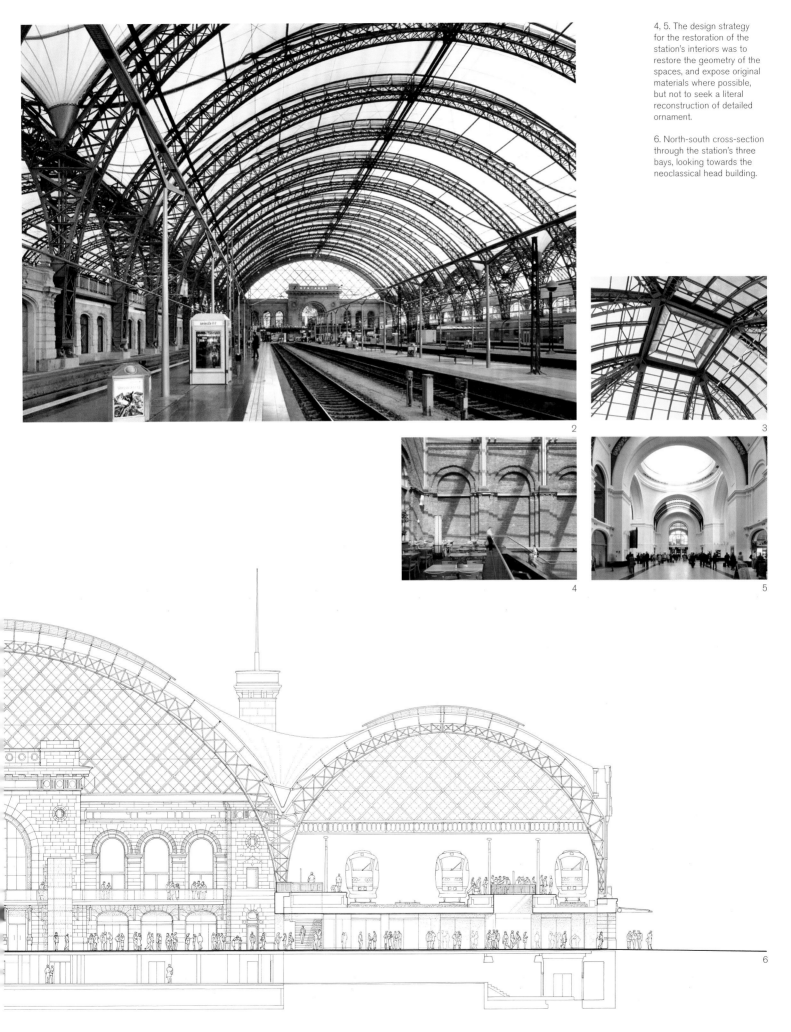

4, 5. The design strategy for the restoration of the station's interiors was to restore the geometry of the spaces, and expose original materials where possible, but not to seek a literal reconstruction of detailed ornament.

6. North-south cross-section through the station's three bays, looking towards the neoclassical head building.

2

3

4

5

6

Willis Faber & Dumas Headquarters

Ipswich, England 1971–1975

The country headquarters for insurance company Willis Faber & Dumas challenged accepted thinking about the office building while maintaining a sense of continuity within its urban setting. The unprecedented use of escalators in a three-storey structure, the central atrium, and the social dimension offered by its swimming pool, roof-top garden and restaurant, were all conceived in a spirit of democratising the workplace and encouraging a sense of community. Outside, the building reinforces rather than confronts the urban grain. Low-rise, with a free-form plan, it responds to the scale of surrounding buildings, while its facade curves in response to the medieval street pattern, flowing to the edges of its site like a pancake in a pan.

The distinctive sheath-like glass curtain wall, which was developed with the glazing manufacturer Pilkington, pushed the technology of the day to its limits. The solar-tinted glass panels, each 2 metres square, are connected by means of corner patch fittings, forming a three-storey-high curtain which is suspended from a continuous clamping strip at roof level. Internal glass fins at each floor level provide wind bracing. By day the glass reflects an eclectic collage of Ipswich's old buildings; by night it dissolves dramatically to reveal the activity within.

Conceived before the oil crises of the mid-1970s and heated by natural gas, Willis Faber was a pioneering example of energy-conscious design, its deep plan and insulating grass roof ensuring good overall thermal performance. Recognising these innovations, over the years it has attracted as many awards for energy efficiency as it has for its architecture. It also pioneered the use of raised office floors, anticipating the revolution in information technology; so much so, that when Willis Faber introduced computerisation, it was able to do so with minimal disruption. Paradoxically, although designed for flexibility, the building now has Grade I listed status: an honour that means it cannot be changed.

1

2

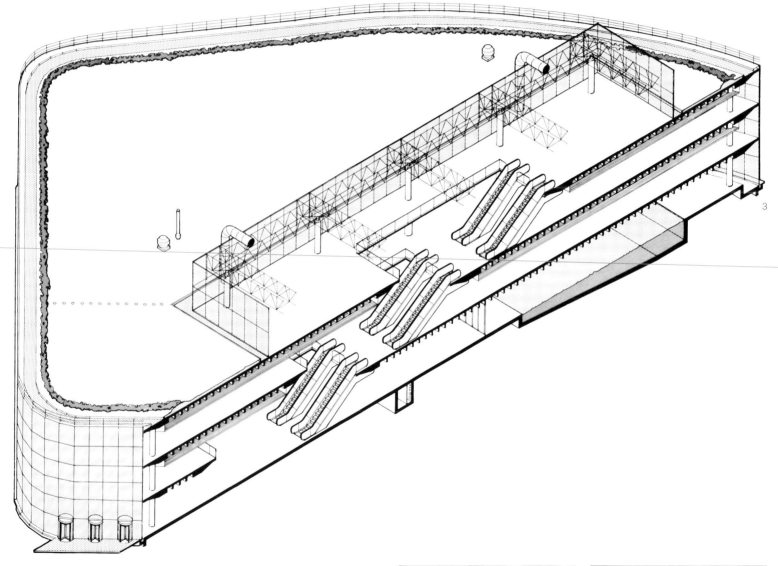

3

4

5

6

7

8

Previous pages, left: sketch by Norman Foster capturing the diagrammatic simplicity of the building. Escalators move up towards the sunlight and the green space of the roof. Right: night view, showing how the facade dissolves to reveal the inner workings of the building.

1. The roof garden – the first of the practice's 'gardens in the sky'.

2. The staff restaurant at garden level.

3. A cutaway axonometric showing the twin escalators rising up from the entrance foyer to the roof.

4, 5. Two images of the ground floor swimming pool (now decked over) with its water level flush with the floor.

6, 7. Two photographs, taken twenty years apart – in 1975 and 1995 respectively – show how the building has adapted easily to dramatic changes in information technology.

8. Looking across the upper floor towards the staff restaurant.

9. Although it has a very deep plan, the heart of the building is bathed in daylight.

10. Early concept sketch by Norman Foster.

9

10

Tower Place
London, England 1992–2002

The low-rise, deep-plan, energy-conscious office building with flexible, full-access floors and improved circulation is a typology pioneered by the practice in the early 1970s with the design of the Willis Faber & Dumas Headquarters in Ipswich. Nearly thirty years after Willis Faber's completion, the practice is continuing to replace obsolete 1960s office towers with lower-rise structures for progressive developers. Although each is particular to its site, the design specifications are remarkably similar to those of Willis Faber. What was once avant-garde has entered the mainstream.

The City of London has traditionally been characterised by relatively small-scale buildings laid out on an essentially medieval street plan. Situated within this context, these seven-storey offices in Tower Place, close to the Tower of London, replace an insensitive sixteen-storey office development that obstructed important view corridors between Greenwich and St Paul's Cathedral and between the Monument and the Tower. The new buildings help to restore the site's traditional urban grain, while reinstating historical views and creating a new public plaza with trees and water in front of All Hallows Church.

The development provides 42,000 square metres of office space in two blocks, broadly triangular in plan. Their stone and glass cladding system is designed to allow maximum daylight penetration, while blade-like aluminium louvres provide solar shading and add a shifting textural layer to the facades. Linking the two blocks is a glazed atrium – one of the largest such spaces in Europe. The engineering of the atrium's glass walls is highly advanced: rows of glass panels are hung like curtains from tension cables stretched between the two buildings. They terminate one storey above ground level, creating an open, naturally ventilated space that forms a covered extension of the piazza outside. This new space incorporates two designated City Walkways, inviting people to use it as a thoroughfare or as a sheltered place to meet friends and colleagues throughout the day.

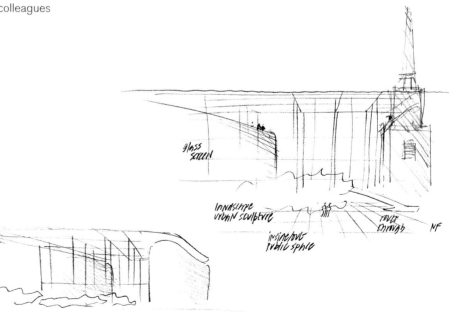

1

2

Previous pages, left: concept sketches by Norman Foster. Right: looking out through the glazed wall of the atrium towards All Hallows Church.

1. Night-time view looking west over Byward Street.

2. The spiralling access ramps on the south side of the building, illuminated at night.

3. The atrium is conceived as very much a part of the public realm – a continuation of the precinct in front of All Hallows Church.

4. Cross-section through the atrium; six floors of offices sit above two floors of parking for cars and tourist buses.

5. View along the executive floor of the east building.

6. Sol Lewitt's mural in the lobby of the west building.

7, 8. The glass wall of the atrium appears suspended in space: the glass panels are hung like curtains from tension cables stretched between the two buildings.

9. Detail of the limestone cladding and aluminium brise-soleil of the east building.

3

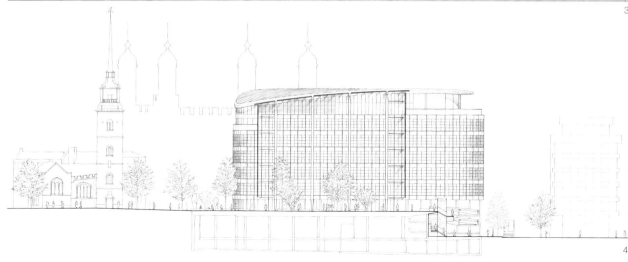

4

5

6

7

8

9

10 Gresham Street

London, England 1996–2003

The City of London and its environs are characterised for the most part by relatively low-rise buildings laid out on an essentially medieval street plan. Designing new buildings in this context is a delicate balancing act between commercial requirements, the need for flexibility, and respect for the area's historical character and traditional materials. This office building is located in a particularly sensitive area of the City, just south of the Guildhall, and close to two nineteenth-century livery halls: Wax Chandlers' Hall and Goldsmiths' Hall.

Rising eight storeys above ground, the building adopts the optimum template for new office development in the City: 18-metre-deep floor plates line a central atrium, which extends below ground level to bring daylight down into the basement floors, dissolving conventional distinctions between ground and subterranean levels. Heightening this sense of light and space, the lifts and lobbies are all glazed so as to cast sunlight around the circulation spaces. Externally, the corner stair towers, which anchor the building visually, are clad in limestone, the stone flank walls wrapping into the building to provide a point of continuity between inside and outside. The ventilated, triple-glazed office facades, which incorporate louvres to control solar gain and glare, are designed to maximise natural light levels, minimise energy consumption and ensure a high level of environmental comfort.

The development takes advantage of a site bounded almost entirely by streets, to create a stand-alone building, a comparatively rare achievement in the City. To the south, it is pulled back from the site boundary to create a more respectful relationship with Wax Chandlers' Hall. The resulting passage between the two buildings opens out into a small public court, used as a cut-through to the adjacent Gutter Lane or simply as somewhere to sit during a lunch break. In this way, the building aims not only to offer a light and flexible workspace but also to reinforce the traditional pattern of streets and alleyways that give the City its charm.

1. Looking across the timber louvres and atrium towards the glazed lift shaft.

2. Standing on the fifth floor beneath the clear glass ceiling of the atrium.

3. Cross-section through the atrium.

Opposite: limestone-clad stair towers anchor the building on Gresham Street.

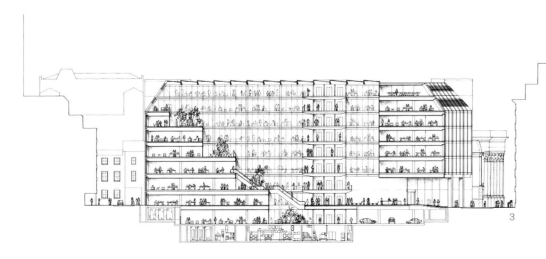

Bishops Square

London, England 2001–2005

The Bishops Square development completes the regeneration of the historically important Spitalfields neighbourhood, which bridges the City and the East End, and provides a major new public space for London – larger than the Piazza at Covent Garden. Comprising a new covered market area, 3,700 square metres of retail space, 72,000 square metres of offices, along with apartments, community facilities, cafés and restaurants, the scheme has transformed a former wholesale fruit and vegetable market into an eclectic, vibrant urban quarter.

The development includes the restoration of the old market buildings along Brushfield Street, with a new covered pedestrian route to the rear. Lined on both sides with shops, this promenade opens up unexpected views of Hawksmoor's magnificent Christ Church Spitalfields. A new headquarters building for Allen & Overy is designed to mediate between the tall commercial buildings on Bishopsgate and the smaller-scale historic fabric around Spitalfields Market. It makes this change in scale in a series of stepped terraces, which form planted gardens overlooking the square below. At ground level the building is transparent and permeable, forming connections to the surrounding network of civic spaces and pedestrian routes; and the northern facade is recessed to create a covered arcade for shops and cafés. Containing the largest commercial photovoltaic installation in Europe, the building harnesses enough energy to power the landscape lighting across the site.

Bishops Square itself lies between the new building and the existing buildings along Bishopsgate and accommodates a sheltered outdoor performance area. An additional public space, Crispin Square, which is covered by a glazed canopy, connects the offices with the old Spitalfields Market. The Charnel House, a twelfth-century chapel discovered during archaeological excavations on the site, has been preserved and exhibited with other artifacts in a sunken courtyard, sheltered beneath a glass pavement. This exhibition is complemented by an ongoing programme of temporary art installations orchestrated by the Spitalfields Development Group, which aims to celebrate Spitalfields' rich history and the ever-changing nature of the area.

1

2

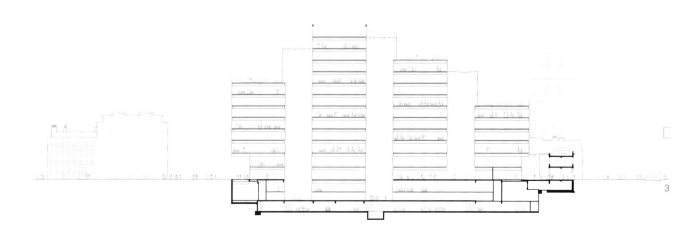

3

1. View of Bishops Square showing the relationship between the public plaza and the Allen & Overy headquarters building.

2. Looking through the preserved Brushfield Street buildings towards Crispin Square.

3. Cross-section through the entire Bishops Square development.

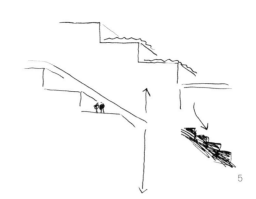

4. The roof garden of the Allen & Overy building – a social space for office staff.

5. Sketch study of the landscaped roof terraces by Norman Foster.

6. The covered shopping promenade along Market Street, with Christ Church visible through the canopy.

7. Looking down into Bishops Square; the tented structure is a venue for concerts and other events.

8. The covered public space at Crispin Square, which forms a connection between the new offices and the old Spitalfields Market.

Electronic Arts European Headquarters
Chertsey, England 1997–2000

Through the design of a number of company headquarters and office buildings, beginning with Reliance Controls in 1966, the practice has consistently encouraged companies to adopt flexible, non-hierarchical working environments. In the design of its European Headquarters, the leading computer-game software development company Electronic Arts wholly embraced this philosophy. The headquarters sets new standards in this fast-moving industry, providing high-quality workspace, a state-of-the-art media centre for presentations, and an extensive range of on-site facilities.

Bound to the north by an eighteenth-century lake, the building comprises a group of three-storey office blocks arranged as three 'fingers', projecting into the landscape. These fingers are linked by a sweeping glass wall that encloses a street-like atrium. As an animated showcase for Electronic Arts' work and the social focus of the building, this atrium provides primary circulation at ground level and forms an environmental buffer between the offices and the landscape. Electronic Arts' staff take pride in working as a family with common values. In keeping with this ethos, a huge range of amenities is provided, including games arcades, a gym and sports pitch, a library, a bar and a 140-seat restaurant. With this wealth of leisure options, staff members have joked that the experience is like 'homing from work'.

The building also satisfies a number of complex technological criteria. In offices equipped with large amounts of hardware, cooling and ventilation are the chief environmental concerns. As a result, the building employs a low-energy environmental strategy and a range of new-technology management systems. Comfortable conditions are maintained by combining displacement ventilation with natural cooling from the high thermal mass of the building's exposed structure. When supplementary ventilation and cooling are required the building management system can simply open the windows or, on the very hottest days, switch on the air conditioning. Heat gain is minimised by extensive use of brises-soleil so that the whole building becomes comfortable and controllable whatever the season.

1

2

3

4

Previous pages, left: sketch by Norman Foster imagining the building's curved lakeside facade. Right: a view of the triple-height internal 'street' that runs along the lakeside.

1-5. Details of the interior, from informal games, meeting, and eating areas, through to the top-floor design studio, and first-floor marketing offices.

6. Looking out through the glazing of one of the building's three 'fingers' of offices.

7. Detail of the main staircase.

8. Night view, looking towards the main entrance.

9. The building as seen across the lake.

10. A cross-section through the atrium, from the car-park entrance on the left, through studio spaces, the main staircase and 'street', to the lakeside terrace on the right.

8

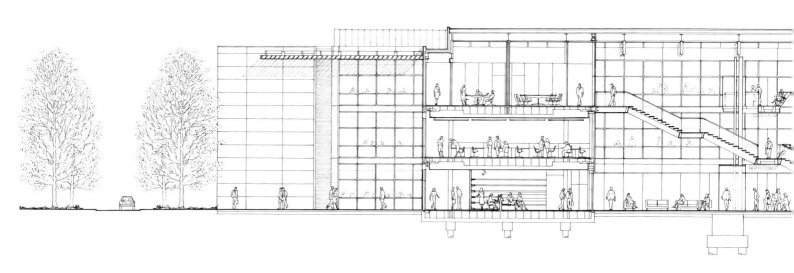

5

6

7

9

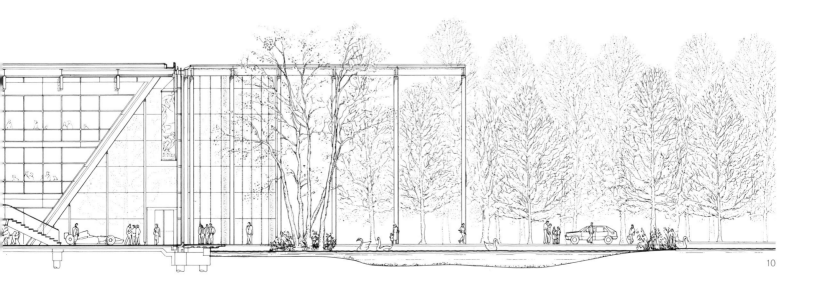

10

McLaren Technology Centre
Woking, England 1998–2004

The TAG McLaren Group is a collection of high-tech companies involved in the design and development of Formula One cars, high-performance road cars, electronic systems and composite materials. Since McLaren began competing in Formula One in 1966, it has established a global reputation as one of the most successful teams in the history of the sport. The Technology Centre provides a headquarters for the group's 850 staff and is designed to reflect the company's design and engineering expertise. It includes design studios, laboratories and testing and production facilities for Formula One and road cars, including the Mercedes-Benz SLR McLaren.

Viewed on plan, the building is roughly semi-circular, the circle being completed by a formal lake, which forms an integral part of the building's environmental cooling system. The principal lakeside facade is a continuous curved glass wall, developed in part using McLaren's own technological expertise, which is shaded by a cantilevered roof. Internally, the building is organised around double-height linear 'streets', which form circulation routes and articulate 'fingers' of flexible accommodation. These house production and storage areas on the lower levels, with top-lit design studios, offices and meeting rooms above. Directly behind the facade is a circulation 'boulevard' which leads to areas for hospitality and to the staff restaurant, both of which look out across the landscape. Other social facilities include a swimming pool and a fitness centre.

A Visitor Centre with educational facilities is located in a separate building at the entrance to the complex. This two-storey structure is buried underground – like the rest of the Technology Centre it is designed to make a minimal intervention in the landscape – and is visible only by its circular rooflight. It houses a temporary exhibition space and lecture theatre and is linked to the main centre by a subterranean building with a permanent display of McLaren's historical racing and road cars.

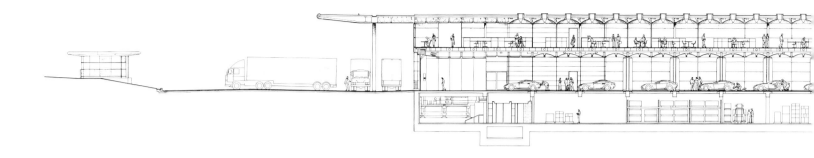

2

Previous pages, left: sketch study by Norman Foster. Right: view of the double-height internal 'boulevard' looking south along the curving lake front.

1. Cross-section through the car assembly line and lake.

2. Looking along the main boulevard with a line of McLaren Formula One cars.

3. The Mercedes-Benz SLR McLaren assembly line.

4. Looking down from one of the reception areas into the boulevard.

3

4

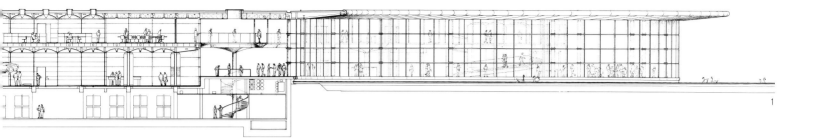

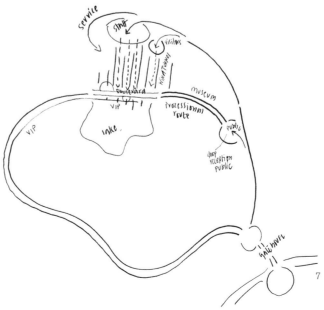

5. The lakeside frontage illuminated at night.

6. Double-height linear 'streets' form circulation routes and articulate the 'fingers' of flexible office/ workshop accommodation.

7. Sketch by Norman Foster, indicating how VIPs, staff, service vehicles and visitors take different routes through the site.

Hongkong and Shanghai Bank Headquarters
Hong Kong 1979–1986

Conceived during a sensitive period in the former colony's history, the brief for the Hongkong and Shanghai Bank Headquarters was a statement of confidence: to create 'the best bank building in the world'. Through a process of questioning and challenging – including the involvement of a feng shui geomancer – the project addressed the nature of banking in Hong Kong and how it should be expressed in built form. In doing so it virtually reinvented the office tower.

The requirement to build in excess of one million square feet in a short timescale suggested a high degree of prefabrication, including factory-finished modules, while the need to build downwards and upwards simultaneously led to the adoption of a suspension structure, with pairs of steel masts arranged in three bays. As a result, the building form is articulated in a stepped profile of three individual towers, respectively twenty-nine, thirty-six and forty-four storeys high, which create floors of varying width and depth and allow for garden terraces. The mast structure allowed another radical move, pushing the service cores to the perimeter so as to create deep-plan floors around a ten-storey atrium. A mirrored 'sunscoop' reflects sunlight down through the atrium to the floor of a public plaza below – a sheltered space that at weekends has become a lively picnic spot. From the plaza, escalators rise up to the main banking hall, which with its glass underbelly was conceived as a 'shop window for banking'.

The 'bridges' that span between the masts define double-height reception areas that break down the scale of the building both visually and socially. A unique system of movement through the building combines high-speed lifts to the reception spaces with escalators beyond, reflecting village-like clusters of office floors. From the outset, the Bank placed a high priority on flexibility. Interestingly, over the years, it has been able to reconfigure office layouts with ease, even incorporating a large dealers' room into one floor – a move that could not have been anticipated when the building was designed.

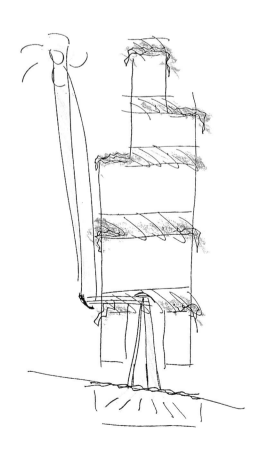

1

Previous pages, left: Norman
Foster's concept sketch
showing how the sunscoop
reflects sunlight down
through the atrium. Right:
looking into the atrium.

1. The north facade as seen
from Statue Square.

2. A cross-section through
the atrium. The division
between the banking hall
and the ground level plaza
is provided by the minimal
intervention of the glass
underbelly.

3. In a city where public
space is rare, the plaza
beneath the Bank provides
a welcome moment of calm,
and a place to shelter from
the heat of the sun.

4. Hong Kong's Filipino
community has adopted
the plaza as a favourite
weekend picnic spot.

5. Looking down through
the atrium into the main
banking hall.

6. Escalators lead from the
plaza up to the banking hall.

7. An early design sketch
by Norman Foster.

Overleaf: A detail of the
Bank's stepping form
on the skyline.

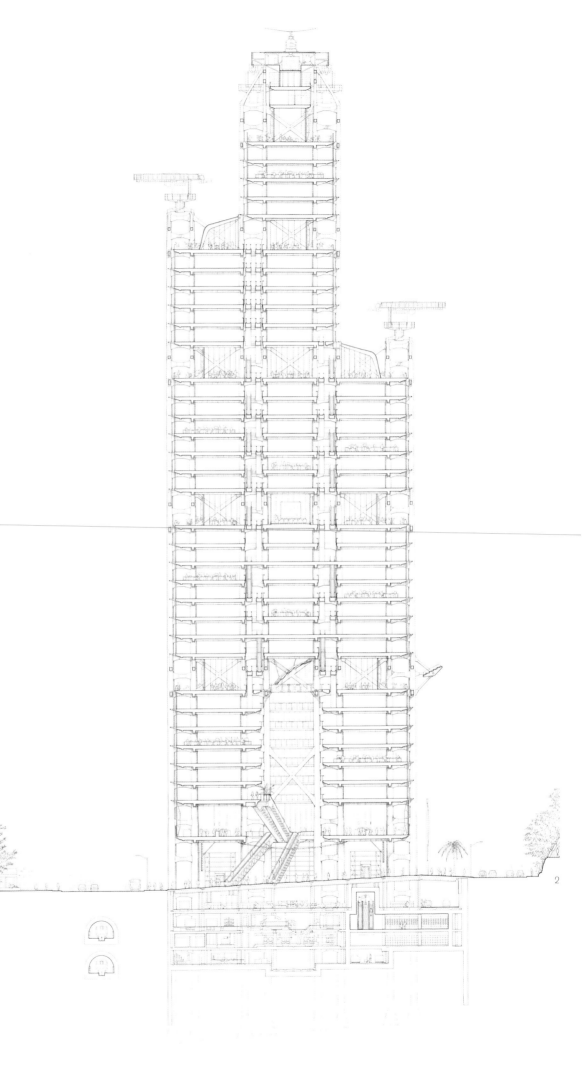

2

3

4

5

6

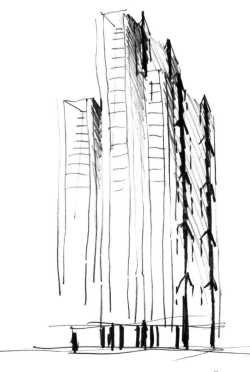

7

Commerzbank Headquarters
Frankfurt, Germany 1991–1997

At fifty-three storeys, the Commerzbank is the world's first ecological office tower and the tallest building in Europe. The project explores the nature of the office environment, developing new ideas for its ecology and working patterns. Central to this concept is a reliance on natural systems of lighting and ventilation. Every office is daylit and has openable windows, allowing the occupants to control their own environment. The result is energy consumption levels equivalent to half those of conventional office towers.

The plan of the building is triangular, comprising three 'petals' – the office floors – and a 'stem' formed by a full-height central atrium. Winter gardens spiral up around the atrium to become the visual and social focus for four-storey office clusters. From the outside these 'gardens in the sky' give the building a sense of transparency and lightness. Socially, they form focal points for village-like clusters of offices, providing places to meet friends or relax during breaks. Environmentally, they bring light and fresh air into the central atrium, which acts as a natural ventilation chimney for the inward-facing offices. Depending on each garden's orientation, planting is from one of three regions: North America, Asia or the Mediterranean.

The tower has a distinctive presence on the Frankfurt skyline but is also anchored into the lower-scale city fabric, through the restoration and sensitive rebuilding of the perimeter structures to reinforce the original scale of the block. These buildings provide shops, car parking, apartments and a banking hall, and help to forge links between the Commerzbank and the broader community. At the heart of the scheme is a public galleria with restaurants, cafés and spaces for social and cultural events, which has become a popular pedestrian thoroughfare. Interestingly, on the day the Commerzbank opened, the Financial Times adopted it as the symbol of Frankfurt, just as it features the Houses of Parliament and the Eiffel Tower as symbols of London and Paris.

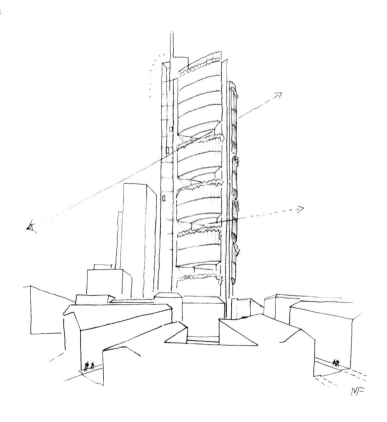

1
2
3

4

5
6

7

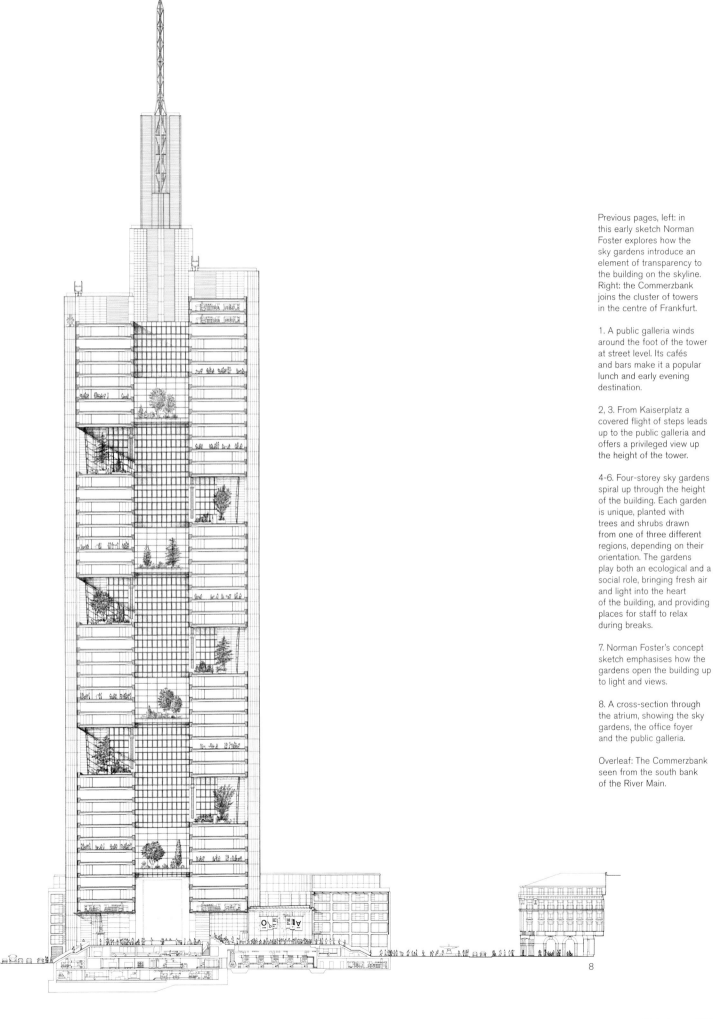

Previous pages, left: in this early sketch Norman Foster explores how the sky gardens introduce an element of transparency to the building on the skyline. Right: the Commerzbank joins the cluster of towers in the centre of Frankfurt.

1. A public galleria winds around the foot of the tower at street level. Its cafés and bars make it a popular lunch and early evening destination.

2, 3. From Kaiserplatz a covered flight of steps leads up to the public galleria and offers a privileged view up the height of the tower.

4-6. Four-storey sky gardens spiral up through the height of the building. Each garden is unique, planted with trees and shrubs drawn from one of three different regions, depending on their orientation. The gardens play both an ecological and a social role, bringing fresh air and light into the heart of the building, and providing places for staff to relax during breaks.

7. Norman Foster's concept sketch emphasises how the gardens open the building up to light and views.

8. A cross-section through the atrium, showing the sky gardens, the office foyer and the public galleria.

Overleaf: The Commerzbank seen from the south bank of the River Main.

8

Swiss Re Headquarters
London, England 1997–2004

London's first ecological tall building and an instantly recognisable addition to the city's skyline, this headquarters for Swiss Re is rooted in a radical approach – technically, architecturally, socially and spatially. It rises forty-one storeys and provides 76,400 square metres of accommodation, including offices and a shopping arcade accessed from a newly created plaza. At the very top of the building – London's highest occupied floor – is a club room that offers a spectacular 360-degree panorama across the capital.

Generated by a circular plan, with a radial geometry, the building widens in profile as it rises and tapers towards its apex. This distinctive form responds to the constraints of the site: the building appears more slender than a rectangular block of equivalent size and the slimming of its profile towards the base maximises the public realm at ground level. Environmentally, its profile reduces wind deflections compared with a rectilinear tower of similar size, helping to maintain a comfortable environment at street level, and creates external pressure differentials that are exploited to drive a unique system of natural ventilation.

Conceptually the tower develops ideas explored in the Commerzbank and before that in the Climatroffice, a theoretical project with Buckminster Fuller that suggested a new rapport between nature and the workplace, its energy-conscious enclosure resolving walls and roof into a continuous triangulated skin. Here, the tower's diagonally braced structure allows column-free floor space and a fully glazed facade, which opens up the building to light and views. Atria between the radiating fingers of each floor link vertically to form a series of informal break-out spaces that spiral up the building. These spaces are a natural social focus – places for refreshment points and meeting areas – and function as the building's 'lungs', distributing fresh air drawn in through opening panels in the facade. This system reduces the tower's reliance on air conditioning and, together with other sustainable measures, means that the building uses only half the energy consumed by conventional air-conditioned office towers.

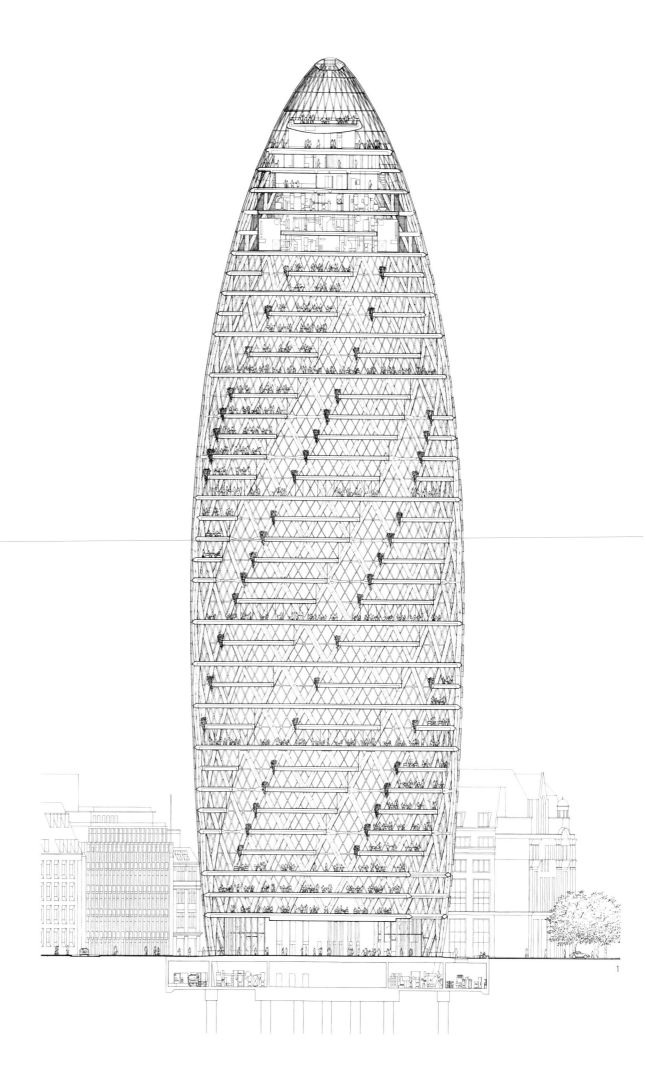

Previous pages, left: Norman Foster's sketch explores how the building sits within the close urban grain of the City of London. Right: the building approached from Leadenhall Street.

1. Cross-section through the tower showing the spiralling sky gardens and upper level restaurant and bar spaces.

2. The club room at the top of the building offers 360-degree panoramic views across London.

3. Sketch by Norman Foster exploring the design of the club room.

4, 5. The external skin is a triangulated geodetic structure, clad entirely in glass panels.

6. Norman Foster's early sketch exploring different colour options for the horizontal and vertical cladding members.

7, 8. Looking into the main entrance and lobby space.

Overleaf: The tower seen on the City skyline at night.

1

2

3

4

5

6

7

8

Deutsche Bank Place

Sydney, Australia 1996–2005

Since the design of the Hongkong and Shanghai Bank, the practice has continued to redefine the nature of the office tower and to explore how it can respond to the context and the spirit of the city in which it stands. This thirty-one-storey building, located on a prominent site close to the harbour, explores new strategies for flexible, column-free office space and creates a new 'urban room' in Sydney's dense central business district.

The building's unusual design and distinctive profile were guided by a number of factors, including the narrow site, the need for large open floor plates, and exacting planning regulations that protected the amount of sunlight falling on two nearby public spaces. The building's orientation exploits a number of environmental factors and maximises views across the harbour. Daylight is drawn into the office levels and down through the building via an atrium, which runs the full height of the tower between the core and the office floors and is crossed by a series of bridges. Movement through the building is clarified and celebrated, the atrium and lobbies being both physically and psychologically removed from the workplace. The main structural core is offset to the lower, western edge of the site and consists of two towers, which provide the main stiffening elements and act as solar buffers. To permit greater flexibility in planning office layouts, curtain walling on the three glazed facades has been turned 'inside out' with mullions and transoms placed externally.

At ground level, the private world of the tower meets the public realm of the city in a four-storey covered plaza – the 'assembly'. This soaring, light-filled space functions as a busy public square. A prelude to the office lobbies, it also contains shops, cafés and a crèche. The central water feature that runs the length of the space can be controlled to enable all kinds of activities, including fashion shows and parties, to take place there at any time of day.

Previous pages, left; early
sketches by Norman
Foster exploring options
for stepping the height of
the building to protect the
amount of sunlight falling on
two nearby public spaces.
Right: the building seen from
the east, with the distinctive
diagonal 'cage' at the
summit.

1. The main lift lobby.

2. Looking down into
the atrium.

3. View of the assembly
from Hunter Street looking
towards the podium building,
with the water feature in
the foreground.

1

2

3

4

5

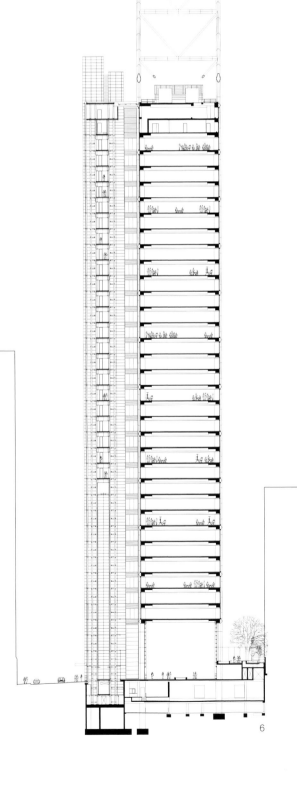

4. The entrance from Phillip Street.

5. Cafés and restaurants spill out on to the assembly.

6. Cross-section looking north, showing the offset core to the left, the full-height atrium and the column-free office floors.

7. The tower seen from the entrance to the Botanic Gardens. The State Library of New South Wales is in the foreground.

6

7

Hearst Headquarters
New York, USA 2000–2006

The Hearst Headquarters revives a dream from the 1920s, when publishing magnate William Randolph Hearst envisaged Columbus Circle as a new media quarter in Manhattan. Hearst commissioned a six-storey Art Deco block on Eighth Avenue, anticipating that it would form the base for a tower, though no scheme was ever advanced. Echoing an approach developed in the Reichstag and the Great Court at the British Museum, the challenge in designing such a tower at seventy years remove was to establish a creative dialogue between old and new.

The forty-two-storey tower rises above the old building, linked on the outside by a skirt of glazing that encourages an impression of the tower floating weightlessly above the base. The main spatial event is a lobby that occupies the entire floor plate of the old building and rises up through six floors. Like a bustling town square, this dramatic space provides access to all parts of the building. It incorporates the main lift lobby, the Hearst cafeteria and auditorium and mezzanine levels for meetings and special functions. Structurally, the tower has a triangulated form – a highly efficient solution that uses 20 per cent less steel than a conventionally framed structure. With the corners cut back between the diagonals, it creates a distinctive faceted silhouette.

The building is also significant in environmental terms. It was built using 80 per cent recycled steel and is designed to consume 25 per cent less energy than its conventional neighbours. As a result, it was the first office building in Manhattan to achieve a gold rating under the US Green Buildings Council's Leadership in Energy and Environmental Design Program (LEED). As a company, Hearst places a high value on the quality of the working environment – something it believes will become increasingly important to its staff in the future – and it is hoped that Hearst's experience may herald the construction of more environmentally sensitive buildings in the city.

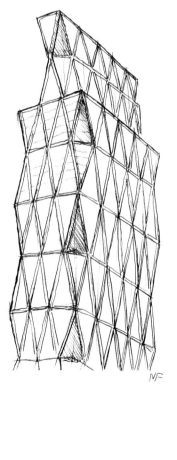

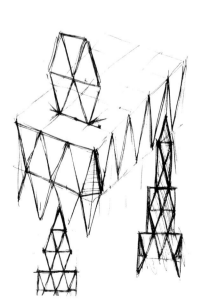

Previous pages, left: early sketches by Norman Foster exploring alternative treatments for the top of the building. Right: a detail of the facade; the diagrid structure provides greater strength and structural redundancy than a conventional post-and-beam structure, using 20 per cent less steel.

1. The tower seen from Central Park.

2. North-south cross-section through the lobby at 959 Eighth Avenue. A bank of escalators rises through sheets of cascading water to deliver visitors into a cavernous, seven-storey volume beneath the forty-six-storey tower.

3. Compositionally, the Art Deco Hearst building acts as a 'plinth' to the tower, an outcome originally envisaged in the 1920s by its architect Joseph Urban.

1

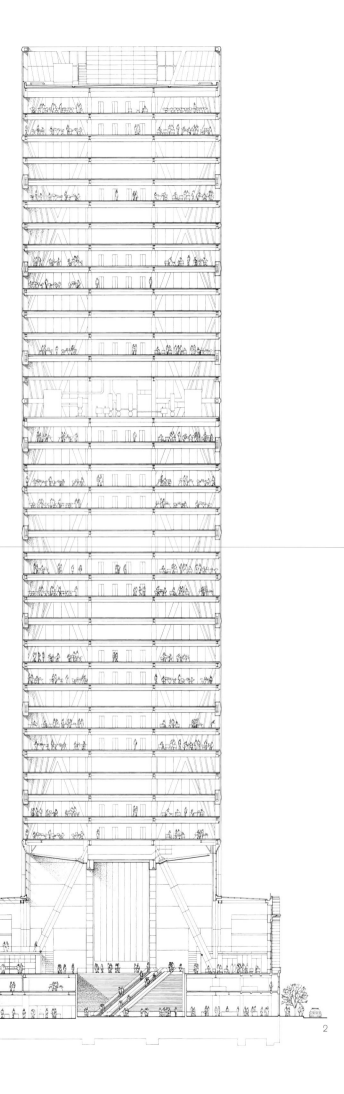

2

4. A horizontal spatial reveal separates the old building from the tower and articulates the transition from the 'heavy' masonry base to the 'light' glass-and-steel superstructure.

5. Detail of the escalators in the lobby which rise up past an environmental water feature – 'Icefall' – designed in collaboration with glass specialist Jamie Carpenter and Jim Garland of Fluidity.

Overleaf: looking across the lobby – a civic space for the Hearst community conceived on the scale of a town square. 'Riverlines', the large-scale wall piece by Richard Long, seen left, is made from mud 'harvested' from the banks of the Avon and Hudson Rivers.

3

4

5

The Practice

Mouzhan Majidi
Chief Executive

1

Every autumn in the studio we stage an exhibition of models and drawings by recent graduates who have joined the practice. It's an opportunity to review their work, to engage them in discussion and to welcome them to our team. Year on year that exhibition grows bigger and more impressive, to the point that last year we had to stage it over two evenings. Norman Foster, our chairman, personally leads the 'crit' with every participant. It's a reminder – should we need it – of how young and talented our team is, and how motivated they are to work hard and excel. Just one indicator of that work ethic, and in turn, how we encourage young architects to develop their skills, is to see how many of those graduates continue studying to gain their ARB qualification – an astonishing eighty-seven in 2007.

Today, with a staff of 1,250, the average age in the studio is just thirty-three – interestingly, the same as when Norman founded the company in 1967. Behind the numbers, of course, lies a depth of experience and forty years of shared endeavour. Like most of my senior colleagues I too joined the office as a new graduate, in my case in 1987. Over more than two decades together we have grown with the practice, helped to shape it, and now guide its future direction.

If our team is young it is also truly international. Collectively we speak some forty-five languages; and at the time of writing, we have twenty offices around the world and projects in sixty-two countries. The diversity and tempo of the London studio reflect this rich mix of cultural connections, which spans six continents and virtually every time zone. Stand at our bar in the entrance hall during lunch or coffee breaks and you are as likely to hear conversations in Chinese, French, German, Russian or Spanish as you are in English.

Although design tends to be focused in the London studio – and management flows out from there – every project, once it shifts from drawing to reality, will be supervised on site by a dedicated project team. That team will remain in place until the project is completed, wherever it is in the world. This means that not only will the architects be based locally but many of them will be able to enjoy a fluent dialogue with the client and the construction team – something that pays real dividends in terms of relationship building and the quality of the end result.

From the very beginning, the practice's relationship with clients has offered a high degree of personal service, reinforced by a commitment to manage the project closely. 'On time and on budget' is not just a mantra – it is part of the practice's mindset. We believe that good design can add value, and that design excellence and its successful execution go hand in hand. Beyond that, we believe that as professionals we have a dual responsibility: first to our clients, but also to the public domain and the people that will use or encounter the building every day.

Over the past four decades, the studio has broadened its horizons to embrace not only architecture but also infrastructure and product design. In the last decade we have undertaken some of the most ambitious projects of modern times, including the new Terminal 3 at Beijing International Airport – currently the largest single building in the world. We could not do that without the resources that only a practice of our size can provide. So in that sense, 'size matters'. However, we also believe that the best work – and the best client experience – comes from the small team. The practice's structure aims to get the best of both worlds.

In 2003 Norman restructured the company to establish six design groups, each with a senior partner as leader. The group leaders are: Grant Brooker (Group 1), David Summerfield (Group 2), Stefan Behling (Group 4), Gerard Evenden (Group 5) and Nigel Dancey (Group 6). I continue to lead Group 3, assisted by Andy Bow, who is also a senior partner. Brandon Haw, another senior partner, with experience in exploring new markets, is responsible for Business Development. Each member of this core group has been with the practice over many years and has been responsible for running large and often complex projects in many different parts of the world. They are supported by a younger generation of partners – and a wider team of associate partners and associates – whose energy and enthusiasm are essential in motivating the office as a whole. The group structure has proved to be highly flexible and adaptable – a key factor in allowing us to respond as the scale, diversity and global reach of our projects has grown.

The groups do not have particular specialisations or geographical focus – quite the opposite. We believe that diversity is an essential ingredient in driving creativity, innovation and motivation. Each group will typically have a rich cross-section of projects – large and small – spread around the world. In the case of Group 3 this ranges from a series of luxury yachts to Russia Tower – the tallest naturally ventilated tower in the world and probably one of the greenest new buildings in Europe.

The design of every new project is reviewed regularly within the studio, both formally and informally. This process takes place under the direction of the design board, which balances the greater spread of design

5

6

7

8

9

2   3   4

1. Norman Foster
2. Mouzhan Majidi
3. Spencer de Grey
4. David Nelson
5. Grant Brooker
6. David Summerfield
7. Stefan Behling
8. Gerard Evenden
9. Nigel Dancey
10. Andy Bow
11. Brandon Haw
12. Paul Kalkhoven
13. Mark Sutcliffe
14. Graham Young
15. Matthew Streets

responsibility in the groups with a broader overview based on shared values and the practice's 'collective memory'. The design board was created in the spirit of 'challenging and being challenged' and can initiate design as well as review it. The board is led by senior partners Spencer de Grey and David Nelson as joint heads of design, and its permanent members include Norman, myself, Armstrong Yakubu, Stefan Behling, Nigel Dancey and Narinder Sagoo. The intention is for the composition and leadership of the design board to develop and rotate over time, with the potential for mobility between groups and the board.

As the six groups develop a design concept and begin to communicate its intentions, they have the support of a range of specialist teams, including materials and environmental research, product design, space planning, interior design, communications, graphics, visualisations, model making, and 3D computer modelling. To use an urban analogy, if the six groups can be thought of as individual buildings, then the network of specialist support teams is the infrastructure that binds them together.

The practice's specialist modelling group has an advanced 3D computer modelling capability that allows architects to explore design solutions rapidly and to communicate data to consultants and contractors. While new technologies have transformed the way we work, traditional model making still plays a crucial role and our state-of-the-art model shop can produce everything from quick sketch models to full-size mock-ups.

As a project moves from the design stage into built reality, the architects are supported by further in-house disciplines that include information technology, contract management and construction. These teams are led by Graham Young, Mark Sutcliffe and Paul Kalkhoven respectively; and the practice's financial direction is guided by Matthew Streets; all four are senior partners.

We also have an information centre, which contains a materials research centre that helps architects to select products and sometimes initiates the use of new materials. It is a key component in our knowledge base, helping us to create inspirational as well as sustainable buildings. Clients are sometimes surprised when we tell them that we have been investigating sustainable technologies since the 1970s – long before the term 'green' was being used. But sustainability is something that we have always been passionate about. Today in the studio we have a sustainability forum that promotes the use of sustainable technologies and methods. The forum is part of the research and development group, whose role is to ensure that the practice remains at the forefront of architectural innovation. It has representatives from the six design groups, the information centre, training, and research departments, and together they provide a crucial link between the resources and knowledge of the forum and the individual design teams.

In order to monitor the sustainability agenda of individual projects, our aim is to establish a sustainability profile for every new project, which allows each team to determine targets and methods from the outset. This information is collated in a database that can be accessed throughout the practice to guide the design of subsequent projects. This methodology is augmented by providing staff training across a range of issues, including sustainability criteria and assessment, renewable energy sources and environmental analysis. By maintaining a commitment to research – one of our great strengths as a practice – we are not only up-to-date with new discoveries and techniques, but are also able to evaluate their relevance for individual projects. We recognise, of course, that architects are essentially only advocates – and that not every project will be able to meet all the desired criteria. But we believe that we have a responsibility to try to persuade our clients to adopt sustainable strategies and that even small steps in the right direction are better than none at all.

In 2007 Norman initiated a small but significant step in reconfiguring the company's structure. We knew that to allow us to expand our range of client services and open up new markets we needed to broaden our financial base. That led us to invite 3i to take a minority shareholding in the company. There is a natural synergy between our two organisations: 3i's profile, global network and long-term interests are complementary to our own. As part of that restructuring of the practice we expanded the company's ownership to include nine senior partners, increasing the number of shareholders from four to fourteen. Later the same year, to coincide with our fortieth anniversary celebrations, we welcomed another thirty-three partners as shareholders; and this is a pattern that will continue in the future.

Significantly, the first year of our new collaboration was the practice's most successful ever. During that period we won thirteen international competitions and forty-one design awards – a record for us – and we opened offices in New York, Istanbul and Madrid. Although the challenges we face as architects are becoming more complex, the future has never been more exciting.

10   11   12

13   14   15

Group 1
Grant Brooker

Group 1 is led by Grant Brooker, who combines a broad understanding of the commercial office market, particularly within the City of London, with wide experience of airport design. Significantly, the group is developing a number of large transport projects, ranging from the new airport terminal at Heathrow East to Spaceport America – the first building in the world to articulate the thrill of space tourism. Another thread is the nature of the modern city. Quartermile, in Edinburgh, reclaims a former hospital site to create a sustainable, mixed-use community, while Walbrook Square in London has the potential to create a vibrant urban quarter and set new standards for the workplace.

1

2

4

3

1. Spencer de Grey in the main studio with Grant Brooker and Mouzhan Majidi.

2. Walbrook Square was a collaborative exercise with Jean Nouvel, seen here with Norman Foster, Grant Brooker and Spencer de Grey.

3. Arjun Kaicker with Tamsin Green and D'Arcy Fenton.

4. Grant Brooker with Norman Foster.

5

6

10. Rob Harrison and Grant Brooker discuss 51 Lime Street, in the City of London.

11. Svetlana Curcic with Ian Whitby and Jonathan Bell.

12. Dan Sibert, Grant Brooker and Daniel Poehner discuss a model for the Tour Signal competition with model maker Gareth Verbiest.

7

9

8

10

11

5. Norman Foster, Grant Brooker, Spencer de Grey and Max Neal in a design review.

6. Spencer de Grey and David Nelson with a model for West Plaza, Auckland.

7. Arjun Kaicker and Antoinette Nassopoulos.

8. Graham Philips, David Nelson, Norman Foster, Spencer de Grey and Grant Brooker in a design review.

9. Joon Paik leads a discussion on Spaceport America.

12

Group 2
David Summerfield

Led by David Summerfield, Group 2 is engaged in the design of tall buildings around the world. Following the completion of the Hearst tower they are building a seventy-nine storey building on the site of the World Trade Center, the sixty-eight storey Shangri-La hotel on Lexington Avenue and a forty-storey apartment tower at 10 UN Plaza, all in New York. Further projects include an office tower in Copenhagen, the newly completed Elephant House in Copenhagen Zoo, a hotel and residences in Buenos Aires, and Yale School of Management. Equally important are projects that embrace infrastructure and urban renewal, notably an urban quarter in Washington DC and mixed-use developments in India.

1. Michael Wurzel in Foster + Partners' New York office.

2. Lindsay Bush, Maddalena Cannarsa and Cristina Segni.

3-5. David Summerfield in a design review with David Nelson and Norman Foster.

6. Rafe Bertram discusses the Four Seasons Hotel in Copenhagen with the client and Armstrong Yakubu.

7. David Summerfield and Mouzhan Majidi.

8. A design review meeting with Mike Jeliffe, Mouzhan Majidi, Armstrong Yakubu, Spencer de Grey and Chris Connell.

9. Nigel Curry.

10. Chris West and Kirsten Scott.

11. Ben Scott and Judy Cheung.

12. Chris Bubb, Maria Norgaard Jensen and Sabrina Friedl with a model of Spinningfields, Manchester.

7

8

9

10

11

12

Group 3
Mouzhan Majidi

Led by Mouzhan Majidi, who has been closely involved in the design of three of the practice's major airport terminals – at Stansted, Chek Lap Kok and Beijing International – Group 3 are currently involved in projects that range in scale from the design of an innovative series of 40-metre, long-range cruising yachts to Russia Tower in Moscow City – a mixed-use, super-dense vertical city that will be home to 25,000 people. In addition to cultural and commercial projects in Russia – where the group has established a strong base – they are developing the Camp Nou Stadium in Barcelona and applying their airport expertise to the development of Queen Alia International Airport, in Amman.

1

2

3

4

5

6

1. Foster + Partners' office in Hong Kong.

2. Alistair Lenczner, Spencer de Grey and Luke Fox.

3. A Group 3 partners meeting.

4. Brian Timmoney in the Beijing office.

5. Luke Fox with Sharon Giffen and Andy Bow.

7

8

10. Michael Gentz and Ricky Sandhu discuss Russia Tower.

11. Angus Campbell and Luke Fox.

12. Norman Foster and Mouzhan Majidi with a model of Beijing Airport.

13. Mouzhan Majidi with Mark Sutcliffe in the London studio; seated left is Suzie Trechman; to the right are Margaret Saunders and Rosie Thomson.

9

10

11

12

6. Mouzhan Majidi with Andy Bow, Ken Hogg and Narinder Sagoo.

7. Angus Campbell chairs a design meeting.

8. Jonathan Parr with Alistair Lenczner, David Nelson and Spencer de Grey.

9. Mouzhan Majidi with Norman Foster.

13

Group 4
Stefan Behling

Stefan Behling, who leads Group 4, has for many years helped to guide the practice's approach to sustainable design and the group's projects naturally reflect this. These investigations span from the urban scale, with a masterplan for a sustainable community in a former industrial area of Milan, to a series of discreet tourist retreats on the Green Mountain coastline of Libya, which form part of a wider goal of achieving carbon neutrality on a regional scale. The group is also involved in a number of major arts projects, including the transformation of the Museum of Fine Arts, Boston and the creation of the Winspear Opera House in Dallas.

1. Michael Jones reviewing a model with Ben Cowd.

2. A Group 4 design review.

3. Stefan Behling, Elena Bertarelli, Luis Matania, Spencer de Grey and Darron Haylock.

4. Stefan Behling with Norman Foster and Christian Hallmann.

5. Stefan Behling with Nikolai Malsch, Lara Thrasher and David Nelson.

11. Luis Matania, Spencer de Grey, Stefan Behling and David Nelson in a design review.

12. Luis Matania working with Maddalena Sanvito.

13. Susanne Popp introduces the Baltimore Tower in a design review.

14. Maddalena Sanvito, Nigel Dancey, Darron Haylock, Stefan Behling and Kate Murphy in a review of the Santa Giulia project.

7

8

9

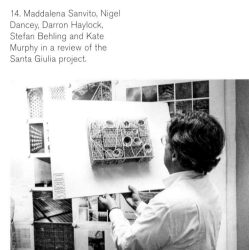

10

11

12

6. Michael Jones and Charles Di Piazza with Ingrid Sölken and Kate Murphy.

7. Stefan Behling, Nikolai Malsch and Josef Kaps.

8. Luis Matania, Stefan Behling and Elena Bertarelli.

9. Kate Murphy in a design review with David Nelson, Michael Jones and Darron Haylock.

10. Stefan Behling examines a study model.

13

14

Group 5
Gerard Evenden

Group 5 is led by Gerard Evenden, who has developed a particular expertise in the design of transport and urban infrastructure, and that theme represents a strong thread within the group. Projects range from the Florence High Speed Rail Station – the latest of the practice's many station projects – to the desert community of Masdar in Abu Dhabi, which offers a benchmark for the carbon-neutral city of the future. The theme of sustainable urban living is further explored in a series of cultural and mixed-use projects, including Central Market in Abu Dhabi and The Troika in Kuala Lumpur, which assume the scale of the city quarter.

1

2

3

4

1. Gerard Evenden with David Nelson.

2. Norman Foster gave a keynote address at the World Future Energy Summit, Abu Dhabi in January 2008. Pictured here at the event are Gerard Evenden, Norman Foster, David Nelson and Simon Wing.

3. Norman Foster with a model for the Al Raha Beach development.

4. Gerard Evenden presents in a design review.

5

6

5. The team with a model of the YTL Headquarters, Kuala Lumpur.

6. Muir Livingstone in a design review.

7. Charbel Tannous, design systems analyst, examining the facade of Central Markets, Abu Dhabi.

8. Norman Foster discusses the design of Central Markets with the team.

7

8

10

9

11

12

9. Model maker, Gareth Verbiest working on a model of Central Markets.

10. A design review for the Sheikh Zayed Museum.

11. Muir Livingstone and Graham Philips.

12-14. Ross Palmer, Edson Yabiku and Jurgen Happ discuss models of Masdar University with Stefan Behling and Gerard Evenden.

13

14

Group 6
Nigel Dancey

Group 6 is led by Nigel Dancey, who has developed research buildings for Stanford University that set a precedent by opening up the private world of the institution to a formative dialogue with the public realm. This process continues in a number of current projects that range from a museum for Johnson Wax in Racine to two buildings within the City of Justice in Madrid, which will be the largest judicial campus in Europe. Other projects with a strong public focus include Motor City in Aragon, Spain, and the Khan Shatyr Entertainment Centre, in Astana, Kazakhstan, which shelters a range of civic, cultural and social amenities within a protective climatic envelope.

1

2

3

4

1. Nigel Dancey, Mouzhan Majidi and colleagues discuss a collaboration between Groups 3 and 6.

2. Katy Roach, Russell Hales and David Moreno prepare a competition model.

3. Nigel Dancey with Tomonobu Hirayu and Filo Russo

4. Nigel Dancey in a design review in the Istanbul office.

5

6

7

8

9. A design review of the Bodrum Sustainable Resort Community, led by David Nelson with Graham Philips, David Summerfield, Michelle Johnson, Niall Dempsey and Todd Hutton.

10. Nigel Dancey prepares for a client meeting.

11. Nicholas Ling in a design review.

12. Nigel Dancey, Norman Foster and Spencer de Grey in a design meeting.

13. Norman Foster with David Summerfield and Nigel Dancey.

9

10

11

12

5. Norman Foster and Nigel Dancey in a client meeting for the Monaco masterplan.

6. Russell Hales with a model of the Al Faisaliah II tower.

7. Eric Stroud and David Moreno preparing for a presentation.

8. Nick Ling discussing the Corniche Bay Resort with David Nelson.

13

Specialist Teams

Within the studio the design groups are supported by specialist teams who provide wide-ranging expertise, including product design, space planning, communications, graphics, visualisations, model making, 3D computer modelling, information technology, and contract and construction management. We also have an information centre, which contains a materials research centre that helps architects to select established products or initiate the use of new materials. The computer modelling techniques developed by the specialist modelling group allow projects with complex geometries to be explored and developed rapidly, while at the other end of the spectrum our traditional model shop can produce everything from quick sketch models to full-size mock-ups.

1

2

3

4

5

1. A product design briefing session at a side table in the main studio.

2. Product design team discussion led by John Small with Claudia Danelon, Mike Holland, Dmitri Warner and James White.

3. Claudia Danelon, John Small, Mike Holland, Dmitri Warner and James White from the product design team review two new Emeco 20-06 chairs.

4. Mike Holland examines drawings of the Ilium light for Italian manufacturer Nemo.

5. John Small and James White discuss the specifications for the interior of a private jet with Norman Foster.

6. The bar and reception in the Riverside Studio.

7. View of the Riverside studio from the mezzanine level above the model shop.

8. The model shop is an integral part of the studio; pictured here are model makers John Dixon, Ryan Mitchell and Robert Turner.

9. Senior model maker Ryan Mitchell with trainee Kayleigh Driver.

10. Model maker Hayley Henry.

11. Looking into the model shop from the main studio.

1

2

3

1. Architectural Illustrator
Neryhs Phillips Kwak.

2. Gamma Basra, who leads
the visualisation team.

3. Matthew Foreman,
researcher and librarian.

4. Stefan Behling, with
Katy Harris, head of
communications, and
presentations manager
Jonathan Cox.

5. Narinder Sagoo, head of
communication design, with
artist assistant, Jon Cambeul.

6. Mark Sutcliffe, who leads
the management group with
assistant project manager,
Genevieve Abeydeera.

7. Fitore Pllana, a research
and administrative
assistant to the workplace
consultancy.

4

5

6

8. Martin Glover of the workplace consultancy, working with plans of a business park in Mumbai.

9. Martin Glover, with Sarah Furniss, interior designer discussing a post-occupancy evaluation project.

10. A workplace consultancy team meeting, with Martin Glover and interior designers Vimal Raghwani and Kerry Knight.

7

8

9

12

10

13

11. Interior designer Sarah Furniss with Arjun Kaicker, who leads the workplace consultancy and strategic consultancy groups.

12. Martha Tsigkari, of the specialist modelling group, at work on the parametric model of a spiral staircase.

13. Graham Young, head of IT with Francis Aish and Hugh Whitehead of the specialist modelling group.

11

The Team

Founder and Chairman
Norman Foster

Chief Executive
Mouzhan Majidi

Senior Executives
Spencer de Grey
David Nelson

Chief Financial Officer
Matthew Streets

Executive Directors
Grant Brooker
Nigel Dancey

Senior Partners
Stefan Behling
Andy Bow
Gerard Evenden
Brandon Haw
Paul Kalkhoven
David Summerfield
Mark Sutcliffe
Graham Young

Design Board
Norman Foster
Spencer de Grey
David Nelson
Mouzhan Majidi
Armstrong Yakubu
Nigel Dancey
Stefan Behling
Narinder Sagoo

Partners
Francis Aish
Mark Atkinson
James Barnes
Gamma Basra
Stephen Best
Toby Blunt
John Blythe
Kimberley Boon
Chris Bubb
Angus Campbell
Martin Castle
Jan Coghlan
Chris Connell
Philipp Eichstadt
D'Arcy Fenton
Luke Fox
Juan Frigerio
Stanley Fuls
Mike Gardner
Michael Gentz
Pedro Haberbosch
Russell Hales
Christian Hallmann
Ulrich Hamann
Katy Harris
Robert Harrison
Richard Hawkins
Darron Haylock
Ken Hogg
Thouria Istephan
Mike Jelliffe
David Jenkins
Reinhard Joecks
Iwan Jones
Michael Jones
Arjun Kaicker
Josef Kaps
David Kong
Paul Leadbeatter
Alistair Lenczner
Nicholas Ling
Muir Livingstone
Nikolai Malsch
Luis Matania
Ricardo Mateu
Robert McFarlane
James McGrath
Laura Morales
Kate Murphy
Antoinette Nassopoulos
Max Neal
Michael WT Ng
Diane Oates
Ross Palmer
Jonathan Parr
Divya Patel
Peter Ridley
Giles Robinson
Filo Russo
Narinder Sagoo
Margaret Saunders
Roland Schnizer
Sven Schmedes
Dan Sibert

John Small
Hugh Stewart
Huw Thomas
Brian Timmoney
Steve Trstenjak
Neil Vandersteen
Juan Vieira-Pardo
Jeremy Wallis
Colin Ward
Chris West
Ian Whitby
Hugh Whitehead
Chris Williams
Michael Wurzel
Edson Yabiku
Armstrong Yakubu

Associate Partners
Zak A Ayash
Alexander Barry
Mike Bass
Aike Behrens
Jonathan Bell
Simona Bencini
Rafe Bertram
Doretta Bevilacqua
Florian Boxberg
Marco Callegaro
Patrick Campbell
William Castagna
Graham Collingridge
Tony Cooper
Hayley Cross
Nigel Curry
Hugo D'Enjoy
Xavier De Kestelier
Ben Dobbin
James Edwards
Tie Fan
Jon Fielding
Morgan Fleming
Colin Foster
Marco Gamini
Anna Garreau
Carolyn Gembles
Sandra Glass
Chris Glew
Martin Glover
Robert Hall
Christopher Hammerschmidt
Peter Han
Joost Heremans
Darryn Holder
Mike Holland
Todd Hutton
John Jennings
Mathias Kerremans
Anton Khmelnitskiy
Jeremy Kim
Edmund Klimek
Angelika Kovacic
Andreas Krause
Hernan Kraviez
Gaby Kunze
Jurgen Kuppers
Ashley Lane
Loretta Law
Giulia Leoni
Mathieu Le Sueur
Randy Liekenjie
Stuart Macalister
Neil MacLeod
Mathis Malchow
Robert Malcolm
Emanuele Mattutini
Bobbie Michael
Tony Miki
Carlo Negri
Gary Owen
Joon Paik
Alpa Patel

Nick Paterson
Brady Peters
Emily Phang
Daniel Poehner
Susanne Popp
Tony Price
Austin Relton
Martin Rolfe
Ricky Sandhu
Diana Schaffrannek
Matthias Schoberth
Ben Scott
Kirsten Scott
Cristina Segni
Gordon Seiles
Danny Shaw
Riko Sibbe
Barry Smith
Neville Smith
Paul Smith
Carlos Sole Bravo
Ingrid Sölken
Digeo Suarez
Iwona Szwedo-Wilmot
Colm Tamney
Pearl Tang
Caroline Tarling
Dara Towhidi
Karsten Vollmer
Vincent Westbrook
Hans-Christian Wilhelm
Simon Wing
Dion Young
Nigel Young

Associates
Omar Al Omari
Amer Altaf
Sofia Arraiza
Marco Belcastro
Karin Bergmann
Elena Bertarelli
Andy Bingham
Beate Bischofberger
Robin Blanchard
Tim Bodinnar
Arthur Branthwaite
Richard Brown
Philippe Brysse
Peter Buche
Thorsten Burgmer
Maddelena Cannarsa
Stefano Cesario
Kevin Chatfield
Ho Ling Cheung
Steven Chiu
Young Wei-Yang Chiu
Fai Chow
Marie Christoffersen
Melissa Clinch
Birgit Clottens
Bryan Cory
Miguel Costa
Alicia Cox
Jonathan Cox
Neil Crawford
Coco Cugat
Svetlana Curcic
Federico D'Angelo
Niall Dempsey
Tony Dennison
Charles Di Piazza
John Dixon
Amy DuVergier
Tommaso Fantoni
Tom Fechtner
Karen Fiano
Matthew Foreman
Michaela Fuchs
Giulia Galiberti
Irene Gallou
Gregory Gibbon
Ei-Kie Giam
Sharon Giffen
Harriet Gillham
Ingo Glatsch
Sebastian Gmelin
Henriette Hahnloser
Michael Haley
Isabelle Hannig
Jurgen Happ
Petra Hartmann
Dominik Hauser
Klaus Heldwein
Joern Herrmann
Carolin Hinne
Tomonobu Hirayu
Jens Hoffman
Andy Hyatt
Sukdev Indra

Perry Ip
Dirk Jantz
Christopher Junkin
Kathryn Keen
Jai Krishnan
Luca Latini
Graeme Laughlan
Clarissa Lenz
Tillmann Lenz
Pablo Urango Lillo
Franquibel Lima
Nina Linde
Sanja Lisovac
Andy Lister
Alistair Macmillan
Consuelo Manna
Gayle Markovitz
Ajit Menon
Gregor Milne
Sam Morgan
Ian Motley
Michael Mueller
Michael Ng
Kristine Ngan
Adrian Nicholas
Rosita Niknafs
Brian Nolan
Chris Nunn
Rachael Oldfield
Taek Park
Damon Pearce
Neryhs Phillips Kwak
Bjorn Polzin
Joe Preston
Enrique Ramos
Salvador Rivas
Damiano Rizzini
Emma Robbins
Riccardo Russo
Maddalena Sanvito
Nicola Scaranaro
Torsten Schlauersbach
Falk Schneemann
Wolfram Schneider
Kathryn Schoefert
Birgit Schoenbrodt
Owe Schoof
Dorothea Schulz
Jonathan Scull
Steve Shaw
Marilu Sicoli Vidal
Joanna Smith
Robert Smith
Sunphol Sorakul
Niall Starling
Laura Stecich
Zoe Stokes
Asli Suner
Laurent Tek
Vincent Thiry
Rosie Thomson
Damian Timlin
Kathryn Tollervey
Stefano Tonelli
Gloria Tsai

Inge Tummers
Stephanie Tunka
Robert Turner
Eva Tzivanaki
Diem Uong
Jorge Uribe
Bram van der Wal
Gareth Verbiest
Raquel Viula
Weina Wang
Dmitri Warner
Lena Wegener
Tony Wenban
Liz Westgarth
David Wettergren
Dave Wicker
Simon Windebank
Jessica Wood
Shyue-Jiun Woon
Richard Wotton
David Yang
Kevin Yiu
Zheng Yu

Group One
Grant Brooker

Hermes-Konstantinos
Adamantidis
Sofia Arraiza
Matthew Austen
Genevieve Baudoin
Aike Behrens
Jonathan Bell
Deborah Benros
Beate Bischofberger
Chad Bishop
Diogo Bleck
Aryeh Brawer
Peter Brittain
Peter Buche
Joyce Chan
Saxbourne Cheung
Alan Chiang
Young Wei-Yang Chiu
Justyna Chuchro
Federica Ciocci
Graham Collingridge
Rachel Collins
Alexander Cook
Francois-Pierre Curato
Svetlana Curcic
Gonzalo de Pablo Fernandez
Shareen Elnaschie
Matthew Fajkus
Matthew Farrer
D'Arcy Fenton
Oliver Flindall
Michaela Fuchs
Andrew Gardner
Rafaelle Gavassa
Ingo Glatsch
Florian Graumann
Tamsin Green
William Guthrie
Hallstein Guthu
Christopher Hammerschmidt
Isabelle Hannig
Andres Harris
Robert Harrison
Takuji Hasegawa
Audun Hellemo
Jens Hoffman
Brandon Hubbard
Rachel Hunter
Jamsyid Idrus
Rony Imad
Dirk Jantz
Przemyslaw Jaworski
Aaron Jessop
Kounikui Karihindi
Tim Kemp
Sanghon Kim
Yu-La Kim
Yongcchun Kim
Vera Kleesattel
Jedrzej Kolesinski
David Kong
Angelika Kovacic

Olivier Krenz
Jürgen Küppers
Theresa Kwok
Mei Law
Ashley Lane
Paul Leadbeatter
Maite Lemogne
Li-Jun Lin
Andy Lister
Daniel Lobo
Connie Yuen Nam Luk
Stuart Mackellar
Milena Marucci
Beth McLeod
Ajit Menon
Katy Hyunjoo Min
Gregor Milne
Javier Montero
Ana Morais
Tiziana Mori
Adeline Morin
Nils Muenker
Premveer Nagpal
Agata Najgebauer
Matilde Napoleao
Kazumasa Naritsuka
Antoinette Nassopoulos
Max Neal
Bahar Nejad
William Newell
Kristine Ngan
Phakorn Nilwong
Nick Norifumi Kasai
Ricardo Ostos
Jolanda Oud
Joon Paik
Prisca Pannone
Sun-Young Park
Nick Paterson
Marta Paz Vitorio
Damon Pearce
Daniel Poehner
Silvia Polito
David Ralph
Enrique Ramos
Merino Ranallo
Madelaine Raposas
Jana Rastemborski
Damiano Rizzini
Victoria Robin
Martin Rolfe
Joana Santos
Julian Sattler
Jan Sauermann
Owe Schoof
Fritz Schroeder
Gianpietro Sciarra
Jonathan Scull
Kauntey Shah
Dan Sibert
Neville Smith
Robert Smith
Hugh Stewart
Rossella Stina
Hiroyuki Sube

Isabel Lopez Taberna
Julia Tabrizi
Harold Tan
Caroline Tarling
Mark Thompson
Alexander Thonicke
Pedro Tiago de Sousa
Sanja Tiedemann
Maria Sagrario M Torres
Lucas Trapa
Yusuke Tsutsui
Hiroko Uchino
Caro van de Venne
Martin Vlnas
Marsyas Von Naso
Nicolas Weiss
Ian Whitby
Ross Whittaker
Sam Wilson
Chi Chung Wong
Tomasz Wozny
Pei-Yao Wu
See Teck Yeo
Antonio Yeregui
Jonathan Yeung
Kevin Yiu
Jack Young

Group Two
David Summerfield

Madeleine Adlercreutz
Caroline Assa
Alessandro Baccari
Dennis Bartolomeo
Susanne Bauer
Antonietta Bavaro
Jacob Bekermus
Adolfo Berardozzi
Rafe Bertram
Christian Brunner
Chris Bubb
Brandon Buck
Lindsay Bush
Maddalena Cannarsa
Constanza Chara
Hui-Cheng Chen
Judy Cheung
Marie Christoffersen
Chris Connell
Carlo Costa
Neil Crawford
Nigel Curry
Federico D'Angelo
Aaron Davis
Dimitri Davoise
Niall Dempsey
Laura Di Chello
Claire Donnelly
Niraj Doshi
James Edwards
Philipp Eichstadt
Dagmar Eisenach
Jeremy Emerson
Oznur Erboga
Tommaso Fantoni
Marco Ferri
James Ford
Erica Freeman
Sabrina Friedl
Juan Frigerio
Marco Gamini
Jurgita Garsvaite
Hanne Gathe
David Gillespie
Jan Glasmeier
Lei Guo
Stefan Hache
Robert Hall
Peter Han
Claudia Hassels
Eduardo Gonzales Hernandez
Rebekah Hieronymus
Nike Himmels
Annabel Hodges
Roland Hoferica
Angel Huerga
Karina Huessner
Todd Hutton
Amer Ismail
Mike Jelliffe
John Jennings
Yerko Jeria

Michelle Johnson
Aphrodite Kavallieraki
Erika Kazama
Agnieszka Klak
Se Kwan Kim
Edmund Klimek
Gino Koenraadt
Andreas Krause
Jai Krishnan
Tillmann Lenz
Eddie Linfield
Geraldine Lo
Anthony Logothetis
Jorge Lozano
Alistair MacMillan
Nazarena Manenti
Consuelo Manna
Karl Mascarenhas
Michaela Matheson
John McCulley
Tim McGinley
Sebastian Mendez
Annie Ming-Yee Lo
Mario Mohan
Louise Munch Kofoed
Maria Norgaard Jensen
Declan O'Donnell
Jean Sebastien Pagnon
Chen-Chen Pang
Elisa Pardini
Taek Park
Jiri Pavlicek
Elke Pedal Baertl
James Pike
Priscilla Pinotti
Neda Pourshakouri
Samuel Price
Jose Restrepo
Marian San Emeterio
John Santoro
Iacopo Sassi
Akil Scafe-Smith
Nina Schippel
Torsten Schlauersbach
Sven Schmedes
Matthias Schoberth
Dorothea Schulz
Ben Scott
Kirsten Scott
Cristina Segni
Martin Seibel
Rie Shiomi
Jonathan Sim
Paul Smith
Sara Smith
Diego Suarez
Wei Sun
Robin Tandavanitj
Damian Timlin
Yasuhiro Tohdoh
Maria Sagrario M Torres
Sergio Valentini
Francesca Venturoni
Manijeh Verghese
Viktor Vrecko

Linjie Wang
Chris West
Christy Widjaja
Dominic Wilson
Tom Winter
Jet Wai Wong
Puikie Wu
Michael Wurzel
Anna Xu

Group Three
Mouzhan Majidi
Andy Bow

Omar Al Omari
Carol Aoun
Thomas Arnhardt
Sabah Ashiq
Mark Atkinson
Roman Auweck
Zak A Ayash
Stephen Best
Doretta Bevilacqua
Cely Bigando
Yazan Bilbeisi
Tobias Bloemeke
Florian Boxberg
Thorsten Burgmer
Elsa Alves Caetano
Angus Campbell
Galo Cazares Fernandez
Stefano Cesario
Kevin Chan
Vincent Chan
Genevieve Chen
Dora Chi
Ilya Chistiakov
Steven Chiu
Shin Hyung Cho
Won Suk Cho
Marina Cisneros Vitoria
Melissa Clinch
Birgit Clottens
Edward Cluer
Georgina Couzens
Coco Cugat Garcia
Fernando Da Col
Jonathan Dallas
Sandra Debbas
Jan-Pieter Deheegher
Sophie Deheegher
Fiona Drago
Nicolas Ecrepont
Piotr Ehrenhalt
Christine Eisenhut
Francisca Estarellas
Tie Fan
Karen Fiano
Felix Fischer
Thomas Foggin
Colin Foster
Luke Fox
Lorena Franco
Etienne Fuchs
Lara Genovese
Michael Gentz
Ei-Kie Giam
Sharon Giffen
Sebastian Gmelin
Marta Gonzalez Del Palacio
Paul Gordz
Joerg Grabfelder
Christopher Gresham
Panos Hadji Christofis
Christian Hallmann

Maheen Hameed
Katrin Hass
Masateru Hatamoto
Richard Hawkins
Pauline Hayward
Jakob Hense
Joern Herrmann
Carolin Hinne
Asa Hjort
Shok Wan Ho
Steven Ho
Ken Hogg
Darryn Holder
Jethro Hon
Timothy Hui
Sang Hyeok Lee
Alessandra Iacovella
Jade Ip
Perry Ip
Takehiko Iseki
Danae Katsiveli
Ewa Kazmierczyk
Raphael Keane
Martin Kehoe
Alena Kereshun
Mathias Kerremans
Himanshee Khanna
Anton Khmelnitskiy
Jeremy Kim
Sejin Kim
Alicja Kiszczuk
David Koenigsfeld
Eirini Kouka
Anna Kowal
Jekaterina Kowaltschuk
Oxana Krause
Hernan Kraviez
Diana Krumbein
Renee Tsuen Yan Kwok
Stephanie Lacriox
Celia Yixin Lai
Astor Lam
Christopher Lam
Christa Lange
Loretta Law
Louis Hok Man Lee
Robert Lee
Sang Hyeok Lee
Alistair Lenczner
Vikki Lew
Dao De Li
Daniel Qing Li
Randy Liekenjie
Da Chun Lin
Yuki Liu
Claudia Llorca
Alex Llusia
Adrian Lombardo
Monika Losos
Benedict Lu
Brian Macken
Paulina Mahorowska
Mathis Malchow
Katja Martini
Maher Matar

Tony Miki
O J Miu
Simon Mok
Marian Moravek
Michael Mueller
Sebastien Muller
Jorge Munoz
Veronika Nebesarova
Carlo Negri
Michael WT Ng
Rosita Niknafs
Mu Niu
Naoto Noda
Kurtulus Oflaz
Kaoruko Ogawa
Claudia Ostwald
Elisa Pagliarani
Daniel Pang
Sophie Panzer
Sang-Kil Park
Woohyuck Park
Jonathan Parr
Siriwat Patchimasiri
Michele Pecoraro
Charles Peronnin
Eduard Petriu
Giada Pilo
Sergio Pineda
Dusanka Popovska
Eliot Postma
Evin Power
Stanley Pun
Ke Quan
Uri Richer Atir
Bettina Richter
Samar Rizkallah
Maria Rodero
Viviana Romani
Lina Ruelas Choza
Nathan St John
Ivo Miguel Sales Costa
Yitzhak-Balfour Samun
Ricky Sandhu
Birgit Schoenbrodt
Jayendra Shah
Bartenis Siaulytis
Riko Sibbe
Richard Simpson
Niall Small
Niall Starling
Petr Stefek
Julia Stumpf
Yang Sun
Pearl Tang
Charbel Tannous
Vincent Thiry
Huw Thomas
Vikrant Tike
Dina Timartseva
Brian Timmoney
Xiaowei Tong
Hiroaki Toyoshima
Charles Tsang
Ivo van Capelleveen
Sam Van Welden

Francisco Vaz Monteiro
Christoph Vogl
Christopher Von Der Howen
Ho Shok Wan
Wiena Wang
Colin Ward
Vincent Westbrook
David Wettergren
Irene Wong
Jeff Tin Long Wong
Lawrence Wong
Shyue-Jiun Woon
Katie Wu
Shu-Hao Wu
Meng Xia
David Yang
Dion Young
Zheng Yu
Xu Yue
Echo Yuen
Alexander Zech
Gongpu Zhao
Jean Wen Yan Zhu

Group Four

Stefan Behling
Michael Jones

Jerome Anton
Benedicte Artault
Alexander Barry
Marco Belcastro
Simona Bencini
Elena Bertarelli
Robin Blanchard
Dariusz Boron
Philippe Brysse
Luca Carraro
William Castagna
Ciriaco Castro Diez
Cristina Cipolli
Gabriele Coccia
Stefan Conev
Graziella Corti
Ben Cowd
Paul-Robert Cristian
Andrea Dallari
Kunal Dalvi
Eike Danz
Hugo D'Enjoy
Federico De Paoli
Charles Di Piazza
Ben Dobbin
Jacopo Fiabane
Jon Fielding
Morgan Fleming
Debbie Flevotomou
Michael Fostiropoulos
Tommaso Franchi
Rebeca Liliana Gonzalez Murillo
Silke Grapenthin
Henriette Hahnloser
Rie Haslov
Matthew Hayhurst
Darron Haylock
Matthias Hehl
Hugh Howley-Berridge
Dmitry Inanoff
Reinhard Joecks
Josef Kaps
Bela Kasza
Judith Kernt
Carl Kessler
Yung A Kim
Kilian Kresing
Gaby Kunze
Graeme Laughlan
Peng Li
Helena Lillo
Wei Jie Liu
Petra Lui
Stuart Macalister
James McGrath
Nikolai Malsch
Tiziano Massarutto
Luis Matania
Alberto Menegazzo
Luigi Montefusco

Kate Murphy
Luigi Orioli
Nicola Pacini
Laszlo Pallagi
Stanimir Paparizov
Pritesh Patel
Daniele Petteno
Birgit Pfisterer
Adeline Piel
Stephan Polatzek
Björn Polzin
Susanne Popp
Shehab Rezk
Il Hoon Roh
Hanna-Li Roos
Varuna Saini
Maddalena Sanvito
Kathryn Schoefert
Gordon Seiles
Alexandra Sgraja
Parul Singh
Ingrid Sölken
Colm Tamney
Diego Alejandro Teixeira
Lara Thrasher
Stephanie Tunka
Luca Vernocchi
Lena Wegener
Leonhard Weil
Kai Wertel
Hans-Christian Wilhelm
Rene Wolter
Sheng-Ming Wu
Syuan-Fu Yu

Group Five

Gerard Evenden

Ahmad Syihan Amir
Matthias Anegg
Massimo Barbera
Jefferson Barnes
Megan Barrett
Dennis Bartolomeo
Joseba Baztan
Matthias Benz
Toby Blunt
John Blythe
Michael Bories
Arthur Branthwaite
Giammarco Bruno
Martin Buchholz
Martin Castle
Annalisa Celani
Darren Chan
Ya-Hsin Chen
Barrie Cheng
Ho Ling Cheung
Assawin Choochottavorn
Fatima Citoula
David Crosswaite
Amy Cruickshank
Miriam Dall'igna
Thomasin Davis
Daniella De Almeida
Francisco Gonzales De Canales
Tiago Lopes De Costa Jorge
Alexander De Fyn
Andrea Desideri
Hanna Diers
Jens Domberg
Markus Elbracht
Natasha Errington
Patricia Fairclough
Olivia Fontanetti
Felix Forthmeijer
Iolanda Fortunato
Fabiano Friedrich
Stanley Fuls
Joliette Gadeken
Giulia Galiberti
Claudia Gentili Spinola
Davide Giglio
Sandra Glass
Christoph Goeke
Maria Golasowska
Marija Gonopolskaja
Vito Gramegna
Andrew Grange
Friso Gros
Silvia Guzzini
Pedro Haberbosch
Dirk Hahn Arellano
Jurgen Happ
Klaus Heldwein
Anja Hilderscheid
Sung Ho Hong
Anja Hoppe
Alexandra Howieson

Marc Iffland
Cordula Jacobi
Yvonne Jendreiek
Vladimir Jovanovic
Christopher Junkin
Hisayo Kaneko
Dorothee Keller
Daniel Keppel
Anastasiya Khranovska
Yong-Bin Kim
Lorain Kok
Angeliki Koliomichou
Kelvin Kong
Krassimir Krastev
Charlotte Krefeld
Shyuan Kuee
Helen Kuo
Javier Lahuerta
Luca Latini
Damien Lau
Wonsuk Lee
Clarissa Lenz
Paul Leo
Giulia Leoni
Franquibel Lima
Kathrin Lind
Jeroen Linnebank
Muir Livingstone
Bridget MacKean
Daniel Madeiros
Thomas Mahon
Robert Malcolm
Emanuele Mattutini
Frank Maurer
Vilda Mazonaite
Miki McBride
Richard McClure
Robert McFarlane
Isabelle McKinnon
Martina Meluzzi
Laura Morales
Jeffrey Morgan
Anuschka Mueller
Candice Naim
Irina Nazarova
Adam Newburn
Israel Nagore Setien
Michael Ng
May Noradee
Chris Nunn
Katriina Nyman
Phil Obayda
James Osbiston
Gary Owen
Ross Palmer
Ill Sam Park
Chan Ik Park
Carlos Bermejo Pascual
Emily Phang
Laura Podda
Luca Poian
Javier Porcel
Johanna Porep
Alison Potter
Gaurav Powale

Anne Rahausen
Rusmir Ramic
Julien Raulet
Austin Relton
Florian Rieger
Ana Maria Robayo
Nielsen Rodrigues
Riccardo Russo
Sonia Carolina Salazar Rojas
Jillian Salter
Andrea Salvucci
Falk Schneemann
Wolfram Schneider
Rafael Schneidewind
Roland Schnizer
Ronald Schuurmans
Christian Schwedler
Carolin Senftleben
Jun Shi
Neha Shrivastava
Marilu Sicoli Vidal
Po Sing Sin
Realrich Sjarief
William So
Hendrik Sokolis
Sunphol Sorakul
Jeppe Sorensen
Nikola Stadler
Anne Starker
Holger Stewering
Gemma Stilwell
Iwona Szwedo-Wilmot
Krzysztof Szymanski
Dara Towhidi
Inge Tuemmers
Viktor Udzenija
Stephan Vahle
Jaime Valle
Bram van der Wal
Natalia Vinuela
Karsten Vollmer
Catharine von Eitzen
Felipe Wagner
Torsten Weber
Lim Keong Wee
Daniel Weiss
Liz Westgarth
Dominic Williams
Simon Wing
Stephanie Winter
Zhongping Wu
Edson Yabiku
Zhenyuan Yang
Munehiko Yokomatsu
Bo Yoon
Soungmin Yu
Hartwig Zehm
Di Zhang
Jenny Xiaoxue Zhou

Group Six

Nigel Dancey

Ana Agag Longo
Angelita Alves
Laura Alvey
Maura Ambrosiano
Annamaria Anderloni
Anna Nga Au
Anna Aversing
Eric Baczuk
James Barnes
Florian Becker
Verena Becker
Jakob Beer
Susanne Bellinghausen
Francesco Benincasa
Karin Bergmann
Besnik Bijo
Jessica Birnbaum
Federico Bixio
Joerg Boettger
Lauren Boulay
Jens Brunner
David Burton
Natalia Busch
Marco Callegaro
Patrick Campbell
Guillaume Chabenat
Sharan Chandola
Charis Charalampous
Claudia Chiappini
Jan Coghlan
Miguel Costa
Hayley Cross
Adam Davis
Kirsten Davis
Maria Dourado
Markus Ehrler
Fatma Elmalipinar
Esra Enhos
Deniz Basar Erol
Corrado Falsetti
Tom Fechtner
Lena Feindt
Jose Fernandez
Manuel Fernandez
Christian Fink
Andreas Fiolka
Andrea Frindert
Luis Fuentes Arambula
Jose Antonio Garcia Ares
Carolyn Gembles
Michail Georgiou
Jennifer Gomes
Jorge Gomez Bernal
William Gordon
Goncalo Guerreiro
Gizem Deniz Guneri
Russell Hales
Ulrich Hamann
Petra Hartmann
Dominik Hauser
Christophe Hellio
Joost Heremans

Mustafa Deniz Hidiroglu
Tomonobu Hirayu
Po-Yuan Huang
Ozgur Ilter
Maria Jara
Beau Johnson
Iwan Jones
Martin Kaftan
Ozkan Karababa
Ivan Kaye
Siobhan Kelly
Andi Kercini
Brenda Kim
Melanie Klaehn
Johanna Knaak
Gulsah Komurcuoglu
Olga Koutantou
Onur Kosedag
Nina Krause
John Krieger
Georgia Krubasik
Kristine Krueger
Kay Kulinna
Binh Le
Mathieu Le Sueur
Heidrun Lehnhardt
Shirley Shee Ying Leung
Mika Liami
Nina Linde
Nicholas Ling
Levin Lo
Sandra Loiseau
Alissa MacInnes
Rachel MacIntyre
Morna McKay
Peter McPherson
Kathleen Mark
Ricardo Mateu
Julia Mauser
David Moreno
Laia Mulet
Santiago Mulinetti
Sabine Muth
Sofia Muzio
Hwee Li Ng
Adrian Nicholas
Emre Ozberk
Marc Palatsi Garcia
Vajini Pannila
Nicholas Papas
Silvia Paredes
Hector Pascalidis
Cristina Perez
Blanca Perinat
Elizabetta Pezzoni
Nike Picon Calvo
Julia Pitschieler
Juraj Pollak
Lorena Prieto
Torsten Radunski
Leyla Rahnavard
Annapaola Ramorino
Taba Rasti
Peter Ridley
Stefano Ricardi

Salvador Rivas
Katy Roach
Giles Robinson
Emma Robbins
Teresa Rodriguez
Jennifer Rubin
Filo Russo
Esperanza Salas
Julian Salt
Ismael Sanchez
Ignacio Sanchez Carrascoso
Canan Saridal
Diana Schaffrannek
Nicola Scaranaro
Tobias Schnur
Declan Sharkey
Danny Shaw
Jimmy Shum
Michaela Smith
Carlos Sole Bravo
Martina Sottile
Artur Stachura
Laura Stecich
Kirstin Steyn
Zoe Stokes
Eric Stroud
Asli Suner
Laurent Tek
Min Ter Lim
Catherine Thiemann
Stefano Tonelli
Steve Trstenjak
Gloria Tsai
Eva Tzivanaki
Jorge Uribe
Pablo Urango Lillo
Bas van Wylick
Benjamin Vancaudenberg
Julia Vidal Alvarez
Juan Vieira-Pardo
Hans von Jagow
Ayca Vural
Casey Nai-Huei Wang
Paul Wang
Simon Weismaier
Eric Werner
Stephan Winn
Natalia Wrzask
Astrid Wulff
Grace Wylie
Huali Zhang
Agnieszka Zych

Specialist Teams

Business Development
Brandon Haw

Communications
Katy Harris
David Jenkins

Laura Barnicoat
Gavin Blyth
Lauren Catten
Isabela Chick
Jonathan Cox
Josephine Cutts
Robert Dunbar
Rani Deshpande
Matthew Foreman
Gregory Gibbon
Ben Hardy
Sarah Kelly
Gayle Markovitz
Victoria McGlade
Jade Niklai
Ian Nurock
Rachael Oldfield
Oliver Pawley
Rebecca Pickering
Zoë Powell
Sarah Simpkin
Kathryn Tollervey
Nigel Young

Construction Review Group
Paul Kalkhoven

Stephan Verkuijlen

Design Communications
Narinder Sagoo

Jon Cambeul
Anita Lau
Richard Miller

Design Systems
Kevin Chatfield

Simon Doyle
Derrol Euling
Amanda Glover
Nuwan Gunawardena
Mohamed Master

Information Centre/MRC
Divya Patel

Huw Bevan
Matthew Burger
Luke Wolfik

Information Systems
Graham Young
Barry Smith

Daniel Adejugbe
Yaseen Ahmed
Olumuyiwa Akin-Kuroye
Amer Altaf
Nicholas Benson
Andy Bingham
Joanne Cassie
Fai Chow
Tony Dennison
Antonio Di Maggio
Barnaby Dick
Kashif Ghafoor
Melissa Grant
Holly Handley
Chris Holgate
Adrian Hughes
Andy Hyatt
Kelvin Lieu
Richard Mark
Michelle Meyer
Alexander McPherson
Bhavesh Patel
Chirag Patel
Mehul Patel
Mark Phillips
Tony Price
Jay Quee
Lee Rance
Chris Rodricks
Neil Snowden
Samantha So
William Thorneycroft
Mark van der Byl
Ryan Watson
Gareth Williams

Management Group
Mark Sutcliffe
Mike Gardner
Thouria Istephan

Genevieve Abeydeera
Andrew Bigwood
Timothy Bodinnar
Julie Davies
Kishani De Silva
Jessica Fung
Neil MacLeod
Darren McFarlane
Ian Motley
Alpa Patel
Inés Puelles Dominguez

Model Shop
Neil Vandersteen
Diane Oates

James Appleby
Richard Brown
Bryan Cory
John Dixon
Kayleigh Driver
Hayley Henry
Henry Landon
Ben Lewens
Lara Lodato
Ryan Mitchell
Sam Morgan
Peter O'Sullivan
Joe Preston
Daniel Rogers
Ralph Seller
Robert Turner
Gareth Verbiest
Karleung Wai
Simon Windebank
Richard Wotton

Product Design
John Small

Claudia Danelon
Mike Holland
Dmitri Warner
James White

Specialist Modelling Group
Hugh Whitehead

Francis Aish
Adam Davis
Xavier de Kestelier
Irene Gallou
Jethro Hon
Stefan Krakhofer
Yuan-Chun Lan
Onur Ozkaya
Brady Peters
Jonathan Rabagliati
Harsh Thapar
Martha Tsigkari
Raquel Viula

Sustainability Research
Stefan Behling
Rafe Bertram

Giovanni Betti
Andrew Haigh

Urban Design
Bruno Moser
Lucie Sarles

Visualisation
Gamma Basra

Zuwi Azuwike Nnadi
Ed Brown
Bartlomiej Chechlowski
Martin Clemie
Hazel Eynon
Luke Gibbs
Chris Glew
Michael Haley
Panos Ioannou
Naveed Mughal
Neryhs Phillips Kwak
Oers Sardi
Leanne Storey

Workplace Consultancy
Arjun Kaicker

Harriet Gillham
Martin Glover
Sarah Furniss
Sarah Jarvis
Chaitanya Jogdeo
Stephen Judge
Kerry Knight
Yeong Jae Kweon
Lucinda Mander-Jones
Catharine Patha
Fitore Pllana
Vimal Raghwani

Administration

Accounts
Chris Williams

Carlyn Aurelien
Colin Chesby
Katie Duffy
Amy DuVergier
Paul Grummett
Simon Hobden
Sukdev Indra
Sanja Lisovac
Fiona McQuillan
Dino Mehdi
Bobbie Michael
Nikki Nicolas
Brian Nolan
Aaron O'Donnell
Chris O'Donnell
Anna Rychlewska
Sinem Sevket
Joanna Smith
Kelly Smith
Bhanumati Soma
Diem Uong

Document Control
Nathan Asare
Garry Fairweather
Maria Farina
Christian Lawrence
Jeff Lewis
Stephen Rock
Agnes Szabo
Jennifer Wassell
Dave Wicker
Edmund Youdeowei

Facilities
Tony Cooper

O'Neil Alexander
Amanda Burns
Len Chappell
Boris Dehalu
Alan Foxwell
David Gadsdon
Mark Hawkins
Norman Johnson
Richard Klewer
Luke Pedliham
Jim-Robert Ulrici

Hospitality
Alicia Cox

Human Resources
Kimberley Boon

Laura Bennett
Claire Fitzgerald
Melissa Giwa
Dora Kocur
Nicola Tarrant

Lord Foster's Office
Richard Dilworth

Emma Campbell Preston
Michaela Flack
Sarah Jayne Makin
Mahima Rawat
Jessica Wood

Porters
Ron Edbrooke
David Gilbert
George Kavanagh
Richard Vaclavek

Postroom
Anne Hone
Andrew Murray
Matthew Wilson

Printroom
Mike Bass

John Driver
Gary Ovenden
Jamie Sinton
James Upton
Tony Wenban

Reception
Anna Garreau

Janet Affran
Elinor Cederlinde
Frida Haraldsson
Laura Ellen Hughes
Natalie Tanjic
Lisa Tapsell

Secretarial
Margaret Saunders

Elisabet Eugenia Barone
Katy Boehm
Mercedes Bouck
Matthew Allan De-Gale
Meriem Derouiche
Maria Gea Velez
Sally Gillison
Simona Gioia
Fahri Gundogdu
Marcelle Gutteridge
Eleanor Hill
Sarah Hilton
Andrea Hutchinson
Kathryn Keen
Michelle Lilley
Cathy Lee Bun
Philippa Mack
Katherine Major
Christina Mann
Laura Manning
Yvonne Matthews
Flora Monro
Andrew Moran
Belinda Mou
Pearl Nute
Asli Oncu
Inma Pedregosa
Arber Pllana
Natasha Pryde
Gillian Reid
Jo Roberts
Silvia Romani
Brooke Rosoman
Rania Samy
Victoria Sanz Luque
Stephanie Sibley
Ulrike Stockhausen
Olga Svintsitskii
Emily Symons
Rosie Thomson
Suzie Trechman
Amy Tsang
Birute Vaitiekunaite
Lavinia Walsh
Sunny Wang
Amy Weight
Hannah Wild
Catherine Wilson

Security
Steve Shaw

Lee Bethal
Geoff Cox
James Cunningham
Roger Da Costa
Antonio De Souza
Al Dionisio
Nigel Griffiths
Tim Hampton
Ross Hancock
Michael Jeffery
Mick Slavin
Luke Wynne-Sutton

Warehouse
Craig Edwards

Peter Porter
Stephen Street
Duarte Vaz

International Offices
Foster + Partners has offices in twenty cities around the world. In May 2008 these were:

Abu Dhabi
Beijing
Berlin
Boston
Buenos Aires
Copenhagen
Dubai
Dublin
Edinburgh
Geneva
Hong Kong
Houston
Istanbul
Kuala Lumpur
London
Madrid
Milan
New York
St Petersburg
Zurich

Personal and Practice Awards

2008
Foster + Partners
   AJ100 International Practice
   of the Year
   AJ100 South East and
   London
   AJ100 Sustainability Initiative
   of the Year
Norman Foster
   AJ100 Most Admired
   Architect
   Britain's Best 2008: Award
   for Achievement in the Arts

2007
Foster + Partners
   AJ100 International Practice
   of the Year
   AJ100 South East and
   London
Norman Foster
   'Der Steiger Award' of North-
   Rhine Westphalia in the Art
   category

2006
Norman Foster
   Madrid Creative Award
   British-German Association
   Medal of Honour for Services
   to Anglo-German relations
   AJ100 Most Admired
   Architect

2005
Foster + Partners
   Building Design Office
   Architect of the Year
   BD Impact 100, Most
   Impactful Architectural
   Practice Working in Britain
   AJ100 10th Anniversary
   Special Award, International
   Practice of the Year
Norman Foster
   Architectural Record
   Innovation Prize awarded at
   the McGraw-Hill Construction
   Innovation Conference (case
   study Hearst Tower, New
   York)
   The British Council for Offices
   President's Award
   World Solar Prize, Solar
   Agency, Switzerland
   Prize of the European Press
   Great Britons 2004 Award in
   the Creative Industries
   category

2004
Norman Foster
   Great Britons Award in the
   Creative Industries category
   Prince Philip Designer's Prize
   Transatlantic Bridge Award

2003
Norman Foster
   City of Rome Lifetime
   Achievement Award and
   Medaglia di Roma 'die
   quadriga' prize for Vision,
   Courage and Responsibility,
   from Werkstatt Deutschland,
   Germany Doctor of Letters
   Honoris Causa University
   of Hong Kong Honorary
   Degree of Doctor of Fine Arts
   from Yale University

2002
Norman Foster
   Honorary Degree of Doctor of
   Design from Robert Gordon
   University
   Honorary Degree from
   Durham University
   Member of the Order 'Pour le
   mérite' for Sciences and Arts,
   Germany
   Praemium Imperiale Award for
   Architecture, administered by
   the Japan Art Association
   International Union of
   Architects, Auguste Perret
   Prize

2001
Norman Foster
   South Bank Show Award for
   Visual Arts
   Honorary Doctorate, London
   Institute, London
   Honorary Doctorate and
   Lifetime Achievement Award
   – Ben Gurion University of
   the Negev, Beer-Sheva, Israel

2000
Norman Foster
   Bentley Systems Lifetime
   Achievement Award

1999
Norman Foster
   Laureate of the 1999 Pritzker
   Architecture Prize
   Life Peerage in the Queen's
   Birthday Honours List
   Commander's Cross of the
   Order of Merit of the Federal
   Republic of Germany
   Le Prix Européen de
   l'Architecture de la Fondation
   Européenne de la Culture
   Special Prize, 4th Internatonal
   Biennial of Architecture, Sao
   Paulo, Brazil

1998
Foster + Partners
   The Building Award,
   Architectural Practice
   of the Year
Norman Foster
   German-British Forum,
   Special Prize

1997
Foster + Partners
   The Building Award, Large
   Architectural Practice
   of the Year
   British Construction Industry
   Awards, A Decade of Success
   1988-1997
   International Association of
   Lighting Designers IALD/
   Hilight Excellence in Lighting
   Award
   European Aluminium Award
   for Architecture
Norman Foster
   Appointed to the Order of
   Merit by the Queen
   Silver Medal of the Chartered
   Society of Designers
   International Academy of
   Architecture Grand Prize '97
   Cristal Globe
   Prince Philip Designer's Prize,
   Special Commendation
   Premi a la millor tasca de
   promoció international de
   Barcelona

1996
Foster + Partners
    The Building Award, Large
    Architectural Practice
    of the Year
Norman Foster
    American Academy of Arts
    and Sciences Award
    The Building Award,
    Construction
    Personality of the Year
    MIPIM Man of the Year Award
    Honorary Doctorate, Doctoris
    Honoris Causa, Technical
    University of Eindhoven
    Honorary Doctorate, Doctor of
    Letters, Honoris Causa,
    University of Oxford
    Honorary Doctorate of
    Literature, University of
    London

1995
Foster + Partners
    The Building Award,
    Architectural Practice
    of the Year
    Queen's Award for Export
    Achievement
Norman Foster
    Gold Medal, Universidad
    Internacional Menedez Pelayo
    Santander, Spain

1994
Foster + Partners
    CICA CAD Drawing Award
Norman Foster
    American Institute of
    Architects Gold Medal
    Officer of the Order of Arts
    and Letters, Ministry of
    Culture, France

1993
Norman Foster
    Honorary Degree, University
    of Manchester

1992
Norman Foster
    Arnold W Brunner Memorial
    Prize from the American
    Academy and Institute of Arts
    and Letters, New York
    Honorary Degree, University
    of Valencia, Spain
    Honorary Degree, University
    of Humberside

1991
Norman Foster
    Gold Medal of the French
    Academy of Architecture
    Honorary Doctorate, Royal
    College of Art, London

1990
Norman Foster
    The Chicago Architecture
    Award
    Knighthood in the Queen's
    Birthday Honours List

1989
Norman Foster
    Grosse Kunstpreis Award,
    Akademie der Künste, Berlin

1988
Norman Foster
    Royal Designer for Industry

1987
Norman Foster
    Japan Design Foundation
    Award

1986
Norman Foster
    Honorary Doctorate,
    University of Bath

1984
Foster Associates
    Honourable Mention, UIA
    Auguste Perret Prize
    for Applied Technology in
    Architecture

1983
Norman Foster
    The Royal Gold Medal for
    Architecture

1980
Norman Foster
    Honorary Doctorate,
    University of East Anglia

Project Awards

2008

Budenberg Haus, Manchester, England
Civic Trust Award, Commendation

Smithsonian Institution Courtyard, Washington DC, USA
Washington Building Congress Craftsmanship Award West London Academy, London, England
Civic Trust Award, Commendation

2007

Beijing International Airport, Beijing, China
Condé Nast Traveller Award for Innovation and Design, Winner Infrastructure category

Budenberg Haus, Manchester, England
Green Apple Residential New Build Gold Award for the Built Environment and our Architectural Heritage
British Homes Awards, Apartment Building of the Year
British Homes Awards, Innovation Award for Building Technology, Commendation
RIBA North West Region Award
IStructE North West Regional Structural Award

Deutsche Bank Place, 126 Phillip Street, Sydney, Australia
Property Council of Australia/ Rider Hunt Award, Overall Winner
Rider Hunt Award for Office Developments

Dresden Station, Dresden, Germany
RIBA European Award
BD International Regeneration Award

Free University of Berlin, Berlin, Germany
contractworld.award, 2nd Prize Education category
Deutscher Architekturpreis, Commendation

Hearst Headquarters, New York, USA
BCI International Award
Business Week/Architectural Record Citation for Excellence for the Interiors
RIBA International Award
Archi-Tech AV Awards, Best Project over $1,000,000
The Greater New York Construction User Council Outstanding Green Project Award
New York City MASterwork Awards, Best New Building
AIA New York Design Honor Award in the Architecture category

Masdar Development, Abu Dhabi, UAE
Global Renewable Energy Awards, Sustainable City of the Year
Cityscape Real Estate Awards, Best Environmental Real Estate Project

New Holland Island, St Petersburg, Russia
MIPIM Architectural Review Future Project Awards, Winner Retail & Leisure category

Petronas University of Technology, Malaysia
Aga Khan Award for Architecture

Quartermile, Edinburgh, Scotland
Scottish Property Awards, Mixed-use Development of the Year
Radial Lighting for iGuzzini
iF Product Design Award

Sainsbury Centre, UEA, Norwich, England
LABC East Anglia Built-In Quality Award,
Best Public Community Project, Highly Commended

Tivoli Four Seasons Hotel, Copenhagen, Denmark
AARETS ARNE Award 'Project of the Year'

Wembley Stadium, London, England
Vodafone Live Music Awards, Best Live Music Venue

20-06 Chair
Good Design Award 2007

2006

Albion Riverside, London, England
Wandsworth Design Award
Civic Trust Commendation

Bishops Square, London
Regeneration Awards, Winner Best Commercial-led Regeneration Project

Central Market, Abu Dhabi, England
MAPIC EG Retail & Future Project Awards, Winner BCSC International Trends category

Deutsche Bank Place, 126 Phillip Street, Sydney, Australia
Australian Stone Architecture Awards, Best Commercial Interior
ASI Steel Awards NSW & ACT, High Commendation Architectural Industrial & Commercial Steel Design category
ASI Steel Awards NSW & ACT, High Commendation

Structural Engineering Steel Design category

Faculty Building, Imperial College, London, England
Civic Trust Commendation

Free University of Berlin, Berlin, Germany
Berlin Architecture Award

The Great Court, British Museum, London, England
Marble Architecture Award, Joint Winner 'External Facings' category

Hearst Headquarters, New York, USA
Build New York Awards, Winner New Project
Emporis 'Best New Skyscraper of the Year for Design and Functionality'

Hong Kong International Airport, Chek Lap Kok, Hong Kong
Skytrax Airport of the Year Silver Award

Leslie L Dan Pharmacy Building, University of Toronto, Canada
Ontario Steel Design Award, Engineering category

Living Wall, Amman, Jordan
Cityscape Architectural Review Awards, Winner Commercial/Mixed-use category

McLaren Technology Centre, Woking, England
Structural Steel Design Award

Millau Viaduct, France
Staalbouwwedstrijd/Concours Construction Acier, Winner International category
IABSE Outstanding Structure Award
The Building Exchange (BEX) Award, 2nd Place Best Use of Architectural or Structural Design in a Regeneration Scheme
Balthasar Neumann Prize, Commendation

Wallpaper Design Awards,
Best New Public Building
National Police Memorial, London,
England
RIBA Award
One London Wall, City of London,
England
LDSA Built-in Quality Awards,
Best Large Commercial
Project
Petronas University of Technology,
Malaysia
PAM Award for Best Public
and Civic Building
Queen Alia International Airport,
Amman, Jordan
Cityscape Architectural
Review Awards, Winner
Transport category
The Sage Gateshead, England
Civic Trust Award
30 St Mary Axe, Swiss Re
Headquarters, London, England
London Architecture Biennale
Best Building Award Civic
Trust Award

2005

Albion Riverside, London, England
National Home Builder
Design Awards, Best
Apartment Building
Asprey, London, England
RIBA Award
Bishops Square, London, England
London Planning Awards,
Best Built Project contributing
to London's Future, Joint Winner
Djanogly City Academy,
Nottingham, England
The City of Nottingham Lord
Mayor's Award for Urban
Design, Commendation
Faculty Building, Imperial College,
London, England
RIBA Award

H M Treasury, London, England
British Construction Industry
Conservation Award
British Council for Offices
London Refurbished/
Recycled Workplace Award
Urban Land Institute (ULI)
Award for Excellence, Europe
competition
Hearst Headquarters, New York,
USA
Global Green USA Green
Building Design Award
Hong Kong International Airport,
Chek Lap Kok, Hong Kong
Skytrax Airport of the Year
Gold Award
AETRA Customer Satisfaction
Survey Best Airport
Worldwide, Special
Recognition Award
James H Clark Center, Stanford
University, USA
Building Design and
Construction (BD&C)
Building Team Project
Platinum Award
McLaren Technology Centre,
Woking, England
Festival Automobile
International Architecture
Prize
British Association of
Landscape Industries (BALI)
National Landscape
Grand Award
BALI National Landscape
Soft Landscaping over 1
Hectare Award and
Grand Award
RIBA Stirling Prize Channel 4
'People's Choice' Award
RIBA Award
The Royal Fine Art
Commission Trust/
BSkyB Building of the Year
Award
RTPI Planning Awards, Award
for Planning for Business

Millau Viaduct, France
Festival Automobile
International Architecture
Prize
Travel + Leisure Design
Award for Best Infrastructure
ECCS European Award for
Steel Structures
RIBA Award
D&AD Gold Award
Moor House, London, England
Deep Foundation Institute
Outstanding Project Award
More London Plot 1, London,
England
LDSA Built-in Quality Awards,
Winner Large Commercial
category
NF1 Housing, Duisburg, Germany
Exemplary Buildings in North
Rhine-Westphalia Prize
Quartermile Masterplan, Edinburgh,
Scotland
Property Executive
Development Award,
Regeneration Award for
Excellence
The Sage Gateshead, England
Roses Design Award for Best
Public Building
LABC Built in Quality Awards,
Best Public/Community
Project
LABC Built in Quality Awards,
Best Access/Disability
Regulations Innovation
The Journal North East
Landmark of the Year Award
The Journal Landmark Public
Sector Award
The Wood Awards, Winner
Commercial & Public Access
category
RIBA Inclusive Design Award
British Construction Industry
Local Authority Award
Retail & Leisure Property
Awards, Best Public Sector-
funded Leisure Development

RIBA Award
Construction Excellence
North East Award
for the Mobile Acoustic
Ceiling Panels
Scottish Gas HQ, Edinburgh,
Scotland
Scottish Design Award,
Commercial Interior
30 St Mary Axe, Swiss Re
Headquarters, London, England
LDSA Built-in Quality Awards,
Winner Innovation category
Tanaka Business School, Imperial
College, London, England
LDSA Built-in Quality Awards,
Winner
Social Commercial category
World Squares for All: Trafalgar
Square, London, England
RTPI Planning Awards,
Commendation for
Planning for City and
Metropolitan Areas

2004

Albion Riverside, London, England
Concrete Society Award
Certificate of Excellence in
the Building category
The Business Academy, Bexley,
England
Civic Trust Commendation
RIBA Award
Capital City Academy, Brent,
England
Civic Trust Commendation
Chesa Futura, St Moritz,
Switzerland
Holzbaupreis Graubünden,
Commendation
ForthQuarter Masterplan,
Edinburgh, Scotland
RICS Awards, Joint Winner,
Regeneration
Foster 500/5 Series
Baden-Württemberg
International Design 'Focus in
Silber' Award

Red Dot Design Award
10 Gresham Street, London, England
The Worshipful Company of Chartered Architects New City Architecture Award, Commendation
Civic Trust Award
Hearst Headquarters, New York, USA
Wallpaper 2004 Design Awards Winner
Best Building Sites
Hong Kong International Airport, Chek Lap Kok, Hong Kong
Chek Lap Kok, Skytrax Airport of the Year
Inner Harbour masterplan, Duisburg, Germany
Renault Traffic Design Special Award 'Harbours'
James H Clark Center, Stanford University, USA
SEAONC Award of Excellence in Structural Engineering
AISC Engineering Awards of Excellence, Merit Award
R&D Magazine Laboratory of the Year Award
RIBA Worldwide Award
Metropolitan, Warsaw, Poland
MIPIM Award, Winner of the 'Business Centres' Category
Construction Investment Journal Awards, Best Overall Project
More London Plot 1, London, England
British Council for Offices, London
Commercial Workplace Award for 1 More London Place
Structural Steel Design Award
The Sage Gateshead, England
ICE North Robert Stephenson Award for Concept and Design
Scottish Gas Headquarters,

Edinburgh, Scotland
British Council for Offices, National and Scotland Commercial Workplace Award
Swiss Re Headquarters, London, England
Wallpaper Design Awards, Winner Best New View
DETAIL Special Award for Steel
Dutch Steel Award, Category A
Emporis Skyscraper Award
IAS/OAS Awards, Best Central London Development
International Highrise Award Honourable Mention
London Architecture Biennale, Best New London Building
RIBA Award
RIBA Stirling Prize
Tower Place, London, England
Civic Trust Commendation
World Squares for All: Trafalgar Square, London, England
Civic Trust Special Award, Hard Landscaping
RIBA Award
RIBA London/English Heritage Award for a Building in an Historic Context

2003
City Hall, London, England
Institution of Civil Engineers London
Association Merit Award
Expo Station, Singapore
Architecture + Cityscape Awards, Winner of the Public Arts and Culture Category
Gerling Ring, Cologne, Germany
Kölner Architekturpreis
The Great Court, British Museum, London, England
The London Borough of Camden Building Quality Awards, Highly Commended
RIBA Award

ECCS European Steel Design Award
Great Glass House, National Botanic Garden of Wales, Llanarthne, Wales
The Dewi-Prys Thomas Prize
HM Treasury, London, England
British Construction Industry Awards Major Project Category, High Recommendation
British Council for Offices – National Refurbished Workplace Award
Public Private Finance Award, Best Design Project
Millennium Bridge, London, England
RIBA Award
Swiss Re Headquarters, London, England
ECCS European Steel Design Award
AR/MIPIM Future Project Prize – Best of Show joint winner
Tower Place, London, England
Construct Award for Innovation and Best Practice
World Squares for All: Trafalgar Square, London, England
Europa Nostra Award, Cultural Landscape Category

2002
British Library of Political and Economic Science, London, England
Civic Trust Commendation
Dark Shadow Yacht (Interior Design)
Show Boats Awards, Best Sailing Yacht under 38 Meters
Electronic Arts European Headquarters, Chertsey, England
Concours des Plus Beaux Ouvrages de Construction Metallique

Expo Station, Singapore
Singapore Construction Excellence Award, Civil Category
Foster 500 Series
Red Dot Design Award
The Great Court, British Museum, London, England
National Heritage Museum of the Year Award 2000/2001
Camden Design Award
Civic Trust Award
Hong Kong International Airport, Chek Lap Kok, Hong Kong
ARCASIA Award for Architecture 2001–2002, Gold Medal in category B-4
Jiushi Headquarters, Shanghai, China
Lu Ban Prize
Millau Viaduct, France
Singapore Construction Excellence Award, Civil Category Newbury Racecourse Grandstand, Newbury, England
Structural Steel Design Awards, Commendation

2001
Bathroom Foster for Duravit and Hoesch
Innovationspreis Architektur und Technik, Sanitaryware Category
Canary Wharf Underground Station, London, England
World Architecture Awards, Best Transport/Infrastructure Building
Citigroup Headquarters, London, England
British Council for Offices, National Corporate Workplace Building Award
Electronic Arts European Headquarters, Chertsey, England
Civic Trust Award
The Great Court, British Museum,

London, England
  British Construction Industry
  Awards Major Project
  Category, Highly Commended
  Institute of Civil Engineers,
  'Special Award' with Buro
  Happold (and Mace)
  DuPont Benedictus Awards,
  Special Recognition
Great Glass House, National
Botanic Garden of Wales,
Llanarthne, Wales
  D&AD Silver Award for
  Environmental
  Design & Architecture
  H & V News Awards,
  Environmental
  Initiative of the Year Award
  Civic Trust Award
Helit Foster Series Desktop
Furniture
  Industrie Forum Design
  Hanover Product Award
  Winner
Hong Kong International Airport,
Chek Lap Kok, Hong Kong
  Architectural Ironmongery
  Specification Awards
  2000/2001, Winner of the
  Overseas Public Buildings
  Category
Kingswood Technical Park, Ascot,
England
  Civic Trust Award
Willis Faber & Dumas
Headquarters, Ipswich, England
  Concrete Society Award,
  Certificate of Excellence in the
  Mature Structures Category for
  Corporate Headquarters

2000

A900 Seating for Thonet
  Red Dot Design Award
  Baden-Württemberg
  International Design
  Award 2000, Focus Working
  Environment
American Air Museum, Duxford,

England
  Celebrating Construction
  Achievement Award
ASPIRE National Training Centre,
Stanmore, England
  Civic Trust Commendation
Canary Wharf Underground
Station, London, England
  RIBA Regional Architecture
  Award
  British Construction Industry
  Awards, Special Award for the
  Pursuit of Engineering and
  Architectural Excellence
  in Public Transport
  Civic Trust Award
  Railway Forum/Modern
  Railways Industry
  Innovation Award
  Royal Fine Art Commission
  Trust Building of the Year
  Award, High Commendation
  AIA UK Design Awards,
  Commendation
Electronic Arts European
Headquarters, Chertsey, England
  RIBA Regional Architecture
  Award
  The Times/Gestetner Digital
  Office Collection Award, Third
  Prize
  Runnymede Borough Council
  Design Award, Commercial
  Category
  Whitby Bird and Partners'
  Structural Award
Expo Station, Singapore
  NRCA Gold Circle Award for
  Innovation
  Metal Roofing and Cladding
  Association of Australia
  Special Achievement Award
  Institute of Engineers
  Australia, High Commendation
Great Glass House, National
Botanic Garden of Wales,
Llanarthne, Wales
  RIBA Regional Architecture
  Award

Architecture in Wales
Eisteddfod
  Gold Medal in Architecture
  Structural Steel Award
  Royal Institute of Chartered
  Surveyors Building Efficiency
  Award
  The Concrete Society
  Building Award
  The 2000 Leisure Property
  Awards, Finalist for Best
  National Scheme
Helit Foster Series Desktop
Furniture
  Architektur und Office 2000,
  Architecture and Industry in
  Partnership
Imperial College, Sir Alexander
Fleming Building, London, England
  Civic Trust Commendation
J C Decaux International
Headquarters, Brentford, England
  RIBA Regional Architecture
  Award
  RIBA Crown Estate
  Conservation
  Architecture Award
  The Concrete Society and
  British Precast Concrete
  Federation Award for
  Excellence in Precast Concrete
New German Parliament,
Reichstag, Berlin, Germany
  Architekturpreis 2000 des
  BDA Berlin Auszeichnung
  Preis des Deutschen
  Stahlbaues 2000
  MIPIM Special Jury Prize
  The Design Sense Corporate
  Award
North Greenwich Transport
Interchange, London, England
  Civic Trust Award
  National Lighting Design
  Awards, Distinction
Room Control Device for
Weidmüller
  Industrie Forum Design Award
Saturn Lighting for iGuzzini

Industrie Forum Design Award
World Port Centre, Rotterdam, The
Netherlands
  Corus Construction Award
  for the Millennium

1999

American Air Museum, Duxford,
England
  Civic Trust Award
  FX International Interior
  Design Award, Best Museum
  Concrete Society Award
  Design Council Millennium
  Product Award
Hong Kong International Airport,
Chek Lap Kok, Hong Kong
  Construction Quality Awards
  International Project of the Year
  Structural Steel Design Award
  International Lighting Design
  Award of Excellence
  Travel & Leisure Magazine
  Critics' Choice Award for Best
  Airport
  Design Council Millennium
  Product Award
  Best Architecture in Hong
  Kong, Second Prize, voted by
  the people of Hong Kong
  Institute of Structural
  Engineers Structural
  Award, Commendation
Hongkong and Shanghai Bank
Headquarters, Hong Kong
  Best Architecture in Hong
  Kong, First Prize, voted by the
  people of Hong Kong
Imperial College, Sir Alexander
Fleming Building, London, England
  RIBA Regional Architecture
  Award
  R & D Laboratory of the Year,
  USA, High Honours
New German Parliament,
Reichstag, Berlin, Germany
  RIBA Regional Architecture
  Award
  RIBA Conservation Category

Award
Deutscher Architekturpreis
ECCS European Award for
Steel Structures
Architects' Journal and Bovis
Europe Grand Award for
Architecture at the Royal
Academy
Summer Exhibition
Eurosol Preis für Solares
Bauen Design
Council Millennium Product
Award
Du Pont Benedictus Award,
Special Recognition
North Greenwich Transport
Interchange, London, England
Aluminium Imagination
Awards Winner
Structural Steel Design
Award, Commendation
Repsol Service Stations, Spain
City Planning, Architecture
and Public Works Award,
Madrid
Robert Gordon Univerity Faculty of
Management, Aberdeen, Scotland
RIBA Regional Architecture
Award
Civic Society Award
Room Control Device for
Weidmüller
Design Plus Award
Valencia Congress Centre,
Valencia, Spain
RIBA Regional Architecture
Award
Willis Faber & Dumas
Headquarters, Ipswich, England
British Council for Offices
Test of Time Award,
Commendation

1998
Agiplan Headquarters, Mülheim,
Germany
Bund Deutscher Architekten,
'Guter Bauten', Ruhr Area
American Air Museum, Duxford,

England
RIBA Stirling Prize
RIBA Regional Architecture
Award
Royal Fine Art Commission
BSkyB
Building of the Year Award
ASPIRE National Training Centre,
Stanmore, England
Harrow Heritage Trust
Observer Award
Bath Road Offices, Slough,
England
Business Industry Agents
Society Award
Bilbao Metro, Bilbao, Spain
RIBA Regional Architecture
Award
Brunel Award, Madrid
Veronica Rudge Green Prize
in Urban Design
British Gas Offices, Thames Valley
Park, Reading, England
RIBA Regional Architecture
Award
British Council for Offices
Award
Carré d'Art, Nîmes, France
Veronica Rudge Green Prize
in Urban Design
Commerzbank Headquarters,
Frankfurt, Germany
RIBA Regional Architecture
Award
Bund Deutscher Architekten,
Martin-Elsaesser-Plakette
Award
Duisburg Microelectronic Centre,
Duisberg, Germany
Bund Deutscher Architekten
Preis, Nordrhein Westfalen
Area
Great Glasshouse, National
Botanic Garden of Wales,
Llanarthne, Wales
BIAT Open Award for
Technical Excellence
Hong Kong International Airport,
Chek Lap Kok, Hong Kong

British Construction Industry
International Award
HKIA Silver Medal
Kingswood Technical Park, Ascot,
England
Business Industry Agents
Society Award
Kowloon-Canton Railway Terminal,
Hong Kong
HKIA Certificate of Merit
Motorway Signage System
Design Council Millennium
Product Award
Wind Turbine for Enercon
Design Council Millennium
Product Award

1997
American Air Museum, Duxford,
England
British Construction Industry
Awards, High Commendation
AIA London Chapter
Excellence in Design
Commendation
British Guild of Travel Writers
Silver Unicorn Award
Bilbao Metro, Bilbao, Spain
Manuel de la Dehesa Award,
Commendation
Cambridge University Faculty of
Law, Cambridge, England
David Urwin Design Awards,
Commendation
Commerzbank Headquarters,
Frankfurt, Germany
British Construction Industry
International Award
Duisburg Microelectronic Centre,
Duisburg, Germany
RIBA Regional Architecture
Award

1996
Duisburg Microelectronic Centre,
Duisburg, Germany
Bund Deutscher Architekten,
'Guter Bauten', Rechter
Niederrhein Area

Linz Solar City, Germany
International Academy of
Architecture Medal and
Honorary Diploma
Solar-Electric Vehicle
ID Design Distinction Award
in Concepts

1995
Bilbao Metro, Bilbao, Spain
Premio Radio Correo Award
Cranfield University Library,
Cranfield, England
Civic Trust Award
Duisburg Inner Harbour
Masterplan, Duisburg, Germany
Disabled Access Award for
Steiger Schwanentor
Joslyn Art Museum Extension,
Omaha, USA
AIA State Architecture Award
AIA Regional Architecture
Award
American Concrete Institute
(Nebraska)
Award of Excellence
Solar-Electric Vehicle
Design Week Award for
Product Design
Design Review Minerva
Award, Commendation

1994
Century Tower, Tokyo, Japan
Intelligent Building Promotion
Award
The Society of Heating, Air
Conditioning and Sanitary
Engineers of Japan Award
Cranfield University Library,
Cranfield, England
British Steel Colourcoat
Award, Runner Up
Duisburg Business Promotion
Centre, Duisburg, Germany
Bund Deutsche Architekten
Bezirksgruppe Ruhr Award
Marine Simulator Centre,
Rotterdam, The Netherlands

Interiors (USA) Award
Architectural Review Best
European Lighting Scheme
Highlight Award
Stansted Airport, Stansted, England
BBC Design Award Finalist

1993
Torre de Collserola
Telecommunications Tower,
Barcelona, Spain
    The Architecture and
    Urbanism Award of the City of
    Barcelona
    The Architecture FAD Award,
    Barcelona
    The Opinion FAD Award,
    Barcelona
    Cultural Foundation of Madrid
    Award
Carré d'Art, Nîmes, France
    Interiors (USA) Award
Cranfield University Library,
Cranfield, England
    RIBA Regional Architecture
    Award
    British Construction Industry
    Supreme Award
    British Construction Industry
    Building Award
    Interiors (USA) Award
    Eastern Electricity
    Commercial Property
    Award, Building of the Year
    Bedfordshire Design Award,
    Special Award
    Design Review Minerva
    Award, Commendation
    Financial Times Architecture
    Award, Commendation
    Concrete Society Award,
    Highly Commended
    Lighting Design Award, Highly
    Commended
Crescent Wing, Sainsbury Centre
for Visual Arts, Norwich, England
    International Association of
    Lighting Designers Awards,
    Citation

Sackler Galleries, Royal Academy
of Arts, London, England
    RIBA Best Building of the
    Year Award
    Design Review Minerva Award
    Marble Architecture Award
Stansted Airport, Stansted, England
    Benedictus Award, USA, for
    Innovative Use of Laminated
    Glass
    Financial Times Architecture
    Award, Commendation
Stockley Park Offices, Uxbridge,
England
    British Council for Offices
Award

1992
Torre de Collserola
Telecommunications Tower,
Barcelona, Spain
    Premio Alcantara Award for
    Public Works in Latin
    American Countries
Century Tower, Tokyo, Japan
    Nikkei Business Publications
    Award for New Technology
    BCS Award Tokyo
    Lightweight Metal Cladding
    Association Award
Crescent Wing, Sainsbury Centre
for Visual Arts, Norwich, England
    RIBA Regional Architecture
    Award
    Civic Trust Award
    Design Review Minerva
    Award, Commendation
ITN Headquarters, London,
England
    RIBA Regional Architecture
    Award
    British Council for Offices
    Best Building Award
    Design Review Minerva
    Award, Commendation
Sackler Galleries, Royal Academy
of Arts, London, England
    RIBA National Architecture
    Award

RIBA Regional Architecture
Award
The Royal Fine Art
Commission and Sunday
Times Building of the Year
Award
Structural Steel Award
Interiors (USA) Award
Institution of Civil Engineers
Merit Award
British Construction Industry
Award, High Commendation
Mansell Refurbishment Award
National Dryline Wall Award
Design Review Minerva
Award, Commendation
Stansted Airport, Stansted, England
    RIBA National Architecture
    Award
    RIBA Regional Architecture
    Award
    Civic Trust Award
    Structural Steel Award
    Royal Institute of Chartered
    Surveyors Energy Efficiency
    Award
    Brunel Award, Madrid for
    British Rail Station
    Concrete Society Award
    English Tourist Board Car
    Park Award
    Design Review Minerva
    Award, Commendation
    Architects' Journal Hilight
    Lighting Award,
    Commendation

1991
Century Tower, Tokyo, Japan
    Institute of Structural
    Engineers Special Award
ITN Headquarters, London,
England
    Aluminium Imagination
    Architectural Award
Stansted Airport, Stansted, England
    Mies van der Rohe Pavilion
    Award for European
    Architecture

British Construction Industry
Supreme Award
Aluminium Imagination
Architectural Award
Business and Industry Panel
for the Environment Award
Colourcoat Building Award
British Gas Energy
Management Award
British Association of
Landscape Industries Award
Royal Town Planning Institute
Silver Jubilee Award
National Childcare Facilities
Award
Stockley Park Offices, Uxbridge,
England
    Aluminium Imagination
    Architectural Award

1990
Willis Faber & Dumas
Headquarters, Ipswich, England
    RIBA Trustees Medal

1989
Stockley Park Offices, Uxbridge,
England
    British Construction Industry
    Award

1988
Esprit Shop, London, England
    Interiors (USA) Award
Hongkong and Shanghai Bank
Headquarters, Hong Kong
    Quaternario Award for
    Innovative Technology in
    Architecture
    PA Innovations Award

1987
Nomos Desking System for
    Tecno
    Premio Compasso d'Oro
    Award
    Design Centre Award
    Stuttgart

1986
Hongkong and Shanghai Bank
Headquarters, Hong Kong
  Structural Steel Award
  R S Reynolds Memorial Award
  Institute of Structural
  Engineers Special Award
Renault Distribution Centre,
Swindon, England
  First Prize, European Award
  for Industrial Architecture,
  Hanover

1984
Renault Distribution Centre,
Swindon, England
  Civic Trust Award
  Structural Steel Award
  Financial Times Architecture
  at Work Award

1983
Hongkong and Shanghai Bank
Headquarters, Hong Kong
  Premier Architectural Award
  at the Royal Academy of Arts,
  London

1981
IBM Technical Park, Greenford,
England
  Financial Times Industrial
  Architecture Award
  RIBA Commendation

1980
IBM Technical Park, Greenford,
England
  Structural Steel Award
Sainsbury Centre for Visual Arts,
Norwich, England
  Sixth Eternit International
  Prize for Architecture,
  Brussels
  Ambrose Congreve Award
  Museum of the Year Award

1979
Sainsbury Centre for Visual Arts,
Norwich, England
  R S Reynolds Memorial Award
  British Tourist Board Award

1978
Sainsbury Centre for Visual Arts,
Norwich, England
  RIBA Award
  Structural Steel Finniston
  Award

1977
Palmerston Special School,
Liverpool, England
  RIBA Award
Willis Faber & Dumas
Headquarters, Ipswich, England
  RIBA Award

1976
Palmerston Special School,
Liverpool, England
  Eternit International Prize for
  Architecture, Brussels
Willis Faber & Dumas
Headquarters, Ipswich, England
  R S Reynolds Memorial Award
  Business and Industry Panel
  for the Environment Award

1974
Modern Art Glass Warehouse,
Thamesmead, England
  Financial Times Industrial
  Architecture Award

1972
IBM Pilot Head Office, Cosham,
England
  RIBA Award
  Structural Steel Award

1971
Air-Supported Office for Computer
Technology
  Financial Times Industrial
  Architecture Award,
  Commendation

1970
Fred Olsen Amenity Centre,
London, England
  Financial Times Industrial
  Architecture Award,
  Commendation

1969
Creek Vean House, Feock, England
  RIBA Award
Fred Olsen Amenity Centre,
London, England
  Architectural Design Project
  Award

1967
Reliance Controls Electronics
Factory, Swindon, England
  Financial Times Industrial
  Architecture Award

1966
Reliance Controls Electronics
Factory, Swindon, England
  Architectural Design Project
  Award

1965
Housing for Wates, Coulsdon
Wood, England
  Architectural Design Project
  Award

1964
Waterfront Housing, Feock,
England
  Architectural Design Project
  Award

Project Credits

Albion Riverside
London, England 1999–2003
Client
Hutchison Whampoa Property
Area
30,000m²
Team
Ove Arup & Partners
Davis Langdon & Everest
Exterior International Plc
CM International
Jolyon Drury Consultancy
Townshend Landscape
Architects

Aldar Al Raha Beach
Abu Dhabi, UAE 2006–
Client
Aldar Properties PJSC
Area
37,000m²
Team
Arup, London
Laing O'Rourke

American Air Museum, Duxford
Duxford, England 1987–1997
Client
Imperial War Museum, Duxford
American Air Museum in Britain
Area
7,400m²
Team
Ove Arup & Partners
Roger Preston & Partners
Davis Langdon & Everest
Aerospace Structural and
Mechanical Engineering
Hannah Reed & Associates
Rutherford Consultants

Banyan Tree, Corniche Bay
Mauritius 2006–
Client
Tatorio Holdings Ltd
Area
859,400m²
Team
Arup
PHA Consult
Manly Development Services Ltd
Gleeds and Hoolooman Project
Services
Mace

Beijing Capital International Airport Terminal 3
Beijing, China 2003–2008
Client
Beijing Capital International
Airport
Area
986,000m²
Team
Arup
NACO Airport Consultants
Beijing Institute of Architectural
Design
Michel Desvigne Landscape
Concept
Speirs and Major Architectural
Lighting

Bilbao Metro
Bilbao, Spain 1988–1997
Line One
1988–1995
Line Two
1997–2004
Client
Basque Government
IMEBISA
Team
Sener
TYPSA
Saitec
Ove Arup & Partners
Büro Aicher
Weiss Design Asociados
Atelier Weidner

Bishops Square
London, England 2001–2005
Client
Spitalfields Development Group
Area
101,521m²
Team
Arup
Davis Langdon
Hoare Lea
Townshend Landscape
Architects
Centre for Accessible
Environments
Emmer Pfenninger Partner AG
Lerch Bates Associates
Montagu Evans

Bodrum Resort
Turkey, 2006–
Client
Capital Partners
Area
60,000m²
Team
PHA Consult
Arup
Arup Fire
Vogt Landschaftsarchitekten

British Museum Great Court
London, England 1994–2000
Client
British Museum
Area
19,000m²
Team
Buro Happold
Northcroft
Mace
Giles Quarme & Associates
Claude R Engle
EPP
FEDRA
Sandy Brown Associates

Camp Nou Stadium
Barcelona, Spain 2007–
Client
FC Barcelona
Area
101,000m²
Team
AFL Architects
Whitby Bird
Gleeds
PHA Consult
Jason Bruges

Canary Wharf Underground Station
London, England 1991–1999
Client
Jubilee Line Extension Project
(JLEP)
Area
31,500m²
Team
Posford Duvivier
Jubilee Line Extension Project
Ove Arup & Partners
Claude R Engle
Davis Langdon & Everest
De Leau Chadwick

Carré d'Art
Nîmes, France 1984–1993
Client
Ville de Nîmes
Area
18,000m²
Team
Ove Arup & Partners
OTH
Thorne Wheatley
Claude and Danielle Engle
Lighting
Jolyon Drury Consultancy

Center for Clinical Sciences Research, Stanford University
Stanford, USA 1995–2000
Client
Stanford University School of Medicine
Area
21,000m²
Team
Fong & Chan Architects
Ove Arup & Partners
Research Facilities Design
Peter Walker and Partners

Central Market
Abu Dhabi, UAE 2006–
Client
Aldar Properties
Area
607,000m²
Team
Halvorson & Partners
EC Harris International
BDSP Partnership
Emmer Pfenninger Partner AG
Lerch Bates and Associates
Systematica

Chesa Futura
St Moritz, Switzerland 2000–2004
Client
Sisa AG
Area
4,650m²
Team
Ove Arup & Partners
Davis Langdon & Everest
Edy Toscano AG
Peter Walker & Partners
Emmer Pfenninger Partner AG
EN/ES/TE AG
R & B Engineering GmbH

Circle Hospital
Bath, England 2006–
Client
Circle/Health Properties (Bath) Ltd
Area
6,367m²
Team
WSP Cantor Seinuk
Davis Langdon
Arup
Plincke
Buro Four
CSJ Planning
IMA Transport Planning
MJ Medical

City of Justice
Madrid, Spain 2006–
Client
Comunidad de Madrid
Area
45,000m²
Team
Buro Happold

Clarence Hotel
Dublin, Ireland 2006–
Client
The Clarence Partnership
Area
20,741m²
Team
J J Campbell & Associates
Bruce Shaw
MacArdle McSweeney Associates
Jason Burgess Studio
Design Group
John Spain Associates

Commerzbank Headquarters
Frankfurt, Germany 1991–1997
Client
Commerzbank AG
Area
100,000m²
Team
Ove Arup & Partners
Krebs & Kiefer
Roger Preston & Partners
Pettersen & Ahrends
Schad & Hölzel
Jappsen & Stangier
Davis Langdon & Everest
Quickborner Team
Ingenieur Büro Schalm
Lichtdesign
Sommerland
Per Arnoldi

Crystal Island
Moscow, Russia 2006–
Client
STT Group
Area
1,100,000m²
Team
Buro Happold
Systematica
PHA consult

Deutsche Bank Place, 126 Phillip Street
Sydney, Australia 1996–2005
Client
Investa Property Group
Area
67,370m²
Team
Hassell
LendLease Design
Rider Hunt Australia
Norman Disney & Young
Lincoln Scott
Roger Preston and Partners
Arup
Stephen Grubits & Associates

Dolder Grand Hotel
Zurich, Switzerland 2002–2008
Client
Dolder Hotel AG
Area
41,000 m²
Team
Itten & Brechbühl
Werner Sobek Ingenieure
Ernst Basler & Partner
Kopitsis Bauphysik AG
Emmer Pfenninger Partner AG

Dresden Station
Dresden, Germany 1997–2006
Client
Deutsche Bahn AG Station & Service
DB ProjektBau GmbH
Area
34,000m²
Team
Arcadis Homola AG
SSF Ingenieure GmbH
Buro Happold
Schmidt Reuter
Kaiser Baucontrol Ingenieurgesellschaft GmbH
Zibell Willner & Partner GmbH

Duisburg Inner Harbour Masterplan
Duisburg, Germany 1991–2001

Steiger Schwanentor 1993–1994
Client
LEG, Düsseldorf
Team
Hans Kolbeck Ingenieur
Büro Klement

Hafenforum 1995–1996
Client
THS, Essen
Team
Architekturbüro Dieter Müller
Ingenieurbüro Cosanne
THS
Glamo GmbH

Canals 1996–1998
Client
  IDE, Duisburg
Team
  ABDOU GmbH
  TUV
  Ingenieurbüro R Knoke
  B-Plan

Housing 1997–2001
Client
  THS, Essen
Team
  Ingenieurbüro Cosanne
  Ingenieurbüro Dr Meyer

Duisburg Inner City Masterplan
  Duisburg, Germany 2007–
Client
  Stadt Duisburg
Team
  Intelligent Space Partnership
  Städtebau Workshop with Prof.
  Dr.-Ing. Franz Pesch, Professor
  für Stadtplanung und Entwerfen
  am Städtebau-Institut, Universität
  Stuttgart

**Electronic Arts European
Headquarters**
  Chertsey, England 1997–2000
Client
  Electronic Arts
  P+O Developments
Area
  24,000m²
Team
  Whitby Bird & Partners
  Oscar Faber
  Wheelers
  Land Use Consultants
  Mark Johnson Consultants
  Recording Architecture
  Jeremy Gardner Partnership
  Claude R Engle
  Rowney Sharman
  Exterior International

Elephant House
  Copenhagen, Denmark 2002–
  2008
Client
  Foundation Realdania for
  Copenhagen Zoo
Area
  2,500m²
Team
  Buro Happold
  Ramboll
  Stig L Andersson Architects
  Davis Langdon & Everest

Eurogate, Duisburg
  Duisburg, Germany, 2006–
Client
  Innenhafen Duisburg
  Entwicklungsgesellschaft GmbH
Area
  41,500m²
Team
  Werner Sobek Ingenieure
  Schmidt Reuter GmbH

Expo Station
  Singapore 1997–2001
Client
  Land Transport Authority
  Singapore
Area
  7,164m²
  Team
  Arup
  Davis Langdon & Seah
  Land Transport Authority
  Singapore
  Cicada Singapore
  Claude R Engle

**Faculty of Law, University of
Cambridge**
  Cambridge, England 1990–1995
Client
  University of Cambridge
Area
  8,500m²
Team
  Anthony Hunt Associates
  YRM Engineers
  Davis Langdon & Everest
  Sandy Brown Associates
  Emmer Pfenninger Partner AG
  Cambridge Landscape Architects
  Ove Arup & Partners
  Halcrow Fox

Florence Station
  Florence, Italy 2003–
Client
  TAV-RFI
Area
  47,000m²
Team
  Arup
  Davis Langdon & Everest
  Land Use Consultants
  Claude R Engle
  ETA

Folkestone Academy
  Folkestone, England
  2003–2007
Client
  DfES and Folkestone Academy
  Trust
Area
  12,282m²
Team
  Buro Happold
  Davis Langdon

Free University of Berlin
  Berlin, Germany 1997–2005
Client
  Free University of Berlin
  Berlin Senate Administration for
  Urban Development
Area
  6,290m²
Team
  Schmidt Reuter
  Pichler Ingenieure
  Kappes ipg GmbH
  Büro Noack
  Höhler + Partner

Furniture

A900 Seating
  1997–1999
Client
  Thonet, Germany

Kite! Chair
  1987–1997
Client
  Tecno SpA, Italy

Foster 500 Series
  2001–2002
Client
  Walter Knoll, USA

20-06 Chair
  2006
Client
  Emeco Inc

Great Glasshouse, National Botanic Gardens of Wales
Llanarthne, Wales 1995–2000
Client
National Botanic Gardens of Wales
Area
5,800m²
Team
Gustafson Porter
Anthony Hunt Associates
Max Fordham & Partners
Symonds
Colvin and Moggridge
Schal International

Green Mountain Regional Plan
Libya 2007–
Client
GTI – Gulf Tourism Investments
Team
Nick Penn Consulting
Clownfish
HRH The Prince of Wales Charity Foundation
JA Stanislaw Group
Model Department – Stuttgart
TRI Hospitality Consulting
BDSP
UNESCO World Heritage Center

200 Greenwich Street
New York, USA 2006–
Client
Silverstein Properties Ltd
Area
291,200m²
Team
Adamson Associates
WSP Cantor Seinuk
Jaros Baum & Bolles Consulting Engineers
Edgett Williams Consulting Group Inc

10 Gresham Street
London, England 1996–2003
Client
Standard Life Investments
Area
34,224m²
Team
Waterman Partnership
Davis Langdon & Everest
Mott Green Wall
Roger Preston & Partners
Charles Funke Associates
Claude R Engle

Hearst Headquarters
New York, USA 2000–2006
Client
Hearst Corporation
Area
79,500 m²
Team
Adamson Associates
Cantor Seinuk Group
Flack + Kurtz
George Sexton
Cerami
VDA
Ira Beer
Tishman Speyer Properties

Heathrow East Terminal
London 2006–
Client
BAA Plc
Area
180,000m²
Team
Ferrovial Agromán
Laing O'Rourke
Vidal Associados
Hoare Lea
Arup
Vanderlande
Gebler Tooth
Siemans
EC Harris
The Design Solution
Motts

H M Treasury
London, England 1996–2003
Client
Exchequer Partnership
Stanhope Bovis and Chesterton
Area
50,000m²
Team
Waterman Partnership
JBB
Hanscomb Partnership
BDSP
Speirs & Major
Gustafson Porter
Ove Arup & Partners
Feilden + Mawson
Per Arnoldi

Hongkong and Shanghai Bank Headquarters
Hong Kong 1979–1986
Client
Hongkong and Shanghai Banking Corporation
Area
99,000m²
Team
Ove Arup & Partners
Roger Preston & Partners
Levett & Bailey
Northcroft Neighbour & Nicholson
Claude and Danielle Engle Lighting
Tim Smith Acoustics
Technical Landscapes Ltd
Quickborner Team
Jolyon Drury Consultancy
Corning Glass
Humberside Technical Services
Project Planning Group
R J Mead & Company

Hong Kong International Airport, Chek Lap Kok
Hong Kong 1992–1998
Client
Hong Kong Airport Authority
Area
516,000m²
Team
BAA
Mott Connell Ltd
Ove Arup & Partners
Fisher Marantz Renfro Stone
O'Brien Kreitzberg & Associates Ltd
Wilbur Smith Associates

House in Kamakura
Kamakura, Japan 1997–2005
Client
Kazuo Akao
Area
1,700m²
Team
Obayashi Corporation
Northcroft
Arup Façade Engineering
Roger Preston & Partners

Imperial College Buildings
London, England, 1994–2004

Sir Alexander Fleming Building
1994–1998
Client
Imperial College and South Kensington Millennium Commission
Area
25,000m²
Team
Schal Construction Management
Claude R Engle
Research Facilities Design
Sandy Brown Associates
Warrington Fire
WSP
Waterman Partnership
Per Arnoldi

Tanaka Business School
   2000–2004
Client
   Imperial College
Area
   6,250m²
Team
   Buro Happold
   Gardiner and Theobald
   Management Services
   Jenkins and Potter
   Davis Langdon & Everest
   Sandy Brown Associates
   Hyder Consulting
   Halcrow Group
   Per Arnoldi

Imperial College Faculty Building
   2001–2004
Client
   Imperial College
Area
   4,000m²
Team
   Buro Happold
   Gardiner & Theobald
   Management Services
   Davis Langdon & Everest
   Jenkins & Potter
   Warrington Fire Research
   Sandy Brown Associates
   Lerch Bates Associates
   Per Arnoldi
   Exterior plc

James H Clark Center, Stanford University
   Stanford, USA 1999–2003
Client
   Stanford University
Area
   8,240m²
Team
   MBT Architecture
   Peter Walker & Partners
   Hathaway Dinwiddie
   AlfaTech
   Middlebrook + Louie
   Cupertino Electric
   Therma

RLS
Charles Salter & Associates
Brian Kangas Faulk
Wilson Ihrig & Associates
Claude R Engle
Davis, Langdon & Everest

Jameson House
   Vancouver, Canada 2004–
Client
   Jameson Development
   Corporation
Area
   33,000m²
Team
   Walter Francl Architects Inc
   Yolles
   Vermeulens Cost Consultants
   Imec Mechanical Ltd.
   PWL Partnership Landscape
   Architects Inc.
   Claude R Engle
   Bridge Electric Corp.
   Piers Heath Associates
   Robert Lemon Architect Inc.

Johnson Wax Company – Project Honor
   Racine, Wisconsin, USA 2006
   2009
Client
   S C Johnson & Sons Inc
Area
   7,432m²
Team
   A Epstein and Sons International
   Inc
   Buro Happold
   Cosentini Associates
   Gilbane
   Gustafson Guthrie Nichol

Khan Shatyr Entertainment Centre
   Astana, Kazakhstan 2006–
Client
   Sembol Construction
Area
   100,000m²
Team
   Buro Happold
   Dr Martin Bepa
   Avi Alkas
   Dr Veli Dogan
   Ergun Tercanly

La Voile
   St Jean Cap Ferrat, France
   1999–2002
Client
   Confidential
Area
   Confidential
Team
   CBM

610 Lexington Avenue
   New York, USA 2005–
Client
   RFR Holdings LLC
Area
   24,155m²
Team
   Hines Interests Limited
   Partnership
   SLCE Architects
   DeSimone Consulting Engineers
   Flack + Kurtz Inc
   Gordon H Smith Corporation

Living Wall
   Amman, Jordan 2006–
Client
   Development and Projects
   Investment Fund, Amman,
   Jordan
Area
   132,275m²
Team
   Maisam Architects &
   Engineers
   Buro Happold

London City Hall
   London, England 1998–2002
Client
   CIT Group
Area
   18,000m²
Team
   Ove Arup & Partners
   Davis Langdon & Everest
   Mott Green & Wall
   Claude R Engle

Lycée Albert Camus
   Fréjus, France 1991–1993
Client
   Ville de Fréjus
Area
   14,500m²
Team
   Ove Arup & Partners
   Roger Preston & Partners
   Davis Langdon & Everest
   Desvigne & Dalnoky
   Claude and Danielle Engle
   Lighting
   Sandy Brown Associates

Masdar
Abu Dhabi, UAE 2007–
Client
Masdar-Abu Dhabi Future
Energy Company
Area
6,000,000m²
Team
Cyril Sweet
ETA
Energy
Ernst and Young
Flack + Kurtz
Transsolar

McLaren Technology Centre
Woking, England 1998–2004
Client
TAG McLaren Holdings
Area
60,000m²
Team
Arlington Securities
Ove Arup & Partners
Schmidt Reuter Partner
Davis Langdon & Everest
Terence O'Rourke
WSP
Intec Management
Claude R Engle
Atelier Dreiseitl

Microelectronic Park
Duisburg, Germany 1988–1997

Telematic Centre
1988–1993
Client
GTT
Kaiser Bautechnik
Area
3,500m²
Team
Ingenieur Büro Dr Meyer
Kaiser Bautechnik
ROM
Oskar Anders GmbH

Microelectronic Centre
1988–1996
Client
GTT
Area
12,000m²
Team
Ingenieur Büro Dr Meyer
Kaiser Bautechnik
Ebert Ingenieur
Emmer Pfenninger Partner AG
ITA GmbH
Höhler & Partner

Business Promotion Centre
1990–1993
Client
GTT
Kaiser Bautechnik
Area
4,000m²
Team
Ingenieur Büro Dr Meyer
Kaiser Bautechnik
Roger Preston & Partners
Oskar Anders GmbH

Millau Viaduct
Gorges du Tarn, France 1993–
2005
Client
French Ministry of Equipment,
Transport, Housing, Tourism and
Sea
Length
2.5km
Team
Chapelet-Defol-Mousseigne
Europe Etudes Gecti
Sogelerg
SERF
Agence TER
Compagnie Eiffage du Viaduc
de Millau

Millennium Bridge
London, England 1996–2000
Client
Millennium Bridge Trust
London Borough of Southwark
Length
320m
Team
Ove Arup & Partners
Sir Anthony Caro
Davis Langdon & Everest
Claude R Engle
Monberg & Thorsen/
McAlpine

Millennium Tower
Tokyo, Japan 1989
Client
Obayashi Corporation
Area
1,040,000m²
Team
Obayashi Corporation

More London
London, England 1998–2008
Client
More London Development Ltd
Area
232,255m²
Team
Ove Arup & Partners
Davis Langdon & Everest
Desvigne & Dalnoky
Space Syntax
Feilden + Mawson

Motor City
Alcañiz, Spain 2007–
Client
La Ciudad del Motor City
Area
85,000m²
Team
Buro Happold
ETA – Renewable Energies
Gleeds Europe Limited
Hoberman Associates Inc
Transsolar Energietechnik GmbH

Motor Yacht *Izanami*
1991–1993
Client
Kazuo Akao
Length
58.5m
Team
Gerhard Gilgenast
Fr Lürssen Werft

**Musée de Préhistoire des
Gorges du Verdon**
Quinson, France 1992–2001
Client
Département Alpes de Hautes
Provence
Area
4,500m²
Team
Bruno Chiambretto
Olivier Sabran
SEV Ingénierie
Davis Langdon & Everest

Museum of Fine Arts, Boston
Boston, USA 1999–2012
Client
Museum of Fine Arts, Boston
Area
510,000m²
Team
George B H Macomber
Childs Bertman Tseckares Inc
Buro Happold
SEi Companies
Weidlinger Associates Inc
George Sexton Associates
Acentech
Gustafson Guthrie Nichols
Hughes Associates Inc

New German Parliament, Reichstag
  Berlin, Germany 1992–1999
Client
  Bundesrepublik Deutschland
Area
  61,166m²
Team
  Kuehn Bauer Partner
  Davis Langdon & Everest
  Kaiser Bautechnik
  Fischer Energie & Haustechnik
  IKP Prof Dr Georg Plenge
  Müller BBM GmbH
  Claude R Engle
  Leonhardt Andrä und Partner
  Planungsgruppe Karnasch-Hackstein
  Acanthus
  Amstein & Walthert
  Per Arnoldi

New Globe Theater
  New York, USA 2003–
Client
  Dr Barbara Romer
Area
  8,333m²
Team
  Cantor Seinuk
  Davis Langdon
  Battle McCarthy
  Arup Acoustics
  Shakespeare's Globe, London
  Theatre Projects Consultants

New Holland Island
  St Petersburg, Russia 2006–
Client
  ST New Holland
Area
  180,146m²
Team
  Waterman International
  Buro Happold
  Davis Langdon
  Anne Minors Performance Consultants
  Sound Space Design

Nomos Table
  1985–1987
Client
  Tecno SpA, Italy

Palace of Peace and Reconciliation
  Astana, Kazakhstan 2004–2006
Client
  Sembol Construction
Area
  35,000m²
Team
  Tabanlioglu Architecture & Consulting
  Buro Happold
  Arce
  GN Engineering & HB Technik
  DS Mimarlik
  Studio Dinnebier
  Brian Clarke
  Sound Space Design

Petronas University of Technology
  Malaysia 1998–2004
Client
  Universiti Teknologi Petronas
Site Area
  450 hectares
Team
  GDP Architects
  Roger Preston & Partners
  Research Facilities Design
  KPK
  KLCCB

Product Design

Alessi Tray
  1994–1998
Client
  Alessi SpA, Italy

Bathroom Foster
  1996–2001
Client
  Duravit and Hoesch

Diplomat Pen
  2007
Client
  Helit/Diplomat

Ilium Light
  2006
Client
  Nemo SpA

NF 95 Door Furniture
  1994–1995
Client
  Fusital (Valli & Valli)

Place Kitchen Furniture
  2004
Client
  Dada SpA

Trapex Door Handle
  2005
Client
  Trapex UK

Pushkin Museum Extension
  Moscow, Russia 2007–
Client
  Foundation for the Pushkin Museum of Fine Arts
Area
  100,000m²
Team
  Davis Langdon
  Systematica Milano

Quartermile
  Edinburgh, Scotland 2001–
Client
  Gladedale Projects
Area
  157,500m²
Team
  Waterman Rennick
  Thomas & Adamson
  Roger Preston & Partners
  Desvigne & Dalnoky

Queen Alia International Airport
  Amman, Jordan 2005–
Client
  Marawed (National Resources Investment and Development Corporation)
Area
  1,300,000m² (site)
Team
  Buro Happold
  David Langdon
  NACO

Repsol Service Stations
  Spain 1997
Client
  Repsol
Team
  Ove Arup & Partners
  David Langdon & Everest
  J Roger Preston & Partners
  Claude R Engle

Russia Tower
  Moscow, Russia 2005–
Client
  STT Group
Area
  500,000m²
Team
  Waterman International
  Halvorson & Partners
  Lerch Bates & Associates

Sackler Galleries, Royal Academy of Arts
  London, England 1985–1991
Client
  Royal Academy of Arts
Area
  312m²
Team
  Anthony Hunt Associates
  James R Briggs
  George Sexton Associates
  Julian Harrap Architects
  Davis Langdon & Everest

Sage Gateshead
Gateshead, England 1997–2004
Client
Gateshead Council
Area
17,500m²
Team
Arup
Mott MacDonald
Buro Happold
Davis Langdon & Everest
Theatre Projects Consultants
Equation Lighting Design
Lerch Bates & Associates
Burdus Access Management
Winton Nightingale
Desvigne & Dalnoky
WSP
Laing

Sainsbury Centre for Visual Arts
Norwich, England 1974–1978
and 1988–1991
Client
University of East Anglia
Area
6,186m²
Team
Anthony Hunt Associates
Hanscomb Partnership
Tony Pritchard

Santa Giulia Masterplan
Milan, Italy 2004–
Client
Milano Santa Giulia SpA, Mr
Zunino
Area
708,000m²
Team
MSC Associati srl
Larry Smith Italia
Progettisti Associati SpA
West 8
Ariatta
Battle McCarthy
Studio Tecnico Zaccarelli
TRM

Silken Hotel
London, England 2004–
Client
Grupo Urvasco SpA
Area
28,070m²
Team
Buro Happold
Davis Langdon
BDSP
Gordon Ingram Associates

Smithsonian Institution Courtyard
Washington DC, USA
2004–2007
Client
The Smithsonian Institution
Area
2,800m²
Team
Smith Group
Buro Happold
Battle McCarthy
Emmer Pfenninger Partner AG
Davis Langdon & Everest
Sandy Brown Associates
George Sexton Associates
Lerch Bates

Spaceport America
New Mexico, USA 2007–
Client
New Mexico Spaceport Authority
(NMSA)
Area
8,865m²
Team
SMPC Architects
Balis and Company
URS Corporation
Consult
Exploration-Synthesis Partner

Stansted Airport
England 1981–1991
Client
BAA
Area
85,700m²
Team
Ove Arup & Partners
BAAC
Beard Dove
Currie & Brown
Claude and Danielle Engle
Lighting
ISVR Consultancy Services

Supreme Court
Singapore 2000–2004
Client
The Supreme Court Singapore
Area
77,609m²
Team
CPG Consultants
TID Associates
Arup Facade Engineering
Tierra Design
Lighting Planners Associates Inc.
CCW Associates
Colt International

Swiss Re Headquarters
London, England 1997–2004
Client
Swiss Reinsurance Company
Area
76,400m²
Team
Ove Arup & Partners
Gardiner & Theobald
Hilson Moran Partnership
RWG Associates
Van Densen & Associates

Thomas Deacon Academy
Peterborough, England
2003–2007
Client
The Thomas Deacon Academy
Area
18,197m²
Team
Buro Happold
Davis Langdon
Townshend Landscape
Consultants
EC Harris
Gardiner & Theobald

Torre de Collserola
Barcelona, Spain 1988–1992
Client
Torre de Collserola SA
Area
Tower platforms 5,800m²
Team
Ove Arup & Partners
Davis Langdon & Everest
MC-2
BMT Fluid Mechanics Ltd
Oxford University Wind Tunnel
Laboratory

Tower Place
London, England 1992–2002
Client
Tishman Speyer
Properties Ltd
Marsh & McLennan Companies
Inc
Area
42,000m²
Team
Ove Arup & Partners
E C Harris
Claude R Engle
Townshend Landscape
Architects
MACE

Trafalgar Square
  London, England 1999–2003
Client
  Transport for London
Area
  48,000m²
Team
  Atkins Design Environment and
  Engineering
  Davis Langdon & Everest
  Peter Walker and Partners
  Speirs & Major
  Feilden & Mawson
  GMJ Data Presentation
  TPS Schaal

Tripoli Marina
  Tripoli, Libya 2007–
Client
  Gulf Tourism Investment
  Consultants
Area
  644,000m²
Team
  BDSP
  DCI Architects
  TRI Hospitality Consultants
  Werner Sobek Ingenieur

The Troika
  Kuala Lumpur, Malaysia 2004–
Client
  Bandar Raya Developments
  Berhad
Area
  95,000m²
Team
  Web Structures Singapore
  Northcroft
  Valdun (Jurutera Perunding
  Valdun Sdn Bhd)
  Seksan Design

U2 Tower
  Dublin, Ireland 2007–
Client
  Ballymore Properties
Area
  35,500m²
Team
  WSP Group
  Hoare Lea Consulting Engineers
  Connolly Mescall

Valery Gergiev Cultural Centre
  Vladikavkaz, Russia 2007
Client
  Style Ltd
Area
  20,000m²
Team
  Buro Happold

Walbrook Square
  London, England 2004–
Client
  Legal & General Life Fund,
  Metrovacesa, and Stanhope plc
Area
  130,000m²
Team
  Ateliers Jean Nouvel
  Adams Kara Taylor
  Davis Langdon
  Norman Disney & Young
  Edward Hutchison
  Charles Funke Associates
  Claude R Engle

Wembley Stadium
  London, England 1999–2007
Client
  Wembley National Stadium Ltd
Area
  170,000m²
Team
  HOK Sport+Venue+Event/
  LOBB
  Mott Stadium Consortium
  Franklin + Andrews
  Nathaniel Lichfield & Partners
  Steer Davies Gleave

Willis Faber & Dumas
  Ipswich, England 1971–1975
Client
  Willis Faber & Dumas Ltd
Area
  21,000m²
Team
  Anthony Hunt Associates
  John Taylor & Sons
  Davis Belfield & Everest
  Martin Francis
  Adrian Wilder
  J A Storey & Partners

Winspear Opera House
  Dallas, USA 2002–2009
Client
  Dallas Center for the Performing
  Arts Foundation
Area
  11,000 m²
Team
  Buro Happold
  Battle McCarthy
  Donnell Consultants Inc
  Theatre Projects Consultants
  Sound Space Design
  Kendall Heaton Associates

World Squares for All Masterplan
  London, England 1996–2002
Client
  City of Westminster
  Department for Culture, Media
  and Sport
  English Heritage
  Government Office for London
  The Houses of Parliament
  London Transport
  The Royal Parks Agency
Team
  Halcrow Fox
  Civic Design Partnership
  Davis Langdon & Everest
  Space Syntax Laboratory
  W S Atkins
  Feilden + Mawson
  Schal Construction Management

  Speirs & Major
  GMJ
  Ricky Burdett

YachtPlus 40 Boat Fleet
  2005–
Client
  YachtPlus UK
Length
  41m
Team
  Rodriquez Cantieri Navali
  Burness Corlett – Three Quays
  Jason Bruges Studio

Zenith
  St Etienne, France 2004–
Client
  Saint-Etienne Métropole
Area
  14,800m²
Team
  Thales
  Cyprium
  Battle McCarthy
  Michel Desvigne
  Changement a Vue
  Peutz
  Safege

Complete Works

Arts and Culture

SC Johnson Tribute Building, Racine, USA 2006–

New Holland Island, St Petersburg, Russia 2006–

Kamakura Museum, Kamakura, Japan 2005

National Arena, Glasgow, Scotland 2004–

Zenith, Saint-Etienne, France 2004–

Palace of Peace and Reconciliation, Kazakhstan 2004–2006

Smithsonian Institution, Washington DC, USA 2004–2007

National Museum, Beijing, China 2003

Avery Fisher Hall, Lincoln Center, New York, USA 2003–2009

New Globe Theatre, New York, USA 2003–

Lenbachhaus, Munich, Germany, 2003

Winspear Opera House, Dallas, USA 2003–

Museum of Fine Arts, Boston, USA 1999–

Musée Quai Branly, Paris, France 1999

Anthony D'Offay Gallery Redevelopment, London, England 1998–2001

Uffizi Redevelopment, Florence, Italy 1998

Cultural Centre, Dubai 1998

The Sage Gateshead, England 1997–2004

Scottish Exhibition and Conference Centre, Glasgow, Scotland 1995–1997

Convention Centre, Perth, Australia 2000

Prado Museum Extension, Madrid, Spain 1996

Cardiff Bay Opera House, Cardiff, Wales 1994

Centre de la Mémoire, Oradour sur Glanes, France 1994

The Great Court at the British Museum, London, England 1994–2000

Congress Centre, Valencia, Spain 1993–1998

Imperial War Museum, Hartlepool, England 1993

National Gallery of Scottish Art, Glasgow, Scotland 1993

Musée de Préhistoire des Gorges du Verdon, Quinson, France 1992–2001

Addition to Joslyn Art Museum, Omaha, USA 1992–1994

Clore Theatre, Imperial College, London, England 1992

Design Centre, Essen, Germany 1992–1997

Congress Hall, San Sebastian, Spain 1990

Trade Fair Centre, Berlin, Germany 1990

Congress Hall, Toulouse, France 1989

Crescent Wing, Sainsbury Centre for Visual Arts, Norwich, England 1988–1991

Sackler Galleries, Jerusalem, Israel 1988

American Air Museum, Duxford, England 1987–1997

Salle de Spectacles, Nancy, France 1986

Sackler Galleries, Royal Academy of Arts, London, England 1985–1991

Carré d'Art, Nîmes, France 1984–1993

Whitney Museum Development Project, New York, USA 1978

Sainsbury Centre for Visual Arts, Norwich, England 1974–1978

Knoxville Energy Expo, Knoxville, USA 1978

Samuel Beckett Theatre, St Peter's College, Oxford, England 1971

Civic Realm

Red to Dead, Jordan 2007

Greystones New Quarter, Co Wicklow, Ireland 2006–

Parliament Square Feasibility Study, London, 2005

Spinningfields Masterplan, Manchester, England 2003–2006

Sovereign Bay, Gibraltar 2004–

Milan Fair Masterplan, Milan, Italy 2003

Boavista, Lisbon, Portugal 2003

Arsta Bridge, Stockholm, Sweden 1995–2005

Folkestone Harbour Masterplan, England 2005–

Drentepark Masterplan, Amsterdam, The Netherlands 2002–

Croydon Gateway, London, England 2002–

Turin University Masterplan, Turin, Italy 2002–

World Trade Center Masterplan, New York, USA 2002

West Kowloon Cultural District, Hong Kong 2001–

Quartermile, Edinburgh, Scotland 2000–

Santa Giulia Masterplan, Milan, Italy, 2000–

Elephant and Castle, London, England 2000

World Squares for All: Trafalgar Square and Environs, London 1999–2003

ForthQuarter Masterplan, Edinburgh, Scotland 1999–

More London, London, England 1998–

Eurogate Masterplan, Vienna, Austria 1997

Getafe Masterplan, Madrid, Spain 1997

National Police Memorial, London 1996–2005

Millennium Bridge, London 1996–2000

World Squares for All Masterplan,
London 1996
Linz Solar City, Austria 1995
Regensburg Solar City, Germany
1995
Telecommunications Facility,
Santiago de Compostela,
Spain 1994
Millau Viaduct, Gorge du Tarn,
France 1993–2005
Torre de Collserola, Barcelona,
Spain 1988–1992
Oresund Bridge, Sweden/
Denmark 1993
Porte Maillot Masterplan,
Paris 1993
Albertopolis Masterplan, London,
England 1993
Lisbon Expo '98, winning
competition entry, Portugal 1993
Spandau Bridge, Berlin,
Germany 1992
Masterplan, Lüdenscheid,
Germany 1992
Imperial College Masterplan,
London, England 1992

Wilhelminapier, Rotterdam,
The Netherlands 1991–2010
Inner Harbour and City Centre,
Duisburg, Germany 1991–2001
Viaduct, Rennes, France
1991–2000
Sagrera Station Masterplan,
Barcelona, Spain 1991
Berlin Masterplan, Germany 1990
Nîmes Masterplan, France 1990
Cannes Masterplan, France 1990
Paternoster Square Competition,
London, England 1989
Pont d'Austerlitz, Paris,

France 1988
Microelectronic Park, Duisburg,
Germany 1988–1997
King's Cross Masterplan, London,
England 1987
Statue Square Masterplan,
Hong Kong 1980
St Helier Harbour, Jersey,
Channel Islands 1976–1977

Regional Planning Study Gomera,
Canary Islands 1975

Education and Research

School, Sierra Leone 2008–
Arizona State University, Arizona,
USA 2004–2009
Corby Academy, England
2004–2008
Langley Academy, Slough,
England 2004–2008
Folkestone Academy, England
2003–2008
Thomas Deacon Academy,
Peterborough, England
2003–2007
Turin University Masterplan,
Turin, Italy 2002–
Centre for Advanced Studies in
the Social Sciences, University
of Oxford, England 2002–2004
Djanogly City Academy, Nottingham,
England 2002–2005

Leslie L Dan Pharmacy Building,
University of Toronto, Canada
2002–2006

London Academy, Edgware,
London 2002–2006
The West London Academy, Ealing,
London 2002–2005

The Business Academy, Bexley,
England 2001–2003
Capital City Academy, Brent,
London 2001–2004
Faculty Building, Imperial College,
London, England 2001–2004
Tanaka Business School, Imperial
College, London, England
2000–2004
James H Clark Center, Stanford
University, USA 1999–2003
Petronas University of Technology,
Malaysia 1998–2004
Flowers Multi-Disciplinary
Research Building,
Imperial College, London,
England 1997–2001
Free University of Berlin, Berlin,
Germany 1997–2005
Economics Department Building,
Faculty of Social Sciences,
University of Oxford, England
1996–2000
Center for Clinical Sciences
Research, Stanford University,
USA 1995–2000

Faculty of Management, Robert
Gordon University, Aberdeen,
Scotland 1994–1998

Sir Alexander Fleming Building,
Imperial College London
1994–1998
British Library of Political and
Economic Science, London
School of Economics,
England 1993–2001
Forth Valley Community Care
Village, Larbert, Scotland
1993–1995
Marine Simulator Centre,
Rotterdam, The Netherlands
1992–1993
Lycée Albert Camus, Fréjus, France
1991–1993
Institute of Criminology, University
of Cambridge, England 1991
Faculty of Law, University of
Cambridge, England 1990–1995

Cranfield University Library,
Cranfield, England 1989–1992
Students' Union Building, University
College, London, England 1980
Palmerston Special School,
Liverpool, England 1974–1975
Special Care Unit, Hackney,
London, England 1971–1973
Newport High School, Newport,
Wales 1967

Government

High Court of Justice and Appeals
Court, City of Justice, Madrid
2006–2009
Palace of Peace and Reconciliation,
Kazakhstan 2004–2006
UN Headquarters, New York,
USA 2003
Supreme Court, Singapore
2000–2005
H M Treasury, London, England
1999–2004

City Hall, London, England
1998–2002
New German Parliament,
Reichstag, Berlin 1992–1999
Police Academy, New York,
USA 1992
Hôtel du Département, Marseilles,
France 1990

Industrial and Product Design
Writing Implements for Diplomat,
2006
Radial Lighting for iGuzzini, 2006
RF1 Stacking Chair, 2006
Door Handle for Trapex, 2005
Three Sixty Table Lamp for
Fontana Arte, 2005
Forward Desk System for
Steelcase, 2004
Place Kitchen Furniture for Dada,
2004
Foster 500 Furniture for Walter
Knoll 2001
Focus Outdoor Lighting for DZ
Licht 2001
Saturn Lighting for iGuzzini 2000

Pylons for ENEL, Italy 1999–2000
NF 98 Door Handles for Fusital
1998
A900 Seating and Table for
Thonet 1997–1999
Airline Seating System for Vitra
1997–1999
Helit Foster Series Desktop
Furniture 1997–2000
Oto Track Lighting System for
Artemide 1997–1999
Ra Lighting System for Artemide
1997
Room Control Device for
Weidmüller 1997
Ceramic Bathroom Range for

Duravit and Hoesch 1996–2001
Taps for Stella 1995–1999
Cladding System for Technal 1995
Library Storage System for Acerbis
1994–1996
NF 95 Door Furniture for Fusital
1994–1995
Tray for Alessi 1994–1998

E66 Wind Turbine for Enercon
1993
Street Lighting for J C Decaux
1993
Tabula Table System for Tecno
1992–1993
Cladding System for Jansen Vegla
Glass 1991–1992
Airport Desking System
1989–1991
Street Furniture for J C Decaux
1989
Contract Carpet and Tile Design
for Vorwerk 1988
Kite! chair for Tecno 1987–1997
Nomos Desking System for Tecno
1985–1987
Systems Furniture for Foster
Associates 1981

Leisure and Sport
Yacht Plus 40 Signature Series
boat fleet
2005–2010
National Arena, Glasgow,
Scotland 2004–2009
Silken Hotel, London, England
2004–2007
Hotel Puerta America, Madrid,
Spain 2004–2005
Beijing Swimming Pool, Beijing,
China 2003
Posthaus Restaurant, St Moritz,
Switzerland 2005–2006

Yacht Club de Monaco, Monaco
2003–2010
Elephant House, Copenhagen Zoo,
Copenhagen 2002–2007
Dolder Hotel Zurich, Switzerland
2002–2008
Asprey New York, New York,
USA 2002–2003

Asprey Store, London, England
2001–2004
London City Racecourse, London,
England 2000
Sitooterie, Belsay Hall, England
2000
Grandstand, Newbury Racecourse,
England 1999–2000
Selfridges, London, England 1999
Wembley Stadium, London,
England 1996–2006

ASPIRE National Training Centre,
Stanmore, England 1995–1998
Clubhouse, Silverstone Racetrack,
Silverstone, England 1995
Great Glasshouse, National
Botanic Garden of Wales,
Llanarthne, Wales 1995–2000
Oita Stadium, Japan 1995
Grand Stade, Paris, France 1994
Space Discovery Museum,
Japan 1994
Medieval Centre, Chartres,
France 1993

Tennis Centre, Manchester,
England 1993
Volcano Theme Park, Paris,
France 1992

Cacharel Shops and Franchises,
Europe 1991–1992
Holiday Inn, The Hague,
The Netherlands 1988
Stage Set for Paul McCartney
1988
Esprit Shop, London, England
1988
Hotel for La Fondiaria, Florence,
Italy 1987
Royal Thames Yacht Club, London,
England 1987
Katharine Hamnett Shop, London,
England 1987
Marina, Battery Park, New York,
USA 1986
Athletics Stadium, Frankfurt,
Germany 1981–1986
Granada Entertainment Centre,
Milton Keynes, England 1979
London Gliding Club, Dunstable
Downs, England 1978
Joseph Shop, London, England
1978
Country Club and Marina for Fred
Olsen, Vestby, Norway 1974
Fred Olsen Travel Agency, London,
England 1974
Lord's Hill Shopping Centre,
Southampton, England 1973
Orange Hand Boyswear Shops for
Burton Group, England 1972–
1973
Pavilion Leisure Centres, Knowsley,
England and Badhoevedorp, The
Netherlands 1972
Pavilion Shopping Centre, Exeter,
England 1971–1972

Mixed Use

Nine Elms, Battersea 2007–
La Margineda, Andorra 2008–
St Paul's Onslow Square, London
    2006–2008
Moscow City Tower, Moscow,
    Russia 2006–
Northgate, London, England
    2006–
Eurogate, Duisburg, Germany
    2006–
The Index, Dubai, UAE 2005–2008
Walbrook Square, London
    2004–2010
Jameson House, Vancouver,
    Canada 2004–2009
The Troika, Kuala Lumpur, Malaysia
    2004–2009
Convention Center Site
    Redevelopment, Washington DC
    2003–2011
Regent Place, Sydney, Australia
    2003–2007
Liverpool Ark, Fourth Grace,
    Liverpool, England 2002
World Trade Center, San Marino
    1999–2004
Apartments and Hotel Extension,
    Zuoz, Switzerland 1999
Millennium Tower, London,
    England 1996

Gerling Ring-Karree, Cologne,
    Germany 1995–2001
Retail and Office Development,
    Zhongshan Guangzhou,
    China 1994
Al Faisaliah Complex, Riyadh,
    Saudi Arabia 1993–2000
Shinagawa Mixed-Use
    Development, Tokyo, Japan 1990

Millennium Tower, Tokyo,
    Japan 1989
Open House Community Project,
    Cwmbran, Wales 1978
Fred Olsen Amenity Centre,
    London 1968–1970

Residential

Glebe Place, London, England
    2006–
Jameson House, Vancouver,
    Canada 2004–2009
The Index, Dubai, United Arab
    Emirates 2005–2008
Santa Giulia Masterplan, Housing,
    Milan, Italy 2004–2009
The Troika, Kuala Lumpur, Malaysia
    2004–2009
The Murezzan, St Moritz,
    Switzerland 2003–2007
21-24 Chesham Place, Belgravia,
    London, England 2003–2006
Regent Place, Sydney, Australia
    2003–2007
The Knolls, Sentosa Resort,
    Singapore 2003–
Leedon Park House, Singapore
    2003–
Budenberg Haus, Altrincham,
    Manchester, England 2000–2006
Chesa Futura, St Moritz,
    Switzerland 2000–2004
Albion Riverside, London,
    England 1999–2003
Kamakura House, Kamakura,
    Japan 1997–2004

Housing 'NF1', Duisburg,
    Germany 1997–2001
Gerling Ring-Karree, Cologne,
    Germany 1995–2001

Private House, USA 1995
Private House, Germany
    1992–1994
Refurbishment of Mendelsohn
    and Chermayeff House,
    London, England 1992–1993
Private House, Corsica 1990–1993

Private House, Kawana,
    Japan 1987–1992
2nd Avenue Apartments,
    New York, USA 1989
Riverside Apartments and Studio,
    London 1986–1990
Autonomous House for
    Buckminster Fuller,
    Los Angeles, USA 1982–1983
Foster Residence, London,
    England 1978–1979
Bean Hill Housing, Milton Keynes,
    England 1973–1975

Transport

Project Voyager BAA Offices,
    London 2006
Heathrow East Terminal, Heathrow,
    London 2006–2013
Stansted Airport Satellite 4
Stansted, England 2005
Queen Alia International Airport,
    Amman 2005–
Heathrow Airport Central Terminal
    Area Masterplan, London,
England 2004–2006
Pier Platform Study, BAA Airports,
    2004–2006
Beijing Capital International Airport,
    Beijing, China 2003–2008
TAV Station, Florence, Italy
    2003–2010
Bilbao Metro line 2, Spain
    1997–2004

Transport Interchange, Parramatta,
    Australia 2000
Motorway Signage System 1998
Repsol Service Stations,
    Spain 1997
Dresden Station Redevelopment,
    Dresden, Germany 1997–2006
Expo Station, Singapore
    1997–2001
St Pancras International Rail
    Terminal and Stratford and
    Ebbsfleet Channel Tunnel
    Stations, England 1996–1997
North Greenwich Transport
    Interchange, London, England
    1995–1998
Bangkok Airport, Thailand 1994
Ground Transportation Centre,
    Chek Lap Kok, Hong Kong
    1993–1998
Platform-Edge Screens, Signage
    and Furniture for Mass Transit
    Railway, Hong Kong 1993–1997
HACTL Superterminal, Chek Lap
    Kok, Hong Kong 1992–1998
Hong Kong International Airport,
    Chek Lap Kok, Hong Kong
    1992–1998

Kowloon-Canton Railway Terminal,
    Hong Kong 1992–1998
Solar-Electric Vehicle 1992–1994
Station La Poterie, Rennes,
    France 1992
Canary Wharf Underground
Station, London,
    England 1991–1999
Motoryacht Izanami 1991–1993
British Rail Station, Stansted
    Airport, Stansted,
    England 1989–1991
Passenger Concourse Building,

King's Cross Station, London,
England 1989
Metro System, Bilbao, Spain
1988–1995
City of London Heliport, London,
England 1988
Turin Airport, Turin, Italy 1987
Stansted Airport, England
1981–1991

Hammersmith Centre, London,
England 1977–1979
Fred Olsen Passenger Terminal,
London, England 1969–1970

Workplace
BCME Branches, Morocco
2008–
Samsung Corporation R&D Centre,
Korea 2008–
200 Greenwich Street, New York,
USA 2006–
EnCentre, EnCana Headquarters,
Calgary, Canada 2006–
The Index, Dubai, UAE 2005–
Walbrook Square, London,
England 2004–

Faustino Winery, Gumiel de Hizan
in Ribera del Duero, Spain
2004–2008
Boulogne Billancourt, Paris,
France 2004–2008
3 More London Riverside, London,
England 2003–2006
4 More London Riverside, London,
England 2003–2006

3 and 4 Hardman Square,
Manchester, England 2003–
2007
Camomile Street, London,
England 2002
Stornoway House, St James,
London, England 2002–2004
Amsterdam Vivaldi Kavel II,
Amsterdam, The Netherlands
2002–2007
6 More London Place, London,
England 2002–2003

Repsol Headquarters, Madrid,
Spain 2002–2008
Bishops Square, Spitalfields
Redevelopment, London,
England 2001–2005
51 Lime Street, London,
England 2001–2007

Scottish Gas Headquarters,
Customer Contact
Centre, Edinburgh, Scotland
2001–2003
France Avenue, Paris, France
2000–2004
Hearst Headquarters, New York,
USA 2000–2006
1 More London Place, Ernst
and Young Headquarters,
London, England 2000–2003
2 More London Riverside, London,
England 2000–2003
Cisco Systems Office Campus,

Munich, Germany 2000
Demag Headquarters, Düsseldorf,
Germany 2000
Farnborough Business Park
Offices, Farnborough, England
2000–2001
The Walbrook, London, England
1999–2010
7-11 Hester Road, London,
England 1998–2008
McLaren Technology Centre,
Woking, Surrey 1998–2004
The Metropolitan, Warsaw,
Poland 1998–2003
Moor House, London, England
1997–2005
30 St Mary Axe, Swiss Re
Headquarters, London,
England 1997–2004

HSBC World Headquarters,
London, England 1997–2002
J C Decaux International
Headquarters, Brentford,
England 1997–2000
Electronic Arts European
Headquarters, Chertsey,
England 1997–2000
50 Finsbury Square, London,
England 1997–2000
Parkview Offices, Singapore 1997
100 Wood Street, London,
England 1997–2000
Green Park Offices, Reading,
England 1997–1999
Deutsche Bank Place, Sydney,
Australia 1996–2005
10 Gresham Street, London,
England 1996–2003

Citibank Headquarters, London,
England 1996–2000
Bath Road Offices, Slough,
England 1996–1998

Kingswood Park Offices, Ascot,
England 1996–1998
Daewoo Electronics Headquarters,
Seoul, Korea 1995
Gerling Ring-Karree, Cologne,
Germany 1995–2001
Multimedia Centre, Hamburg,
Germany 1995–1999
IG Metall Headquarters, Frankfurt,
Germany 1995

Jiushi Corporation Headquarters,
Shanghai, China 1995–2001
World Port Centre, Rotterdam,
The Netherlands 1995–2000
Samsung Motors Office and
Showroom, Korea 1995–1998
LIFFE Offices, London, England
1995

Index

Credits

Photographs and Visualisations
© Ambient Images Inc / Alamy: 25 (1)
© Jean – Philippe Arles / Reuters/Corbis: 159 (2, 3)
Arcaid / © Richard Bryant: 195 (9), 227, 272 (2), 273, 279, 313 (4, 7, 8), 370 c3 (t),
© Robert Canfield: 9 (5, 6), 174 (2, 3), 175 (4 – 8), 177, 178 (1 – 4), 179 (7, 9)
© Carlos Carcas: 259 (4)
© Mario Carrieri: 272 (1), 293 (5, 9),
© Chuck Choi: 14, 129, 130 (1), 131 (6), 323 (4, 5), 324 – 325
© Stéphane Compoint: 158 – 159 (4)
© Peter Cook / VIEW: 95 (5, 6)
© Richard Davies: 16 (1), 28 (1), 31 (4), 59 (3, 4), 61 (4), 80 (1), 95 (7), 134 (1), 135 (6), 249 (5, 6, 8), 266 (4), 368 c1, c3, 372 c1 (t)
© Dbox: 89
Courtesy of Duravit: 210 (3)
© Georg Fischer: 207
Norman Foster: 301 (3, 4), 373 c4
© Ti Foster: 174 (1)
Foster + Partners: 12 (3), 13 (6), 16 (2), 17 (3 – 5), 21 (2, 3), 23 (2, 3), 27 (1, 2, 4), 29 (2 – 4), 33 (1, 2), 37 (3), 39 (5), 40 (1, 2), 41 (4), 43 (3, 4), 44 (1 – 3), 45, 47 (1, 3, 5, 6), 48 (1, 2), 49 (3, 4), 50 (1, 2), 51 (6), 52 (1), 53 (6), 54 (1), 55 (3 – 6), 56 (4, 5), 57 (3, 6), 58 (1, 2), 59 (11, 12), 61 (2, 3), 63 (3 – 6), 64 (3, 4), 65 (2, 5), 67, 68 (1, 2), 69 (4), 70 (1), 71 (3, 4), 72 (1, 2, 4), 73 (5), 75 (2 – 5), 76 (1), 77, 78 (1 – 3), 79, 80 (2), 81 (3 – 5), 82 (1, 2), 83, 85 (2, 4), 87 (5), 100 (2), 133, 136 (1), 137 (6, 8 -10), 148 (11), 182 (3), 210 (1), 245, 330 (1), 332 (1), 336 (3), 338 (3, 4), 341 (11), 368 c2 (t), 370 c1, 372 c1 (b), c2 (t)
© Fu Xing Photo: 259 (7)
© Yukio Futagawa: 326 (1)
© Dennis Gilbert / VIEW : 99, 100 (3), 105, 106 (1 – 3), 107 (8), 134 (4, 5), 161 (6), 166 (2), 170 (2, 3), 247, 248 (4), 252 (2, 4), 253 (5, 7), 254 – 255, 269, 271 (5), 285 (5, 8), 314 – 315, 369 c3 (b), c4, 370 c4, 372 c4 (m)
Spencer de Grey: 101 (5)
© Reinhard Görner: 185, 186 (3), 187 (5), 194 (7), 277 (2, 5)
© Hayes Davidson, Paul Raftery Photography: 87 (2, 4)
© Hayes Davidson, Simon Hazelgrove Photography: 87 (1)
© Kerun Ip: 10 (1), 371 c4, 372 c4 (b)
© Ben Johnson: 107 (5 – 7), 115 (8), 148 (8, 10), 251
© Ken Kirkwood: 93, 248 (3), 249 (7), 280 (4), 281 (9), 373 c3
© K L Ng: 71 (5, 6), 181
© Ian Lambot: 206 (1, 2), 299, 300 (1), 301 (5, 6), 302 – 303, 305, 306 (1 – 3), 308 – 309, 371 c3
© James Edward Linden: 147, 148 (9), 166 (1), 167 (5), 173, 267 (10)
Mclaren Marketing Ltd / © Paul Grundy: 297 (5)
© Rudi Meisel: 101 (4, 6), 186 (1), 187 (6, 7), 195 (6, 7), 196 – 197, 281 (7), 326 (6, 7), 327 (3, 4, 12, 13), 328 (1, 5), 329 (8), 333 (12), 336 (1), 341 (6)

© Miller Hare Limited: 35
© James H Morris: 102 –103, 160 (2), 170 (4)
© Michel Porro: 253 (6)
© Paul Raftery / VIEW: 160 (1, 3)
RIBA Library Photographs Collection / © John Donat: 94 (4), 281 (6), 280 (5)
© Jeremy San Tzer Ning / Stzern Studio: 201 (2)
© Tim Soar: 15 (3), 119 (6)
© Dirk Soboll: 135 (8)
© Tim Street Porter: 280 (1, 2), 281 (8)
Courtesy of St. Petersburg Government: 29 (4)
© Peter Strobel: 209 (3 – 6, 8), 211 (5, 8), 213 (7)
© Edmund Sumner / VIEW: 231
Tecno / © Pietro Carrieri: 208 (2), 209 (7)
Courtesy of Tishman Speyer © Nick Wood: 284 (1, 2)
Courtesy of Vitra: 213 (6)
Courtesy of Walter Knoll: 212 (1)
© Jens Willebrand: 306 (4)
Courtesy of Taylor Woodrow: 167 (4)
Nigel Young: 8 (2), 9 (3, 4), 11 (5), 13 (4, 5), 15 (1, 2, 4), 34 (1), 39 (2), 42 (1), 47 (2), 53 (3 – 5, 7, 8), 58 (4, 6, 10), 59 (7), 94 (2, 3), 96 – 97, 107 (9, 10), 109, 110 (1 – 3), 111 (4 – 8), 113, 114 (1 – 3, 5), 115 (6, 7), 117, 118 (1, 3), 119 (4, 5, 7, 8), 120 – 121, 123, 124 (1 – 4), 125 (5 – 7), 126 – 127, 130 (2, 3), 131 (4, 5, 7), 134 (2), 135 (7, 9, 10), 137 (4, 5, 7), 139, 140 (1), 141 (3 – 5), 140 – 141 (6), 143, 144 (1, 3 – 5), 145 (6 – 10), 148 (2, 3), 149 (4 – 7), 151, 152 (2), 153 (3 – 6), 154 –155, 157, 163, 164 (1 – 4), 165 (6, 8 – 10), 169, 171 (5 – 12), 179 (6, 8), 182 (4 – 6), 183 (7 – 10), 186 (2), 187 (4), 188 – 189, 190 (1 – 3), 191 (5 – 8), 193, 194 (1), 195 (8, 10), 199, 200 (4), 201 (3, 5, 6), 203, 204 (1, 3), 205 (5 – 8), 210 (2), 211 (6, 7), 212 (3), 213 (4, 8), 215, 216 (2 – 4), 217 (5 – 6), 219, 220 (1, 3, 4), 221 (5 – 7), 222 – 223, 225 (3 – 5), 228 (1 – 3), 229 (5, 6, 8), 232 (2 – 5), 233 (6 – 8), 235, 236 – 237 (4), 237 (2, 3), 239, 240 (2, 3), 241 (4), 242 – 243, 248, 257, 258 (2, 6), 259 (3), 260 – 261, 263 (2, 3), 265, 266 (1 – 3), 267 (6 – 9, 11), 270 (1 – 4), 271 (6 , 7), 275, 276 (1), 277 (3, 4), 283, 284 (3), 285 (6, 7, 9), 286 (1, 2), 287, 288 (1, 2), 289 (4, 6–8), 291, 292 (1 – 4, 8), 293 (6, 7), 295, 296 (2 – 4), 297 (6), 306 (5, 6), 311, 313 (2, 5,) 317, 318 (1 – 5), 319 (7), 321, 322 (1), 323 (3), 326 (5, 8, 9), 327 (2, 10, 11, 14, 15), 328 (2 – 4, 6), 329 (7, 9 – 12), 330 (2 – 4), 331 (5 – 11), 332 (2 – 6), 333 (7 – 11, 13), 334 (1 – 6), 335 (7 – 14), 336 (2, 4 – 6), 337 (7 – 14), 338 (1, 2 5, 6), 339 (7 – 13), 340 (1 – 5), 341 (7 – 10), 342 (1 – 6), 343 (7 – 13), 368 c2 (m, b), c4 (t, b), 369 c1, c2 (b), c3 (t), 370 c2, c3 (b), 371 c1, c2, 372 c2 (b), c3, c4 (t), 373 c1 (t, m, b), c2

Drawings and Diagrams:
Birds Portchmouth Russum: 94 – 95 (1), 95 (8), 100 – 101 (1), 106 (4), 110 – 111 (9), 115 (9), 118 –119 (9), 124 – 125 (8), 130 _ 131 (8), 144 (2), 152 – 153 (7), 160 (4), 164 – 165 (5), 167 (6), 170 (1), 174 – 175 (9), 178 (5), 186 – 187 (9), 195 (11), 200 – 201 (1), 204 (2), 216 – 217 (1), 220 (2), 225 (6), 228 (4), 229 (7), 232 – 233 (1), 236 (1), 240 (1), 248 – 249 (9), 252 – 253 (1), 258 – 259 (8), 270 – 271 (8), 272 (3), 276 – 277 (6), 284 (4), 286 (3), 292 – 293 (10), 296 – 297 (1), 300 (2), 307 (8), 312, 322 (2),
Birkin Haward: 12 (1, 2), 369 c2 (t)
Darron Haylock: 162
Norman Foster: 8 (1), 11 (4), 18 – 19, 20 (1), 22 (1), 36 (1), 38 (1), 40 (3), 42 (2), 58 (8), 59 (5), 60 (1), 62 (2), 72 (3), 90 – 91, 92, 98, 104, 108, 112, 114 (4), 116, 118 (2), 122, 128, 134 (3), 135 (11), 136 (2), 138, 140 (2), 142, 146, 148 (1), 150, 152 (1), 156, 161 (5), 166 (3), 168, 172, 180, 184, 187 (8), 190 (4), 192, 194 (2, 4, 5), 198, 202, 205 (4), 208 (1), 210 (4), 211 (9), 212 (2), 213 (5), 214 , 218, 224 (2), 226, 234, 238, 241 (5, 6), 244 (1), 246, 248 (1), 250, 252 (3), 256, 258 (1), 259 (5), 262 (1), 264, 274, 278, 281 (10), 282, 289 (5), 290, 294, 297 (7), 298, 301 (7), 304, 306 (7), 310, 313 (3, 6), 316, 320
Foster + Partners: 10 (2, 3), 24 (4), 25 (5), 26 (3), 28 –29 (5), 30 – 31 (5), 32 – 33 (4), 34 (2), 37 (2), 39 (3), 46 (4), 48 – 49 (5), 51 (7), 55 (2), 62 (1), 65 (1), 66 (3), 68 (3), 74 (1), 76 (2), 84 (3), 86 (3), 88 (1), 149 (12, 13), 158 (1), 165 (7), 182 (1), 183 (2), 206 (3), 221 (8), 244 (2), 266 (5), 280 (3), 288 (3), 319 (6)
David Nelson: 52 (2), 70 (2), 176, 230, 268
Narinder Sagoo: 24 (2), 25 (3), 30 (1, 2), 31 (3), 33 (3), 39 (4), 51 (3 – 5), 57 (1, 2), 65 (6), 66 (1, 2), 82 (3), 85 (1), 88 (2), 132, 224 (1)
Space Syntax: 137 (3),

Every effort has been made to contact copyright holders. The publishers apologise for any omissions which they will be pleased to rectify at the earliest opportunity.

Editing: David Jenkins
Writing: Isabela Chick, Gayle Markovitz, Sarah Simpkin
Design: Thomas Manss & Company: Thomas Manss, Joana Niemeyer
Picture Research: Kathryn Tollervey
Research: Matthew Foreman, Ben Hardy
Proofreading: Julia Dawson
Index: Christine Shuttleworth
Production Supervision: Martin Lee
Reproduction: Mondadori
Printed and bound in Italy